The Recovering Catholic's Guide to Spirituality

John C. Davis

ISBN: 979-8-9920287-2-0

Acknowledgements

The Recovering Catholic's Guide to Spirituality

Let me first say that I respect anyone's beliefs. Belief is a very personal thing. For many people, Catholicism has been a marvelous thing, and they have created wonderful lives under its doctrines. For me, it had too many inconsistencies and far too much guilt, judgement and fear.

Special thanks to all who have given me my life experiences, both good and bad. You have shown me a better way to be. I strive each day to live using the knowledge you have afforded me, and to live a truly spiritual life that Jesus, Moses, Mohammed, Buddha, Krishna, and other teachers, would be proud of.

John C. Davis

Foreword

When I started *Next Level Soul* my goal wasn't to preach or convert anyone – it was to create a safe space for seekers of all backgrounds to explore life's biggest questions. I wanted to talk about what it means to be human to be awake and to reconnect with that spark inside us that's been buried under fear guilt and dogma.

Over the years I've sat across from mystics, scientists, healers, and everyday people who've had extraordinary spiritual awakenings. And one truth keeps showing up: spirituality isn't about belonging to a religion – it's about belonging to yourself, to the universe, and ultimately to love.

That's why this book matters. *The Recovering Catholic's Guide to Spirituality* isn't about tearing down anyone's faith. It's about reclaiming it – *your* faith, your connection to the Divine without guilt shame or the belief that you have to earn love.

John Davis writes with the honesty of someone who's lived both sides – the structured world of organized religion and the freedom of waking up to spirit on his own terms. He's not here to tell you what to believe. He's here to help you remember what's already within you.

If you've ever questioned the rules but still hungered for something greater... if you've ever wondered why love sometimes felt conditional... if you've ever suspected that spirituality might be simpler and more personal than what you were taught – this book is for you. John reminds us that recovery doesn't mean rejection – it means reclamation. It means moving from fear into love. From separation into unity. From silence into the kind of truth that no institution can give or take away.

This isn't just a book, it's a lifeline. It's for anyone ready to step out of the shadow of shame and into the light of a self-empowered spirituality. I believe books like this are part of a larger awakening happening all over the world – a movement toward wholeness authenticity and love. My hope is that as you read these pages, you'll feel the same spark of freedom and peace as I did.

Because in the end this journey isn't about leaving something behind – it's about coming home to who you truly are.

Welcome home.

– Alex Ferrari, Founder of *Next Level Soul*

Introduction

I had been a keynote speaker for corporate conferences and spiritual centers, but for twenty-five years prior to all that, I was a sword-fighting comedian at renaissance festivals across the U.S., and sixteen countries abroad (including Iraq and Afghanistan) with the USO. That's right, for over two decades I was wearing tights (try not to visualize). Several years ago, my life shifted when I became a "YouTuber" after creating the very popular YouTube channel called "Expanding Spirit" (formerly known as the "John of New" channel).

It was during my years living the glamorous life of porta-potties, beat-up vans, and low pay that I began to question a lot of my beliefs. You see, I was raised Catholic, number six of an eventual seven kids. My mother, an Irish-Catholic of the highest standing, was so faithful that she got her master's degree in liturgy. That degree landed her the position of head of liturgical doctrine at her church, which basically meant that when the priest wanted to do a sermon, he had to pass it by my mom. She then would give her blessing and the priest, after kissing her ring, would happily run off to deliver his message.

As a good Catholic, I was an altar boy and went to C.C.D. for twelve years (Confraternity of Christian Doctrine for you heathens). If it snowed, the church sidewalks were always cleared by my trusty shovel and aching hands. All those years of Catholic upbringing led me to a major change: I became an atheist. You see, the fear of God didn't sit well with me. I remember a time in my most evil youth that my even more wicked brother swayed me from the faith by taking me for ice cream and putt-putt golf instead of church one Sunday morning. My career as a brazen blasphemer began that day in my eighth year.

The Sunday morning after "the alleged incident," I sat in the choir loft next to Mom, who also played the organ for the Mass. The parish, in forty-part disharmony, ended a hymn, and the priest launched into his pre-approved sermon. "Mortal Sin..." he began. His sermon went on to tell of the severity of the punishment that would be laid upon any soul that would dare to sin against God. In the middle of his sermon, the priest, who I knew well for his weekly visits to our home, mentioned that knowingly missing Mass was a sin. I was doomed. Who knew that the ice cream and putt-putt would be so costly? I burst into tears and confessed to a higher power (Mom) what my brother and I had done.

Mom tried to console me, but I knew it was over, and my short life passed before my eyes. I'm not sure, but I think that my brother's life also passed before his eyes later that day. I was an eight-year-old sinner, and I knew it.

After years of feeling lowly, unworthy, and afraid, I decided there had to be a different way. I became an atheist, and though I am no longer an atheist I am grateful that I went that route. By becoming an atheist, I experienced the true fear of a world without faith. I became morbidly curious about the possibility of nuclear war and knew that we were on our way to global Mass destruction. I began having what I now know was depression. You see, when you have nothing to put faith in, there is no hope. You are accessing your experience only through information at hand, and most information we as a society generate is negative, so I believed we were headed to a negative place. In reality, my time as an atheist was a great base line for finding my eventual faith, a spiritual faith though not a religious one.

How I came to that faith is another story, which I tell you as a means of conveying a message. Along the path of finding my personal spirituality, I made several very profound realizations. Each realization built upon the last until they unveiled a simple Spirituality, and there I found a divine simplicity to my life. It was so simple and yet so completely powerful.

I had found the awareness spoken of by the avatars of old: Jesus, Buddha, Krishna, Mohammed, and many more unnamed enlightened beings. I also found the same teaching in modern teachers as well, Tony Robbins, Wayne Dyer, Neale Donald Walsh, Napoleon Hill, Wallace Wattles, and more. To fully show the realizations as I discovered them, I must tell you some of the stories that transpired.

My history from the beginning was much like a lot of people's. After my sojourn through many spiritual belief systems, I had settled into being a seeker. I had always been looking for the next teacher, the next guru, the next person who would take me to the next rung of the ladder. I was now in a place of just experiencing the world through spiritual eyes.

The stories ahead are meant to teach, not in the style of a classroom, but in the style of the enlightened ones of old. Through realization of the principles we'll discuss, you can take inspired action and begin to see the simple path before you. As then, you step out onto that path you will witness your own spiritual truth unfold.

Part One

My Catholic Story

Chapter 1: I Puked on the Altar

Sunday morning. I was 14 years old and an altar boy. My alarm didn't go off that morning and I was late. This was my day to serve the Mass. What had I done?!! I quickly dressed and ran upstairs from my basement bedroom. My mother was already at the church, as she was the organist for the earlier Mass. In a panic, I ate my Cheerios with a generous amount of milk. Running out the back door, I grabbed my bike and threw it over the back fence. It was the fastest route to the church, which was five miles away. Panicked, I pedaled furiously to the back door of the church.

I arrived just as Mass was getting ready to start. Father Cornelly, seeing me rush in, gave me "the Look" (the disapproving glance over his half lenses reading glasses). He was not only our priest, but he was my mom's best friend. That made it worse. Still panicked about how bad I was for almost missing Mass, I hurriedly prepared everything for the Mass and it began.

My brother was the reader that day and was on the altar with me. After he did his two readings, Father Cornelly took the pulpit. He began his, as I remember it, overlong gospel that I had to stand for the entire time. The altar lights were hot that day. Deep within my stomach my anxiety mixed with my milk-laden Cheerios...not a good combination.

My stomach started to gurgle. The saliva started to flow in the back of my mouth. I started feeling that familiar feeling that no one ever wants to feel and I was standing on a church altar in front of a full congregation! My panic increased. How bad was I that I was not only late and disrespectful to the church, but now my breakfast was going to protest as well. My only thought was I can't throw up on the altar. I cupped my hands in front of me, caught the upcoming attraction and backed through the door from the altar. Running outside so I would not throw up in the church, I delivered the rest of my "penance" to the bushes.

When recounting the tale later that day my brother shared his version. As Father Cornelly was delivering his sermon, a woman from the front pew came to the side of the altar and whispered to my brother, "That young boy doesn't look well." My brother witnessed my dramatic game saving catch, waited for Father Cornelly to finish the gospel and sermon, and during the moment of reflective silence after afterwards he whispered to Father Cornelly, "John threw up." The caring Catholic leader responded," Where?" "In his hand," my brother informed him.

Just as Jesus would have said (*sarcasm*), Father Cornelly responded, "Good." My brother found this hilarious and told that story for years.

Jesus left one commandment: Love one another. That's what the Bible tells us. I was never asked how I was feeling that day. I was admonished for being late and for eating within an hour of Mass, which was forbidden at the time. I deserved what I got in "God's eyes." I felt like the wretch "Amazing Grace" trained me to think I was. Later that night I got the guilt-filled Catholic mom talk. I must be a horrible person. That baptism and confirmation must not have taken hold. I was not worthy of the Love Jesus spoke about. That is what I learned that day.

It is said that the person you will become is mostly determined by the age of seven. My experience with Catholicism during those seven years was that I was an unworthy wretch. To add insult to injury, at home my father had decided that of his eventual seven children I was the one he disliked. His nickname for me was "the worthless bum." Later in this book I will tell you why that was. Spoiler: it was my fault.

Love. What is Love? The most esoteric book of the Bible, the Gospel of John, states that, "God is Love." That is why the word, "Love," is capitalized throughout this book, much to the chagrin of the editor.

God <u>IS</u> Love. When you step outside of the Bible and start studying the religious and spiritual doctrines of the world, you find one commonality. Love in its many forms is the core foundation of spirituality. Saint John, in stating that "God is Love" is clearly stating that we should hold Love above all else.

That morning on the altar, "God" showed up. She showed up when she whispered to my brother that I didn't look well. God whispers to us all the time. It is up to each of us to listen.

My brother reacted fearfully and did not disrupt the sacred service. He chose to set Love aside and stay in line. I don't in any way blame my brother. He was taught this, just like I was.

Father Cornelly was no better in his "Christian" response. Again, I hold nothing against Father Cornelly and remember him quite fondly. He was demonstrating a Pavlovian response. He was conditioned to react exactly as he did. That is what Catholicism taught them both. Obedience to a God figure over anything else is the doctrine of Catholicism. The Ten commandments start that way. You can't blame them.

Let me ask a question. If "God is Love," where in that first commandment is Love mentioned? Translated, this commandment simply says, "You owe me and so you must serve me and no one else." Doesn't sound too much like Love to me. The other thing this commandment does is delineate "God" from "Gods."

I Believe in One God

Let me give a little historical perspective here. As Catholics, we have a "profession of faith" that is drilled into our heads like propaganda. The first involves this one-God belief.

Only one? The Catholic profession of faith starts off with a statement based in clearing away all possibilities of more than one God. Personally, I believe that there is only one God, Source, Universal Energy, whatever moniker you want to give it. To "profess" a belief, I believe you should study and understand what it is you are signing on for. Monotheistic religions have been around for a LONG time.

Many of you know the young Pharoah named King Tutankhamun. (Steve Martin brilliantly depicted his life in song for us all to glory in his magnificence. "Buried with a donkey, he's my favorite honky, King Tut.") Tut Ankh Amun is well remembered more for the discovery of his tomb rather than his life.

As with many ancient cultures, his name is a depiction of his history. The last name of "Amun" literally means "one God." He has this title because his ancestor Akhenaten declared that Amun Ra was the one God over all Gods. Akhenaten was an Amun Ra Cultist. His belief was based in the biases that his God was better than all others. Over time "The One God" became "One God." This began a monotheistic belief in ancient Egypt, and the succeeding Pharaohs took the name "Amun" to profess their belief in the One God, Tutankhamun being one such devotee.

Not too far away, Abraham, the foundational prophet of the top three monotheistic religions (Christianity, Islam, and Judaism) professed the belief in one God. This one God belief is the basis of the first profession you must make as a Catholic.

Each of the top three religions has their belief based in an ever-evolving system.

The western culture tends to believe that the Hindu faith has many Gods. Before my trip to India a few years ago, I actually had never given it any thought. I was on an amazing trip to help someone in need. On the trip, I discovered a wonderful country and a beautiful people. I was surprised to discover that all the beautiful statues are not different Gods, but aspects of the one God. When you have a need in a certain area of your life, you focus on the aspect of God you most need help from.

In the modern metaphysical community. "One God" has been replaced with the Source or The Universe and other singular statements. Either way, the belief is in One Energy Source in which faith is placed.

Science has a unique way of interpreting the "One Source." As science is based on empirical evidence, they do not make statements based on faith. They make statements based on facts at hand, and scientific facts state that everything we perceive is an image of neutrons and electrons firing off at an atomic level. Atoms are the basis of all life, but atoms have nothing solid within them. They are an "energy event." So science states that everything we perceive is made of pure energy.

The label we put on this energy is where faith begins. Noetic science is trying to bridge that gap. We know through noetic science experiments that our thoughts can affect the energy. We also know when that energy is affected the results can be measured. But what *is* the energy? Here is where science cannot go.

Scientists believe that it is within this one energy source that everything we perceive is expressed. In Christianity, the first tenet is to believe in One God. In later chapters we will discuss this in further detail, but you can see here a similarity in faith and science.

I highly respect scientists. I like that fact that they don't take things on faith. I find that their impartial declarations over time have solidified my personal faith.

I do believe in One God. I profess that freely. I believe that the energy the scientists have identified is God. I respect that they can't make that jump, but my label is not based on Amun Ra or the one God of Abraham. "God" is my preferred label for the energy that everything is made from. So I can profess that without reservation and do so. I personally like to believe what the Apostle John stated: God is Love. Love is a wonderful way to think when labeling the One energy that all is made from. I tend to think that the world we live in is predominately positive.

Think about it. Let's say you commute to work daily. On your drive to work you probably see a thousand or more cars on the road. You might see one accident. Tonight on the news what will the story be? Will it be the miraculous fact that thousands of people made it safely to their destination without an incident, or will it be the anomaly to that fact?

We come from a source that 99% of the time is positive. So not only do we come from the one energy/God, but that deity is positive.

It's interesting to watch how each person can affect so many others. In the holiday film, "It's a Wonderful Life," Jimmy Stewart's character George Bailey is given a glimpse of how he personally affected the lives of everyone in the little town of Bedford Falls. Without the small kindnesses he expressed, the entire town would have fallen into disarray. This clearly demonstrates our interconnectedness, our oneness. Each person directly affects those around them and each person clearly witnesses what they put their faith in.

I enjoy when I go to a restaurant and get a grumpy server. It gives me the opportunity to show how interconnected we all are. During my time with the server, I make a concerted effort to change their mood. I usually can make them smile within a couple minutes. I remember one time when I was out to dinner with a friend, and we each had different experiences based upon our own beliefs.

As he walked into the restaurant, my friend stated how much he disliked it,

"I hate this place! Why do we always come here?"

"What do you mean? I love this place," I responded.

As we sat down at the table, the server came over and asked if we wanted something to drink. I could immediately tell she was in a bad mood. I went to work making her smile. Within a minute she was laughing and flirting and enjoying her day. My friend, still grumpy, grumbled that he'd have water to drink. We each ordered our meal and waited for our salad to arrive.

When our salads arrived, it was striking how different they were. My salad was beautiful with all fresh vegetables and looked like it was made with gentle loving care. My friend's salad, on the other hand, was the core of a head of iceberg lettuce with a scattering of other vegetables and a glob of salad dressing splattered on top. "What is this?!" He grumbled as he glanced at me for an approval of his dissatisfaction.

The server gave him an equal look of dissatisfaction, grumbled under her breath, and took the salad back to the kitchen. Minutes later, she returned. It was glaringly obvious that she had taken it to the kitchen and cut up the core of the iceberg lettuce with a knife and brought it back out.

My friend's expectations were met that day. His meal was exactly as he expected. The energy that he put out was the energy received. When our entrées arrived, mine was perfectly cooked and beautifully arranged and I enjoyed every single bite. My friend's meal was undercooked in some parts and overcooked in others. Again he grumbled.

When looking at the concept of oneness with God, I tend to believe that we witness it on a daily basis. Jesus declared that the Father and he were one. He also declared that whatever we ask we shall receive if we have faith. I believe our oneness with the one true God is expressed by the materialization of our belief. If the one God is truly Love, as the Apostle John states, then He/She lovingly gives us what we put faith in and lets us experience exactly what we ask for. My friend had his experience because the energy of the universe, God, gave him exactly what he believed he would get. So believing in one God, means we must believe that the one source Loves us and supplies us with all we believe.

That day on the altar, the "Cheerios Revolution," represented a realization of what each of us put faith in. The "one God" took our faith and expressed it in our reality. Father Cornelly and my brother expressed their obedience and saw it all very differently from the caring woman who expressed her loving concern for the altar boy turning green under the hot lights. I was putting my faith in my guilt and fear, which the one God expressed in the disgusting outcome I received.

Chapter 2: The Priest Ran Giggling Out of the Gay Bar

I grew up in a beautiful beach town. Rehoboth Beach, Delaware, sits on the coast three hours east of the nation's capital, Washington D.C. Over the years Rehoboth has become known as the "Nation's Gay Summer Capital," as many have found its relaxing atmosphere a place they can safely express their love openly. The Catholic church owned a mansion in one of the most expensive areas in town. Across the street was the beach, and the picturesque boardwalk and its attractions were few steps away. The mansion became a vacation spot for many priests in the diocese.

I love to sing. My hometown has many casual night spots with small stages for entertainment, my favorite of which was "The Front Page." On Tuesdays, their stage was an open mic night. My friends and I formed an acapella group called "The Acafellers" and each week we looked forward to the Tuesday night event to try out new music.

One Tuesday, a couple hours before the show, we all went to a local pizza shop for dinner. While eating, the diners at one table in the restaurant were obviously having a great time. They were laughing, joking, and standing out. It was a group of obviously gay men enjoying each other's company, not an uncommon sight in Rehoboth. As I ate my last slice of juicy Italian goodness, I suddenly heard a very familiar laugh. I glanced over to see the latest parish priest at the head of that table. It wasn't a surprise to anyone. We all knew he was gay and thought nothing of it, but it did serve as another confirmation.

We finished eating, paid our check, and started to walk over to the Front Page. On the same street as the Front Page was the Blue Moon, a well-known gay bar in town. As we passed, its front door swung open and two men came out the door holding hands and giggling loudly. As they ran by me, I said, "Good evening, Father," to one I recognized as one of the other parish priests. I felt bad as his face went pale at my greeting. He was keeping that title on the down low.

As I stated earlier, I put great stock in the Apostle John's statement that "God is Love." The Catholic faith, in my opinion, has missed this point. God IS Love. If St. John is right, then who are we to judge how God is expressed? I truly believe Love in any form is not wrong. What would be wrong is *judging* Love being expressed. Catholicism was quick to judge and those priests were hiding their natural way of expressing their Love.

The second line in the first profession of faith calls God, "The Father Almighty." Here is where I begin to step away from taking the full profession of faith. One of the biggest issues I see in the faith is its adherence to a patriarchal hierarchy that has its origins in a bronze age society that no longer exists.

I am a firm believer in equality. In my childhood home, the most influential person was Mom. When surveyed, most Americans would say that their mothers ruled the roost. My mother had the position of being head of liturgical doctrine at her church, yet my mother would never have been allowed to be a priest.

The concept of a One God being male bothers me. I prefer to believe that gender is not involved. If God is Love, as stated above, is Love gender specific? We often hear the phrase, "Only a mother could love" in our society. As a father of an amazing son, I will say that I have never experienced a Love like I have for my son. I am sure that his mother feels the same way. That expression of Love that we feel towards our son is not in any way hindered by me being a male nor her a female. The Love we feel is an expression of the source we come from.

Many religions in the world marginalize people by their gender or sexual orientation. Pope Francis has made great strides in being inclusive with the LGBT community, however, it is still "not allowed under Christian doctrine." If God IS Love, is Love meant for an exclusive few?

In my many years working in theater, I have been fortunate enough to make some very dear friends. Many of those friends were gay. Most of those gay friends were in better relationships than my straight friends. I witnessed their loving expressions towards each other, and it made me smile. I smiled because I like seeing God expressed in such beautiful ways.

The patriarchal veil that most religions are based on is a two-millennium old paradigm. That was a different time. Over the many years, we have come to discover that diversity is an asset not a hindrance. In my life I have known men, women, gay, straight, and alternative lifestyle, who were wonderful people, terrible people, smart people, dumb people, different people and boring people. All of them Loved in their own way. Male and female alike have the desire for Love. No one gender does it better than the others. As John and Paul said, "All you need is Love" (yat da da dat da).

I find it interesting that the image of God often used to depict the "Father Almighty" resembles the Greek God Zeus. This ancient belief that Zeus was "The Mightiest of Gods" closely matches Akhenaten's theory of Amun Ra. In fact there is a theory that Amun Ra (also spelled "Ammon") was the basis for Zeus.

These male images were based on the patriarchal system of their time. They were both an evolution of the multiple deity system just as the eventual dropping of their unique personas to become the "One God" was an evolutionary change.

In my personal experience with Catholic churches, it is usually the women who make them operate. Even though this is pretty standard at most churches, women are not allowed to be priests. The idea that woman are meant to be the vessel for creating new Catholics is as ancient as the idea that the world is flat. Evolution is a part of spirituality, not an argument against it.

As time has passed, we keep evolving. Some evolve more slowly, and none more so than the Catholic church. It took until 1986 for the Catholic church to act progressively and forgive Galileo for making the heretical statement that the world is round.

And in 2015, the Pope apologized to Central America for what the conquistadors did over 500 years ago. A little late, don't you think? I don't blame the church for the delay. I simply believe that the bureaucracy of the church is outdated and unable to keep up with the ever-changing times.

I feel profoundly blessed to live in a time when equality is beginning to be the norm. Many new laws protect the rights of individuals. The Pope recently said it wasn't for him to judge homosexuals for their lifestyle, yet he did not move forward in changing church doctrine towards true equality. The reality of it is as we move forward into these times of equality, we are truly expressing Love more freely, openly, and in a timely manner.

I believe that, like trying to steer a giant ship, it takes a long time to turn the Catholic faith towards the right direction. If the belief is that God is Love, should we hinder it in any form?

Chapter 3: The Nun Said I Was Fat

After high school, I had a job working for a landscaping company. The company's owner was a very well-built bodybuilder. He had several employees who were also bodybuilders. One of them owned a local gym, and I owned a sweatshirt that advertised his gym.

One day while sitting in a fast-food restaurant with the crew of bodybuilders, I noticed across the restaurant was the head nun from my church. She knew who I was. She didn't like my mother. After finishing her meal, she took the long way around the dining room so she would pass my table. Here I was, a portly guy, sitting with a table of Adonis-like figures. The loving, caring, Catholic nun took her time to walk up to me at that table, read my shirt, and say, "I don't believe you go to a gym," The bodybuilders all found that hilarious. I felt worthless.

In that first profession of faith, after the "One God" and the "Father" thing was the phrase, "The Maker of Heaven and Earth, of all that is seen and unseen." So God is the maker of all things. Who is it that puts in the order to be made? Let's ask an authority on God: Jesus.

In the New Testament, Jesus says, "Whatever you ask in God's name is granted if you have faith." He also said, "If you have faith as small as a mustard seed, you can ask a mountain to move and it will move. Nothing will be impossible for you." In those two sentences from that son of a carpenter was the word "you," five times. So it follows that you must take responsibility for what you are asking for in "God's name."

What is God's name? Is it a mystery? Not really. In the Old Testament, there was a guy named Moses. He was the guy who didn't like swimming and split the Red Sea so he could walk instead. On the other side of that sea, he climbed Mt. Sinai and had a deep conversation with a "burning" bush. After talking to the bush for quite some time, he asked for God's name so that he could share it with those who asked. "I Am that I Am," the bush responded (not to be confused with Popeye's, "I ams what I ams").

The phrase "I am that I am" has a couple of meanings and many different interpretations of it have been posited. When you look at it grammatically, it can be broken down to simply "I AM." That said, if

God's name is "I AM," then when we declare who we are with "I AM" statements, we are asking God for an outcome. As promised, God responds in kind and gives us what we put our faith in.

In our lives we are constantly bombarded with "you are" statements. If we put faith in what others say about us, then we ask God for that experience with I AM statements. The Bible never says that God only gives positive outcomes. The Bible says that whatever you ask for in God's name you will receive, if you have faith.

Have you ever known a negative person? (If you don't, you better do some self-reflection and make sure you're not the person people thought of when they read that.) Have you ever noticed that a negative person always has something to be negative about? That is the product of putting faith and believing, "I AM living in a negative world."

When my son was five, we had favorite songs. His personal favorite was the lovely hymn, "There Was an Old Lady Who Swallowed a Fly." (If you don't know this song, turn to page 44 of your hymnal.) In the song, this "old lady"...wait for it...swallowed a fly. She then swallowed a bird to catch the fly. The song progresses with larger and larger animals until it culminates in the closing line of, "She swallowed a horse. She's dead of course." My son and I liked the song so much that we just kept adding larger and larger things that she swallowed instead of her usual equestrian demise.

One day while driving Kynan to kindergarten, we went from horse to dump truck. (Did I mention he was five?) From dump truck we went to the earth. Each time I would ask Kynan for the next larger thing. After the earth he said the sun. After the sun he said the galaxy. I then said to him, "Well that must be it, Kynan, there is nothing bigger than the galaxy."

"Nuh uh, Daddy," Kynan responded. "There are two things bigger than the Galaxy."

I was over-dramatically aghast and said, "Two things are bigger than the whole galaxy?!"

"The universe and God," he confidently declared.

"Is God bigger than the whole universe?!" I snapped back."

"Yup, 'cause he told me he is in everyone and everything and we control the God-part inside of us." I was floored. *"We control the God-part inside us."* Isn't that exactly what was promised, but said very simply? Ask and you shall receive. You are the one asking.

I promised you back in Chapter Two that I would tell you why it was my fault that my father referred to me as the "worthless bum." I feel he saw something in me that made him look at his own life in a negative way. Rather than taking responsibility for his own life, he lashed out at me. It was I, however, that put faith in his words. It was I who asked God to be a worthless bum with that faith, and I struggled with self-worth for a large part of my life.

As a child I didn't understand that I was in charge of my creation. That was the greatest gift that God gave us: Ask and *you shall receive*. The problem is that we didn't understand how we were asking. In fact, the way we ask is too simple. It is not some esoteric mantra, method of praying, or affirmation. It's our own thoughts, words and deeds that are doing the asking. That said, it was my fault that I was a worthless bum because I asked God for it.

When we ask, our belief goes out to God, and God creates what we put faith in, because that is what was promised. What does God create from?

As I said earlier, science has proven that all that is seen is made of energy. Hold up your hand. (Go ahead...do it! No one will judge you.) Look at the back of your hand. Now realize that the hand you are looking at is attached to the wrist bone and the wrist bone is connected to the... well, realize that that hand is nothing but pure energy. There is nothing there but an energy event that shows us our hand. (Now put your hand down...you look ridiculous.)

I believe that energy is God, as I said before. We are literally "made IN God's image." We know that everything we see is made of that energy. Understanding that God is the "Maker of Heaven and Earth" is definitely a big leap of faith, but this new understanding of the energy of the universe explains a lot. As science closes the gap between itself and faith, I find great comfort in the validation of what I've been taught. Catholics are told that in those gaps are the mysteries of faith. "Because it is a mystery," George Carlin used to say with a smug smile and a raised eyebrow in his comedy routines. The space must be filled with faith. So where does that faith originate?

Faith is another word for belief...or maybe more appropriately, *confident* belief. In the religious world, faith is based on the oral traditions of nomadic people.

Have you ever played the telephone game? If not, here is the gist of the game: Line up ten people in a row. The first person in line whispers some information into the ear of the second. Then the second whispers it into the ear of the third and so on. By the time the tenth person receives the information, it is usually completely different than the original information. This is because each person brings their own belief system and experiences into hearing the information.

This game is played in a matter of mere minutes. Imagine playing the telephone game for years, generations, decades, or centuries before the information is even written down. Then imagine that what is written is then translated into another language and then another and so on. Then you have many interpretations that various people added or subtracted from the text.

That is what every religious text is today, and none have been more altered that the current Bible used in the Catholic church.

I'm sure many of you have a crazy family member who can really tell a great story. That relative toys with the story to make it more interesting and enjoyable, like the tale of the whale-sized guppy that fishermen tell on a daily basis in every country around the world.

As Catholics, we are putting our faith in the information, the story, from the last person in the telephone game.

I one time was discussing the Bible with a very devoted Christian. I asked him if the gnostic texts that didn't make it into the Bible were just as valid as those that did. His response was that they weren't. He "had to believe" that "God's hand was involved in the choosing."

At the Nicaean Council, books were chosen and compiled into the one Bible, with many books being deleted. These men who chose decided what was to be spread as doctrine and what was to be discarded as unworthy to be considered.

Yet the concept of their infallibility in the choices was yet another leap of faith. Building a faith upon the skewed judgements of others builds a questionable foundation and is risky, to say the least. I don't believe that any carpenter would begin to build a house without seeing what it was he was building upon. In fact, that carpenter couldn't even start building without a very solid foundation.

Chapter 4: The Priest Said: "The Hell If I'm Going to Let You Quit"

As with all children, altar boys can be real jerks. As I said earlier, my self-worth had been severely damaged by the treatment from my father. Being overweight with low self-worth makes you a target for bullying. At our church, the other altar boys loved picking on me. As we prepared for Mass they would tease me, poke me, and laugh at me. It was truly a terrible experience, and I mustered up the courage to talk to my mother.

"I don't want to be an altar boy anymore," I told her.

"You have to tell Father Byrolly yourself," she said, disapprovingly.

I was scared. I didn't want the confrontation. Father Byrolly was a very stern man with a harsh, disapproving glare that made one avert their eyes to not experience it. Sunday came and I was one of the altar boys that served that morning. I decided to wait until after the service to tell the priest.

As a Mass came to an end and we processed out the back door of the church, I turned to Father and said, "I don't wanna be an altar boy anymore."

"The HELL if I'm going to let you quit," Father Byrolly snapped back with his piercing glare. The other altar boys thought this was hilarious and the good Father did not correct them for thinking so.

Being a child can be difficult, especially in a world that is supposed to be unconditionally loving and isn't. If God is Love, was the priest's response loving? What is his refusal to correct the other altar boys loving? Jesus told us, "You are the children of God." If we are the children of God then we are the children of Love. That makes me and my brothers sons of God and my sisters daughters of God.

The profession of faith says, "we believe in one lord Jesus Christ, the only son of God." How can I be? Jesus told us that we are the children of God, so if we are the children of God, how can he be the only son when I am also male?

We each came into this physical world through the natural reproduction process of our parents. We are "begotten" of our parents. After the line in the profession, "we believe in one lord Jesus Christ the only son of God," comes the line, "eternally begotten of the father." So by the mere definition, Jesus arrived here through the reproductive cycle of his "father." After some descriptive phrases like, "God from God, light from light, true God from true God," it reiterates, "begotten, not made." (Father Byrolly was also a child of God, but being a church elder gave him an ego that was way out of balance. He truly felt that he walked closer to God than anyone else.)

I believe that we are all equal in God. No part is greater, or less than, any other part. The priest was exerting power. He was drunk with it. He felt it should be his way, and no one else had a choice. He didn't care if one of his altar boys was miserable. He only cared that he had his way. The Bible says, "The love of money is the root of many evils." I believe that money is power. And the currency of power can be very intoxicating. I believe just like a land baron drunk on making the next million, Father Byrolly was drunk with the power of the priesthood. That intoxication was the root of many evils.

I remember Father Byrolly's greeting very well. He always used your first and last name, "John Davis, and how are you today?" Before you could answer, he would snap out, "now ask me how I am." This was really annoying; he assumed you had no social graces and condescendingly dictated how you should respond. My father hated him and used to tell us we should respond, "Frankly, Father, I don't give a shit!" Of course he himself would never say that to him in fear of the wrath of Mom.

One of my core beliefs is that we are here to represent God. We are here to be Love, show Love, and spread Love. I found very few good examples of God in any of the priests that we knew. Most were "mightier than thou" and looked down upon the parishioners as people they were "saving." For them to have that belief, they had to believe that we were not their equal. Jesus said, "greater works than I have done you will do." He did not set himself apart as greater than us. Yet within the Catholic faith the priests often do. It is rare to find one who does treat the parishioners equally.

Imagine two people leaving for a trip to the same destination. One of the travelers leaves two hours before the other. Is the person who left early "better" than the person who hasn't left yet? Obviously, the answer is no. The person who left early does, however, have a new responsibility: they need to communicate back to the person who hasn't left yet the pitfalls and challenges along the roadway to make the travel easier for the one coming behind. This is how I see Jesus: he was our equal, but he was a little further down the road. He was showing us the pitfalls and challenges and making the journey easier.

The hierarchal structure of Catholicism automatically sets people apart and above others. I believe this is antithetical to what Jesus taught us. The Bible says that Jesus washes his disciples' feet. He did this to show that he was no better than they were. This demonstration shows his Love, humility and kindness, and is an example to those of us who are coming up behind him on the journey.

Chapter 5: "The Police Aren't Going to Call Us Anymore"

As you can tell by now, Catholicism was not a loving place for me. In fact it left me feeling scared and alone. I was sure I was a terrible person and sometimes acted out that way. I had no positive guidance from the Church; instead, my experience was judgment and fear. In my life I never did drugs, and I did not let alcohol pass my lips until I was 21 years old. I also was never in trouble with the law nor had anyone at school call my parents to say I was acting out. In fact, I was a complete introvert due to my lack of self-worth. So when I turned 18 and my mother said to me, "You're 18 now, so the police aren't gonna call us anymore. You're on your own," it hurt. This was a product of my own belief. Yes, that belief came from my upbringing and my religion, but I was the one asking God for more judgment and fear through my belief in my lack of self-worth.

One of the moments that stands out as pivotal in my spiritual growth came in a conversation with my mother after announcing that I had decided I wasn't going to go to church anymore. I basically had become an Easter/Christmas Catholic. I would go on Easter mainly to please my mom. I would go on Christmas because I liked the incense, the music, and the candlelight service.

After I turned 21, it became a tradition to go have a couple drinks before midnight Mass to make the guilt part a little easier. So, while talking with my mother, we were discussing that I didn't go to church. She wasn't in any way judging me, but she said, "You're an adult now; it's your choice. Spirituality is a personal journey and you must find what you believe." I know in her heart she really hoped I would come back to Catholicism, but that was definitely not in the cards.

Catholicism had been so difficult that not only did I not want to attend church, I decided I didn't believe in God and became an atheist. This was a near catastrophic choice for me. I found very quickly that a world without a faith of any kind was depressing. I began looking at the world only through empirical evidence or what was shown to me by the news. This led to an obsession with war and suffering.

When you don't have faith in something better and you only judge the world by what is being shown to you, then you will see the darkness. Faith depends upon what you don't see. That is why there is such a divide between science and spirituality. Spirituality is based in faith. As such science will often mock the spiritual for its lack of evidence.

Over the next few years, I became more and more depressed. I saw nothing good in the world and was living like there was not going to be a tomorrow. It was during this time I was traveling on the weekends to perform at Renaissance festivals and had an eye-opening experience that made me start a new spiritual journey.

I had a multi-week contract with a medieval fair in New Orleans. I would work Monday through Friday in Maryland and Friday night I would fly out to New Orleans to perform on the weekend. Strangely, New Orleans had fallen into a distinctive weather pattern that year. During the week New Orleans would have normal temperatures, but on the weekend it had well below average temperatures, often dropping into the 30s at night.

I was sharing a tent with my comedy partner. After the first weekend of freezing in that tent, and before the second, I was watching 60 Minutes on television. They had an article on a group of Buddhist monks who could go into a freezer and meditate with cold towels on their shoulders. During their meditations, they would increase their body temperature so much that those towels would become hot, well above the normal temperature of 98.6°.

The following week I found myself back in that tent and again the temperature was in the 30s. Perhaps it was naïveté that was the jumpstart of my spiritual growth, but whatever it was, in that tent I had a huge experience. Lying in the tent freezing I decided that if those monks could do it so could I.

Lying there on my back in that tent, shivering, I decided I was going to warm my body with my mind. I focused on my feet. I thought, "my feet are getting warm." Oddly enough my feet felt like they were getting warm. So once my feet felt warm, I decided to bring the heat up my legs. I focused on my ankles, and my ankles were getting warm...and I slowly felt the heat move from my feet and my ankles. I followed up with my shins and then my knees and then my thighs. My legs were entirely warm. Next was my pelvic region and then my abdomen. They got warm. My lower half of my body was completely warm. I could not feel the cold at all.

I then moved up to my chest and the heat rose. For some reason at that point I could not get the heat to rise any higher. I mentally struggled with moving it but it became more and more difficult. Then I had my first very strange experience in this encounter.

In my head I heard a thought, but it wasn't *my* thought. It was like hearing someone else's thought. "Relax into it." So rather than struggle with raising the heat into my chest, I focused on just relaxing and breathing. Suddenly the heat rushed into my head and down my arms, and a burst of heat encompassed my whole body. My eyes, though they were closed, saw pure bright white light and I felt as if the heat was flowing out of me in all directions. At that moment I felt like I was one with everything.

The next morning, I woke up wondering, "What the hell was that?!"

I got dressed and made my way to the stage where my comedy partner was already eating breakfast. I sat down next to him and explained to him what happened the night before. He looked at me, cracked a smile, and said, "you had a kundalini rising." I responded, "Gesundheit." I truly did not understand what he meant. Those words meant nothing to my Catholic/Atheist mind. He explained to me the very basic rudiments of the chakra system and that the root chakra is known as the kundalini chakra. What I had done that night, according to him, was bring my kundalini root chakra energy up through my other chakras. Hindus call this a "kundalini rising," an awakening.

My comedy partner had been a long-time practitioner of transcendental meditation. He had knowledge of the experience but had never experienced it himself. He then told me, "Now that you've had that experience, you're gonna have all kinds of cool things happen."

The whole thing really kind of freaked me out. I didn't remember anything like this in the Bible or in any CCD class I ever took. Being at that time an atheist and much more science based, I wanted to know what had happened. Since I was spending the next night in that tent again, I decided to have another go of it. My comedy partner had gone out on a date and I was alone in the tent. I began warming my feet. The heat again slowly began to rise up my legs.

Suddenly I heard the tent zipper open. I opened my eyes and watched my comedy partner step over me and lie down. I turned, looked around and saw myself lying on the tent floor with my eyes closed. I was in awe! The whole time this experience was happening I was hearing a loud deep humming sound. It shocked me immeasurably. Within minutes, I opened my eyes and everything was back where it was supposed to be. I explained to my partner what had just happened and he responded, “Did you hear the humming noise?

“YES!” I belted out.

“You were out of body. I told you you'd be having more experiences now,” he said with a grin.

One of the things that intrigued me about all of this was that my comedy partner, who had been so knowledgeable about them, was not having them himself. How could this be? The difference I found was that I *believed* I was doing it. I *believed* I was warming my body. I was relaxing into the warmth rather than intellectualizing the concept of a kundalini rising. These were the first of many very profound spiritual experiences I had in my life.

But...this book is not about me, it's about recovering Catholics finding their way to an understanding of spirituality that is practical, joyful, and easy. I will be sharing my other big spiritual experiences in a separate book. For now let's stay on topic and talk about how I overcame my Catholic upbringing and how you can too.

Part Two

The Recovering Catholic's Guide to Spirituality

From Story to Guide

Why I Use "Jeshua" Instead of " Jesus"

Before we go any further, let me explain one choice that may already have caught your eye: throughout this part of the book, I call him **Jeshua** rather than "Jesus."

Why? Because names matter. "Jesus" is the name wrapped in centuries of Catholicism – a name weighed down with doctrines, dogmas, creeds, and institutional agendas. "Jesus" is the figure held up by priests and bishops as the divine exception, the one we must worship, the mediator we must obey. "Jesus" is a theological construction, often stripped of his humanity and weaponized to keep others small.

Jeshua is different. Jeshua was the man. Jeshua was the flesh-and-blood human being born in a dusty village, walking among fishermen and tax collectors, laughing at dinner tables, crying at graves, and daring to confront corrupt powers. Jeshua discovered and lived his divinity – not as an unreachable exception, but as a demonstration of what it means to be human in alignment with Love.

Jeshua's message was not, *Worship me."* It was, *Follow me."* His point was not, *I alone am divine."* It was, *The kingdom of God is within you."* Jeshua was not showing off his uniqueness. He was showing us our own.

That's why I use the name Jeshua. Because this guide isn't about building bigger churches or inventing new doctrines. It's about rediscovering what Jeshua revealed: that Love is the center, presence is power, and every human being carries divinity within.

Why a Guide is Needed

When you walk away from Catholicism (or any rigid system), there's a gap. You know what you no longer believe, but you don't always know what you *do* believe. You know what you want to leave behind, but you're not sure what to carry forward.

That's where many people get stuck. They leave the church but never build something new. They deconstruct but never reconstruct. They end up spiritually homeless, carrying baggage without a new path to walk.

This guide is my attempt to fill that gap. Not with another system of rules, not with rituals to replace old ones, but with simple truths and practices that lead to freedom. These chapters are not theology lectures. They are invitations — to release guilt, to embrace forgiveness, to live in presence, and above all, to embody Love.

What This Part Covers

Part Two unfolds like a journey:

- We begin by naming the burdens of doctrine and authority — showing how religion layered rules upon rules until the simple message of Love was buried.
- We trace how ideas like original sin twisted human identity into shame, and we dismantle those lies.
- We confront the heavy weights of guilt and shame, revealing how they distort not only religion but also psychology and relationships.
- We step into forgiveness, not as obligation but as liberation, freeing both self and others, day by day.
- Finally, we arrive at Love — the true center of Jeshua's teaching and the heartbeat of authentic spirituality.

Each chapter builds on the last, peeling back the layers of fear and revealing the freedom of Love. Each section includes not only ideas but practices — because spirituality isn't about theories. It's about lived experience.

Humor as Companion

If you've read this far, you know I use a great deal of humor. Why? Because humor is holy. Religion often told us to be solemn, to keep a straight face while drowning in guilt. But humor cracks open fear. It loosens shame's grip. It helps us exhale. Jeshua himself had a spark of humor — calling religious leaders "whitewashed tombs," pointing out the absurdity of worrying about specks in other people's eyes while ignoring planks in your own. Humor frees us to laugh at the systems that tried to chain us.

So don't be surprised if this guide makes you chuckle as often as it makes you think. Laughter is part of liberation.

The Point Isn't Belief – It's Life

Catholicism often measured people by belief: did you affirm the creed? Did you obey the catechism? Did you check the right doctrinal boxes? But Jeshua never said, *"By this all will know you are my disciples: that you signed the right statement of faith."* He said, *"By this all will know you are my disciples: that you Love one another."*

Belief systems divide. Love unites. This guide is not about getting your beliefs "right." It's about living your life well. Not after death. Not in some distant heaven. Now.

My Hope for You

My hope is that as you read these chapters, you'll begin to feel lighter. That you'll laugh at the absurdity of doctrines that once terrified you.

That you'll discover forgiveness as release, not as duty. That you'll start noticing Love in ordinary places – in conversations, in meals, in nature, in silence.

I hope you'll stop outsourcing your authority and start trusting your inner voice. I hope you'll recognize your own divinity, not as ego, but as alignment with the Love that pulses through everything.

And I hope that when you finish, you won't just close the book. You'll live it.

So welcome to Part Two – *the guide.* You've heard my story. Now let's walk the path together. Let's recover not just from Catholicism, but from fear, guilt, and shame. Let's learn from Jeshua – not the "Jesus" of dogma, but the *Jeshua* of Love – who showed us not only who he was, but who we are.

This isn't about starting a new religion. It's about living a new life. A life where the weight is lifted, forgiveness flows, and Love stands at the center.

Are you ready? Then let's begin.

Chapter 6: Recognize the Weight of Doctrine

The Burden of Religious Layers

You know that feeling when you open your closet one day, and you realize you've got seventeen shirts you don't even remember buying, a jacket that looks like it was made for a 1980s extra in Miami Vice, and a pile of shoes that could supply a small nation? That's a little bit what it's like to grow up Catholic. Except instead of shirts and shoes, you've got doctrines, dogmas, rituals, feast days, fast days, and sins (mortal or venial, take your pick) stacked on your spiritual shelf until the closet door won't close. And God forbid (literally) if you take something out of order and the whole pile comes crashing down on you in a guilt avalanche.

For me, the dawning realization hit one day in Mass when the priest was droning on about some obligation or another, and I caught myself thinking, "Why does this feel less like a path to God and more like I accidentally joined a spiritual tax-preparation seminar?" Because that's what Catholicism, at least in its fully loaded doctrinal form, really is: an ongoing accounting system. How many times have you sinned this week? Was that thought lustful or merely appreciative? Was that lie mortal or venial? Is eating meat on Friday this week a ticket to hell or just a stern look from Sister Agnes? You practically need a spiritual CPA to get through it.

And here's the kicker: none of this was the message of Jeshua. *None of it.* The guy's entire gig was simple: Love one another, recognize the spark of God within yourself, and live in that present moment awareness. But apparently that wasn't complicated enough for the rest of us. Somewhere along the line, the simplicity of "God is Love" got translated into "God is Love... plus here's a 900-page instruction manual, a complicated rewards system, and a few hidden fees."

When I really started to notice the absurdity was when I compared it to my actual lived experience. Jeshua's teaching felt light, free, expansive. Every time I sat in presence, or what I now call "sitting in Love," I felt peace. But every time I sat in Mass, I felt weighed down by a bureaucracy of heaven that made the DMV look efficient. And if you've ever been to the DMV, you know that's saying something.

The burden of doctrine is exactly that — a burden. Instead of liberating the soul, it loads it down with conditions, caveats, and clauses like a bad cell phone contract. And once you're in it, you can't even question it, because questioning is itself considered rebellion against authority. So not only do you carry the weight, you also carry the fear of putting it down. It's like being forced to wear a backpack filled with bricks but also told that taking it off will get you struck by lightning. No wonder so many people spend their whole lives bent double under the weight.

I used to imagine Jeshua walking into one of these heavily ritualized services. I think he'd probably sit down, listen for a few minutes, and then say something like, "Wait... you guys turned my three-point sermon into a 2,000-year franchise? With outfits?" And then he'd laugh, because the irony would be too rich. But beneath that laugh, there would be sorrow too, because every extra layer of doctrine is like an onion — peel enough of it, and instead of getting to the center, all you get are more tears.

That's the burden I had to recognize for myself: the difference between a living truth and a layered doctrine. The living truth is simple, freeing, and always points you back to your own experience of presence. The layered doctrine is complex, restrictive, and always points you to an external authority to double-check if you're "doing it right." Once you notice the weight of it, you can't un-notice it. It sits on you, nags you, and at some point you either collapse under it or you shrug it off and walk free.

I chose to shrug it off. And I can tell you, nothing feels lighter than realizing you don't have to keep carrying someone else's spiritual luggage.

The Problem with External Authority

If Catholicism were a company, it would have the most bloated org chart in history. At the bottom, you've got the faithful — that's you, me, Grandma with her rosary beads, and Cousin Tony who only shows up at Christmas Mass and Easter Sunday but swears he's "very devout." Above us are the priests, above them the bishops, then the cardinals, and finally the pope. The hierarchy is so top-heavy it makes a Jenga tower look stable. And here's the kicker: this whole structure is built around the idea that you can't actually access God directly. Nope. You need an intermediary — a spiritual middleman — to file the paperwork.

Now, I don't know about you, but I've never liked middlemen. They're the people who jack up the price without adding any real value. Car dealers, cable companies, airline booking fees — and yes, in this case, priests. The whole thing reminds me of one of those old mob movies: "Nice little soul you got there. Be a shame if anything happened to it. Don't worry, for a small fee of obedience and confession, we'll keep the Big Guy off your back."

The problem with external authority isn't just inconvenience — it's dependency. From the moment you're baptized, you're told that you can't trust yourself. You're broken, sinful, prone to error, and in desperate need of someone holier, wiser, or better dressed in a robe to set you straight. And you swallow it, because everyone around you is swallowing it too. Before long, you find yourself in a spiritual game of "Mother, May I?" — except instead of a childhood game, it's your eternal soul on the line.

I remember sitting in confession as a kid, rattling off my list of "sins," which usually included things like stealing cookies, talking back to my mom, or imagining what the girl two rows up in class looked like without her sweater. The priest, half-asleep behind the screen, would mutter something about saying ten Hail Marys and one Our Father.

And I remember thinking, "Wait a second — God, the Creator of the Universe, is keeping tabs on my cookie theft? And you're the one who gets to decide if I'm forgiven?" It felt like going to court for jaywalking and finding out the judge also sold the tickets.

And the fear! Let's not forget the fear. If you rely on external authority to get it "right," then you also live in terror of getting it "wrong." What if you forget a sin? What if you eat meat on the wrong day? What if you skip a Mass because you had the flu? Suddenly, you're not just living your life — you're tiptoeing through a minefield of invisible spiritual infractions, praying you don't step in the wrong spot. That's not empowerment. That's paranoia dressed up in stained glass.

Now contrast that with Jeshua's actual words. Luke 17:21: "The Kingdom of Heaven is within you." He didn't say, "The Kingdom of Heaven is within your local parish priest," or "The Kingdom of

Heaven can be accessed by papal decree." *Within you.* That's as direct as it gets.

The Buddha echoed it: "Do not believe in anything simply because you have heard it." In other words, stop outsourcing your truth.

Lao Tzu chimed in with: "When you realize there is nothing lacking, the whole world belongs to you."

None of these great teachers said, "Find someone holier than you and do whatever he says." They all pointed inward, not upward through a chain of command.

The trouble with external authority is that it creates spiritual adolescence. You never grow up, because you're always waiting for the next adult in the room to tell you what's right. And the Church loves that arrangement, because spiritual teenagers are easy to control. Tell them the rules, scare them with punishment, and they'll line up to follow. But the cost is enormous: you never develop your own direct connection. You never trust your inner compass. You never experience what it feels like to walk into the Kingdom that's been sitting inside you all along.

I'll put it this way: relying on external authority for your spiritual life is like going to a restaurant, ordering a meal, and then letting the waiter eat it for you while describing the flavors. Sure, you might get a sense of what it's like, but you'll always leave hungry. And worse, you'll convince yourself you weren't worthy to eat the meal in the first place.

At some point, I had to ask myself the obvious question: if God is truly Love, why would He/She/It set up such a convoluted system? Why would the Infinite Source of All That Is require an access code, a membership card, and a weekly attendance record? It made no sense. And that's when it hit me: external authority wasn't God's idea. It was ours. Or more accurately, it was the institution's idea — because nothing keeps an institution running smoother than convincing its members they can't live without it.

And let me tell you, once you start sniffing out the absurdity, you can't un-smell it. You start noticing all the ways external authority keeps you small. The way priests stand on a higher platform, literally above you, while delivering the homily. The way bishops wear hats that look like they stole them from a medieval parade float. The way the pope sits on a golden throne while claiming to represent a man who washed people's feet. It's theater, and not even good theater. Broadway has better costumes and at least a coherent plot.

Here's the truth: the real authority is within. It always has been. Jeshua knew it, Buddha knew it, Muhammad knew it, and deep down, you know it too. That quiet voice inside you, the one that whispers peace when you stop the noise — that's authority. That's the Kingdom. The rest is window dressing.

So here's my challenge to you: start paying attention to where you've outsourced your power. Notice the moments you wait for permission, validation, or approval before taking a spiritual step. Ask yourself, "Whose voice am I really following here?" And then remember Luke 17:21. Remember Buddha's warning not to believe something just because you've been told. Remember Lao Tzu's reminder that nothing is lacking.

Because at the end of the day, the problem with external authority isn't just that it's unnecessary. It's that it robs you of the greatest treasure you'll ever own: your direct, unmediated connection with the Divine.

And trust me — once you taste that for yourself, you'll wonder why you ever let someone else hold the spoon.

How Doctrine Disconnects from Experience

Let's talk about ritual, because I have a love/hate relationship with it. Ritual, at its best, is beautiful. It can focus the mind, open the heart, and create a sense of sacred space. Lighting a candle with intention, singing a song of gratitude, sitting silently in meditation — those things can be profound. But once ritual turns into doctrine, once it becomes a "must" instead of a "may," it loses its spark and becomes, well, boring. Empty. Like a spiritual treadmill where you're sweating but not actually going anywhere.

When I was a kid in CCD, we prayed the rosary a lot. And by "a lot," I mean so often that I could rattle off Hail Marys like a trained parrot. "HailMaryfullofgracethelordiswiththee..." all the way around the beads. Did I feel closer to God afterward? Honestly, no. I mostly felt closer to recess. The rosary, for me, wasn't a mystical tool — it was a stopwatch between me and fun.

And this is the heart of the problem: **doctrine substitutes repetition for experience**. Instead of feeling the presence of God, you're performing the gestures that supposedly *lead* to God. It's like reading the ingredients of a recipe aloud every night and convincing yourself you've eaten dinner.

Now, this isn't unique to Catholicism. Every major religion has fallen into this trap. In Buddhism, you've got people bowing and prostrating hundreds of times, counting beads, memorizing chants. In Hinduism, you have elaborate pujas where you can't miss a single step. In Islam, you've got debates about whether your prayer mat was angled 2.7 degrees too far east. In Judaism, you've got people memorizing halakhic details about how many steps you can take on the Sabbath before it counts as "work." It's like every tradition has a committee dedicated to turning the living flame of Spirit into a checklist.

Why? Because human beings love certainty. And certainty is easier to sell than mystery. If you tell someone, "The way to God is simple: sit still, breathe, listen, Love," you'll lose them in five minutes. They'll ask, "But how many breaths? Which words? Facing which direction? On what days?" And before you know it, a ritual is born. Then the ritual calcifies into doctrine, and now we've got an institution that can enforce the rules.

But here's the rub: every time you enforce a rule, you risk losing the *experience* behind it. Presence is replaced by performance. Joy is replaced by obligation. And people begin to mistake the map for the territory.

I remember one particular Lent when I was a teenager. The priest reminded us that eating meat on Fridays was forbidden. I didn't care much — fish sticks in the cafeteria were fine with me. But one day, I forgot. I grabbed a slice of pepperoni pizza at a friend's family pizza shop. Halfway through, I realized it was Friday in Lent. Cue panic.

Was I going to hell? Would God strike me down with indigestion? I spent the rest of the evening sweating over the cosmic consequences of pepperoni.

Looking back now, I laugh. Do we really believe the Creator of the Universe, the Infinite Mind that birthed galaxies, is sitting there keeping score of my lunch meat? "Sorry, John, I was going to grant you enlightenment, but you had pepperoni on a Friday." That's not divine wisdom — that's un-divine micromanagement.

This is exactly how doctrine disconnects from experience. Instead of tuning into the *essence* of Lent – self-reflection, sacrifice, compassion – I was trapped in fear over breaking a food rule. Instead of experiencing Spirit, I was experiencing anxiety.

And this doesn't just happen with food. Think about confession. In theory, it's a powerful practice: releasing guilt, finding forgiveness, starting fresh. But in practice, it became a weekly checklist: "Bless me, Father, for I have sinned..." followed by the same grocery list of minor infractions. I'd confess, get my Hail Marys, rattle them off like a speed-reader, and walk out. Was I transformed? Not really. I just felt like I'd gotten my hall pass signed.

Doctrine takes what should be alive and makes it mechanical. It's spiritual bureaucracy. Imagine if Love worked this way. "Honey, I love you, but just to make it official, please fill out these forms, recite this declaration in the proper tone, and make sure you only say it at the approved times of day." That wouldn't be Love, that would be HR compliance.

The worst part is that over time the rituals actually inoculate you against real experience. Because when you go through the motions long enough, you convince yourself that's all spirituality is. You never stop to ask, "Wait – am I actually *feeling* anything?" You just assume the act itself is enough. And when you don't feel Spirit, you blame yourself. "Maybe I'm not worthy. Maybe I didn't do it right." No one ever tells you, "Maybe the ritual itself has lost its juice."

And here's the kicker: Jeshua warned about this. Over and over, he pointed out that the Pharisees were obsessed with rules, while forgetting the heart behind them. He healed on the Sabbath, scandalizing the rule-keepers. He touched the untouchable, spoke to women, and forgave sinners without demanding ritual sacrifice. He was constantly breaking doctrine in favor of experience. His whole message was, "Don't get so lost in the performance that you miss the point."

I sometimes imagine Jeshua sitting in on a modern Mass. The robes, the incense, the Latin chants. I picture him shaking his head and saying, "You know, I was just trying to tell people to Love one another. Where did you guys get all...this?"

So how do we reconnect with experience? By stripping back the layers. Instead of rattling through rote prayers, pause. Breathe. Feel the words. Instead of obsessing over feast days and rules, ask: "What is the spirit behind this practice?" Instead of letting doctrine dictate your worth, turn inward and listen to your own heart. That's where God lives, not in the checklist.

Because in the end, spirituality isn't about doing it right. It's about being real. And once you've tasted the real thing — the presence, the stillness, the Love — you'll never again mistake the menu for the meal.

The Simplicity of the Inner Voice

Here's the most scandalous truth that religion doesn't want you to know: God's not hiding. The Divine isn't tucked away in the Vatican, or the Holy of Holies, or inside some scroll kept under lock and key. The Kingdom isn't up in the clouds waiting for you to die before you get a glimpse. It's right here. Right now. And the access point? Your own inner voice.

Now, when I say "inner voice," I don't mean the neurotic chatter that reminds you to buy milk or replays embarrassing conversations from fifteen years ago. I mean that deeper voice, the one that surfaces in stillness, the one that feels more like a knowing than a thought.

Jeshua called it the Kingdom of Heaven within. Muhammad called it God closer than your jugular. Buddha called it the lamp unto yourself. Same truth, different packaging.

The simplicity of the inner voice is its biggest threat to organized religion. Because once you realize you can access the Divine directly, you don't need a middleman. You don't need an institution. You don't need a priest with fancy vestments telling you whether or not God approves of your choices. You can check in yourself. That makes you spiritually independent, and institutions don't thrive on independence — they thrive on dependency.

Let me give you an example. When I was younger, I used to agonize over decisions. Should I do this? Should I do that? I'd consult people, weigh pros and cons, sometimes even pray the "Hail Mary, full of grace, give me a sign already" prayer. But the real clarity only came when I sat in stillness. No rosary beads, no rituals, just me and the silence. And in that silence, the answer would rise up — not in words, but in a felt sense of peace around one option. That's the inner voice. That's the Kingdom whispering back, "You already know. Be still and know THAT I Am God."

And here's the kicker: the inner voice never shames you. It doesn't call you unworthy or sinful. It doesn't threaten you with eternal damnation. That's the programming of doctrine, not the essence of Spirit. The inner voice nudges you toward Love, toward compassion, toward truth. It doesn't need incense or choirs or dogmas. It just needs your attention.

Of course, religion doesn't like that setup. Simplicity doesn't pay the bills. Can you imagine if a priest got up on Sunday and said, "Hey everyone, good news: God's within you. Go home and listen to that voice. That's the whole sermon." They'd be out of a job. The collection plate would stay empty. Simplicity isn't profitable. Complexity is.

But life itself keeps pointing us back to simplicity. Watch a child play. Watch someone laugh with their friends. Watch the way you feel when you're present with someone you Love. No doctrine needed, no ritual required – that's divine connection in action. That's the inner voice showing up as experience.

The real question is this: can you trust it? Because after years of conditioning, trusting yourself feels rebellious. You've been told over and over, "You can't trust your own understanding." You need the Church, the priest, the catechism, the approved interpretations. So when you first start listening inward, it feels almost... illegal. Like sneaking out at night as a teenager.

But the more you practice, the clearer it becomes. That simplicity is the heart of spirituality. You don't need to climb mountains or memorize creeds. You just need to listen. And the more you do, the more you realize the inner voice has been speaking all along.

It's like tuning a radio. Doctrine is static – loud, insistent, distracting. But if you dial past the noise, you'll find a clear channel, and on that channel is the truth: simple, direct, and yours.

The Cost of Carrying Doctrine

Doctrine is heavy. Let's just call it what it is. And not heavy in the "deep wisdom" way. Heavy like a suitcase filled with bricks that you didn't pack but somehow got stuck carrying.

Imagine you're starting your spiritual journey. Ideally, you'd want to travel light — maybe just a walking stick and a good pair of shoes. But Catholicism hands you a backpack stuffed with guilt, shame, fear, and obligation. "Here you go," they say. "Carry this if you want to reach heaven." And the cruel trick is that the heavier the bag gets, the more you're told it proves your devotion. If you're exhausted, weighed down, bent double under the rules — good news! You're holy.

Let's break down some of the bricks in that bag.

- **Guilt Brick #1**: Original sin. You're broken before you even begin. Congratulations, you've failed at existence.
- **Fear Brick #2:** Hell. An eternal torture chamber waiting for even the smallest slip-up.
- **Shame Brick #3**: Sexuality. Basically every natural impulse you have is suspicious at best and damnable at worst.
- **Obligation Brick #4**: Ritual. Miss Mass, miss heaven. Forget a Holy Day of Obligation? Add another brick.
- **Doubt Brick #5**: Don't even think about questioning. Inquiry itself is a sin.

Now try walking with all that strapped to your back. No wonder so many people end up crawling through life, spiritually exhausted.

Catholic guilt isn't just installed — it's factory software. Comes preloaded at baptism. There's no uninstall option. Every time you try to move forward, the pop-up appears: "Warning: you are not worthy."

The cost of carrying doctrine is more than just exhaustion. It robs you of joy. It turns your relationship with the Divine into a ledger sheet, with debits and credits, sins and indulgences. It makes God into an accountant instead of a Lover. And that's tragic, because joy is the surest sign of Spirit. If your religion steals your joy, it's not pointing you to God — it's pointing you to chains.

I carried that backpack for years before I realized something radical: I could set it down. And when I did, I swear I grew three inches taller.

Life got lighter. Love flowed freer. And the God I discovered on the other side wasn't scolding or tallying my mistakes. It was a presence, simple and kind, saying, "Welcome home. Took you long enough to drop that bag."

Simple Practices

Alright, enough of the rant. How do we actually move forward? Here are some practices to help you step out from under doctrine's weight and reconnect with presence:

1. **Write it Down.** Write down the doctrines or rules that felt heavy to you. Which ones made you feel guilty? Which ones disconnected you from joy? Which ones felt more about control than Love? Naming them is the first step to releasing them.
2. **Visualization Exercise.** Close your eyes. Picture yourself carrying that giant backpack full of guilt, fear, and obligation. Feel the weight on your shoulders. Then, imagine walking up to the institution that gave it to you – the Church, the doctrine, the authority figures – and hand it back. Say, "Thanks, but no thanks. I'll walk light from here." Then step forward, lighter, freer.
3. **Declaration.** Whenever possible, declare: *"The Kingdom of Heaven is within me."* Let it sink in. Not within Rome. Not within rituals. Not within doctrine. Within *you.*
4. **Sitting in Love.** This is my favorite. Sit quietly, breathe, relax and just feel Love – no agenda, no words, just Love. That's the practice Jeshua modeled. No checklist needed.

So where does that leave us? We started by recognizing the burden of layers. We saw how external authority keeps us dependent. We named the ways doctrine disconnects us from real experience. We rediscovered the simplicity of the inner voice. We acknowledged the exhausting cost of carrying doctrine. And we tried on a few practices to lighten the load.

Here's the big takeaway: doctrine is optional. Presence is not. Doctrine weighs you down. Presence sets you free. Doctrine demands obedience. Presence invites Love. Doctrine builds walls. Presence opens doors.

The choice, in the end, is yours: keep lugging the backpack of fear and guilt or shrug it off and walk light into the Kingdom that's been inside you all along.

And once you do set it down, you'll be ready to face the next big lie head-on: the doctrine of original sin. Because if doctrine is heavy, original sin is the lead brick at the bottom of the bag. And that's where we're headed in Chapter 7.

Chapter 7: Original Sin

The Invention of Brokenness, the Birth of a Problem

If religion were a traveling salesman, "original sin" would be the deluxe vacuum cleaner it pushed at every door. It's the big-ticket item, the one that keeps the whole business afloat. Without it, the rest of the inventory doesn't make sense. Confession, baptism, indulgences, purgatory, salvation – none of these "products" sell if people don't first believe they're defective. And nothing says defective quite like being guilty before you even take your first breath.

Let's start with the story. You know the one. Adam and Eve, two naked people in a garden, hanging out with a talking snake. God tells them not to eat from the Tree of Knowledge of Good and Evil. The serpent says, "Come on, live a little." Eve eats, Adam follows, and suddenly the whole human race is screwed. Because apparently, eating fruit was not just bad dietary planning – it was the cosmic crime of the millennium.

From that moment, so the doctrine goes, every human being is born under the shadow of this "original" mistake. Not just Adam and Eve, but everyone who ever came after. You, me, your sweet grandmother, that squirming baby in the delivery room – all guilty of treason against heaven before we even take our first breath. Congratulations, you've failed at existence before you've started.

Now, when I was a kid, I didn't question this story. Nobody around me did either. It was presented as fact. That's the insidious power of doctrine: it doesn't arrive as "one interpretation." It arrives as "the way it is." Like gravity. You don't question it. You just assume, "Yep, I'm guilty because two ancient people couldn't control their appetite."

But then I got older, and I started asking the obvious questions. Like, why should I be guilty for something I didn't do? That's not justice – that's spiritual nepotism in reverse. Imagine if the law worked like that today. "Sorry, kid, your great-great-great-grandfather stole a horse, so you're under arrest." Absurd, right? And yet, that's exactly what original sin teaches.

And let's talk about the fruit. It wasn't the Tree of Murder, or the Tree of Genocide, or the Tree of Really Bad Haircuts. It was the Tree of Knowledge of Good and Evil. Knowledge! God's supposed to be all about wisdom, right? So why punish people for wanting to know the difference between right and wrong? It's like punishing your kid for reading a book. The moral of the story seems to be: "Obedience matters more than wisdom." And that, my friends, is the seed of every authoritarian religion that followed.

Now, here's where it gets interesting. Jeshua never mentioned original sin. Not once. His teachings were all about Love, presence, and empowerment. "The Kingdom of Heaven is within you." "You are the light of the world." That's not brokenness – that's wholeness. The whole concept of inherited guilt came later, mainly from St. Augustine in the 4th century. Augustine had his own issues – he famously struggled with lust and guilt – and decided humanity must share his torment. If therapy had been around back then, the Church might not have had to carry Augustine's baggage for 1600 years.

Why did the idea stick? Because it was brilliant for business. If you can convince people they're broken by birth, you've got customers for life. They'll come for baptism to wash away sin. They'll come for confession to scrub off new sins. They'll come for Mass to stay on God's good side. It's a perfect cycle of dependency. The Church positioned itself as the only authorized repair shop for the soul. You're guilty, they've got the cure – at a cost, of course.

Think about it. Without original sin, there's no urgency. Why baptize a baby if they're already innocent? Why confess if guilt isn't your default state? Why fear hell if you were born whole? The doctrine of original sin creates the problem so the Church can sell the solution. It's like inventing a disease and then opening the only pharmacy that carries the cure.

But let's set aside the theology and look at lived experience. Have you ever held a newborn? Did you look down at that tiny, squirming miracle and think, "What a guilty little sinner"? Of course not. Babies radiate innocence. They don't arrive with sin. They arrive with life. The only people who think otherwise are those who've been taught to see through the lens of guilt.

That's the tragedy of original sin: it poisons perception. It takes something pure and convinces you it's tainted. It makes you doubt your own worth before you can even spell the word "worth." It disconnects you from the truth Jeshua actually taught: that you are already connected, already divine, already Loved.

Here's the humor in it all: somewhere out there in the cosmos, if there is a Creator, do we really believe they're holding an eternal grudge over a fruit salad gone wrong? That galaxies, stars, and entire universes were created only to be undone by a snack? If it weren't so damaging, it would be hilarious. And honestly, maybe it still is.

The birth of this problem — original sin — wasn't divine revelation. It was human invention. A story crafted out of fear, guilt, and control.

And like all stories, once you recognize it as a story, you can decide whether to keep telling it or to tell a new one.

The Psychology of Guilt

If original sin were just a dusty old doctrine in a theology book, it wouldn't matter much. But it's not. It's psychological dynamite. It seeps into the mind, warps the way you see yourself, and sets up guilt as your default operating system.

Think about how early it begins. A baby is baptized not as a celebration of life but as a rescue mission: "Quick, wash away the stain before God notices!" The priest pours water over the infant's head, and everyone sighs with relief — the baby has been "saved" from the crime of simply being born. What a way to start life! Before you even cut your first tooth, you've been branded guilty.

Now, guilt is one of the most effective control mechanisms humans have ever invented. Why? Because it's sticky. Fear you can shake off once the danger passes. Shame you can sometimes escape by proving yourself. But guilt lingers. It's like a barnacle on your soul — you can't see it directly, but it slows you down everywhere you go. And the Catholic system knows how to keep it stuck. Weekly confessions. Regular reminders from the pulpit. Holy Days of Obligation. Every element of the system is designed to keep guilt alive.

When I was a kid, I didn't question it. Guilt was just the water we swam in. Skip a prayer? Guilty. Daydream during Mass? Guilty. Have an unwholesome thought about the cute girl in math class? Guilty and possibly doomed. And the kicker: if you forgot to confess something, you were guilty of that too. It was guilt wrapped in guilt, like a spiritual turducken.

Over time, guilt changes how you think. It makes you second-guess your joy. That little voice that says, "Don't laugh too loud, it's not holy. Don't enjoy too much, it's selfish. Don't trust yourself, you're flawed"? That's not God. That's programming. And original sin is the root.

Let's call it what it is: a virus of the mind. It installs a lie that says, "You are unworthy." From that lie grows a hundred others: "You can't be trusted." "You must obey." "Your natural desires are dangerous." Before long, you're not living your own life — you're living as an inmate in a prison of invisible bars. And you don't even notice the cage, because you've been in it since birth.

Now, guilt does serve a function when it's healthy. If you harm someone, guilt can be a signpost that says, "Hey, that wasn't loving. Make it right." That kind of guilt is corrective. But original sin replaces healthy guilt with existential guilt. It tells you you're wrong *for existing.* That's not corrective. That's corrosive.

And let's talk about Augustine, the man who gave guilt its golden throne. Augustine struggled with his own impulses, particularly sexual ones. He wanted to be holy, but he also wanted women and men. He lived in torment, swinging between indulgence and shame. Finally, he decided the problem wasn't him — it was humanity itself. If *he* couldn't control himself, then clearly all humans were corrupt from birth. And voilà! The doctrine of original sin. Augustine's therapy session became Church law.

Imagine if therapy had existed back then. Augustine on the couch: "Doc, I keep lusting." Therapist: "That's called being human." Augustine: "So I don't need to condemn the entire human race?" Therapist: "Nope, just work on your own stuff." Boom. Sixteen centuries of guilt avoided.

But therapy didn't exist, and so Augustine's hang-ups became humanity's burden. And the Church ran with it, because guilt is institutional gold. People wracked with guilt don't rebel. They don't trust their own voices. They cling to the authority that promises absolution. And the Church positioned itself as the only absolution dispensary in town.

The psychology of guilt works in subtler ways, too. It makes you distrust pleasure. A meal tastes too good? Probably sinful. A laugh feels too hearty? Probably frivolous. Sex? Don't even get me started. Entire lives have been spent repressing joy because people thought their very humanity was suspect. That's the cruelest part: original sin teaches you to be suspicious of yourself. And once you doubt yourself, you're easy to control.

Let's pause and consider Jeshua. Did he ever shame people for being human? No. He ate with sinners. He enjoyed dinner parties. He forgave freely. He called people into Love, not into guilt. He never once said, "You're broken from birth and only I can fix you." That was never his message. His life was proof that humanity and divinity aren't at odds. They're two sides of the same coin.

But guilt blinds you to that truth. It tells you to suppress the very impulses that could lead you to connection: joy, curiosity, desire, creativity. Instead of seeing them as sparks of life, you're taught to see them as traps. You spend your energy fighting yourself instead of living fully.

Here's the big question: who benefits from that? Not you. Not God. The only one who benefits is the institution that profits from your insecurity. If you feel guilty, you'll confess. If you confess, you'll obey. If you obey, you'll tithe. It's a closed loop, powered by guilt.

So what's the antidote? Awareness. The moment you see guilt as programming, not truth, it starts to lose its grip. The moment you realize you weren't born guilty, but born divine, the virus begins to die. It takes practice, sure. Years of conditioning don't fall away overnight. But each time you choose Love over guilt, joy over shame, presence over programming, you reclaim a little more of your true self.

Original sin wasn't just a theological mistake. It was a psychological wound. But here's the healing: guilt isn't who you are. It's what you were taught. And what can be learned can be unlearned.

Jeshua's Actual Message

If you step back for a moment and set aside everything the Church has told you, it becomes glaringly obvious: Jeshua never taught original sin. He never once said, "You were born guilty." He never once suggested you needed a priest, a bishop, or a pope to act as an intermediary between you and God. In fact, his words and actions dismantle the very idea that humanity is broken. If Augustine gave us a legacy of guilt, Jeshua gave us a legacy of empowerment. The problem is, the Church chose Augustine (and Paul) over Jeshua.

Let's start with the basics. Jeshua's most repeated theme was *the Kingdom of Heaven is within you.* Not in Rome. Not in the Temple. Not in a ritual or a doctrine. Within *you.* That's a radical statement. If the Kingdom is already within, then you're not missing anything. You're not broken. You're not guilty by default. You already have access. The only work to be done is remembering and awakening. That single sentence, if taken seriously, completely dismantles the doctrine of original sin.

Yet somehow, by the time the Church was done building its theology, Jeshua's teaching got buried under Augustine's angst. Instead of hearing "You are divine," we were handed "You are depraved." Instead of empowerment, we got dependence. Instead of presence, we got penance.

And it's not just Luke 17:21. Jeshua's words are littered with reminders that humanity is already connected to the Divine. Think about when he told his listeners, "You are the light of the world." Not, "You are a dim bulb unless I fix you." Not, "You are depraved and I'll throw you a bone of grace." No – *you are the light of the world.*

Already shining. Already whole.

Or take the woman caught in adultery. The religious authorities were ready to stone her, armed with doctrine. They had rules on their side. But Jeshua looked at her and said, "Neither do I condemn you." He didn't say, "Well, you are inherently guilty because of Adam and Eve, so you're lucky I'm in a good mood today." He released her from guilt, reminded her of her freedom, and called her back into Love. That's not a message of original sin – that's a message of original innocence, "you must become as a child enter the kingdom of heaven."

Even in his parables, Jeshua told stories of restoration, not condemnation. The prodigal son wasn't guilty by nature; he was lost by choice. And when he returned home, the father didn't scold him or tally up his sins. He threw a party. That's the Divine response: not guilt, but celebration. The entire story makes no sense if you start from the premise that the son was rotten from birth. Jeshua's whole point was that Love never stops welcoming you home.

Now, repetition here matters, because I want to drive it home: Jeshua never taught original sin. He taught original blessing. He taught that life itself is infused with divinity. He taught that Love fulfills the law, not ritual or guilt. And he demonstrated it over and over again, not just in words but in actions – touching the untouchable, forgiving the unforgivable, lifting burdens rather than adding them.

Contrast that with Augustine's invention. Augustine told us our very desires were corrupt. Jeshua told us, "Ask, and it will be given." Augustine said humanity is fallen. Jeshua said, "You will do even greater works than I." Augustine said we are guilty at birth. Jeshua said, "Unless you become like little children, you cannot enter the Kingdom." For Augustine, children were born stained. For Jeshua, children were the very model of innocence.

Let's pause and laugh a little. Imagine Jeshua listening in on a medieval sermon about original sin. Some priest stands up, booming, "All of humanity is depraved from the womb! We are worms, unworthy of God's Love!" Jeshua leans over to the guy next to him and says, "Worms? Did I say that? I thought I told them they were the light of the world. How did they get worms out of that?"

This is the danger of doctrine: it replaces lived experience with someone else's projection. Jeshua's lived message was empowerment. But Augustine's projection of his personal struggles became doctrine, and that doctrine drowned out Jeshua's words for centuries. It's like tuning a radio to the wrong frequency – the song is still being broadcast, but all you hear is static.

The beauty is that the message of Jeshua never actually went away. It's been there the whole time, waiting for us to tune back in. Every time you sit in stillness and listen for that inner voice, you're living Jeshua's message. Every time you choose Love over fear, you're embodying what he taught. Every time you recognize your worth instead of collapsing under guilt, you're walking in his Way.

And here's the kicker: Jeshua's message wasn't unique to him. Buddha said, "Be a lamp unto yourself." Lao Tzu said, "When you realize there is nothing lacking, the whole world belongs to you." Muhammad said, "God is closer to you than your jugular vein." All of these point inward, to the same truth: you are not broken, you are already whole. Original sin is the outlier here. It's the one message that doesn't belong in the great symphony of spiritual wisdom. It's the off-key trumpet ruining the orchestra.

So why did the Church pick the off-key trumpet? Because empowerment doesn't build empires. Dependency does. If you believe Jeshua — that you are divine, that you already have access to God, that Love is enough — then what do you need the Church for? You don't. And that's the real scandal of Jeshua's message: it made the middlemen irrelevant. No wonder they buried it.

Here's where I'll repeat myself one more time, because this book isn't about filling pages, it's about breaking chains: Jeshua never taught original sin. He taught original blessing, original Love, original wholeness. If you take only one thing from this section, let it be this: you are not guilty for existing. You never were. You never will be.

That is Jeshua's actual message.

How the Church Profited from Sin

If this were a courtroom drama, this would be the moment where the prosecutor stands up, clears his throat, and says, "Ladies and gentlemen of the jury, here is the smoking gun." Because once you understand the economics of original sin, everything else clicks into place. The doctrine wasn't just a theological misstep or an honest misunderstanding of scripture — it was a financial jackpot.

Let's go back to the basics of marketing. Rule number one: create a need. Rule number two: make yourself the exclusive supplier of the solution. Rule number three: keep people hooked.

Now tell me that doesn't sound like the Catholic Church's business model for 1600 years. The need? You're guilty from birth. The solution? Baptism, confession, penance, sacraments — all conveniently provided by the Church. And the hook? Fear of eternal damnation if you miss a payment, metaphorically or literally.

Think about baptism. Without original sin, baptism could be a beautiful ritual of community and belonging. But with original sin, it becomes a cosmic emergency. "Don't wait! Get that baby to the font before God notices they were born!" The Church created the crisis, then positioned itself as the ambulance service. And parents, terrified of their child's eternal fate, lined up. Every baby born became another guaranteed customer. Talk about job security.

Confession worked the same way. Imagine a subscription service where you constantly generate the product you're buying. That's confession. You sin, you feel guilty, you confess, you're absolved – until you sin again. Rinse and repeat. And because original sin framed humanity as fundamentally flawed, you could never escape the cycle. Even if you lived like a saint, you were still guilty by nature.

Confession became less about healing and more about renewing your spiritual subscription before it lapsed.

And then came indulgences. Now, indulgences were where the Church really got creative. "Sure, you've confessed, but let's hedge our bets. For a small donation, you can shave time off purgatory. Why suffer for centuries when you can pay now and upgrade to first-class salvation?" People handed over fortunes, not because they wanted to, but because fear made them feel they had to. Cathedrals like St. Peter's in Rome weren't built out of pure generosity. They were built on centuries of guilt-fueled fundraising.

Here's the humor in all of this: it's basically the spiritual version of AppleCare. You buy a shiny new soul at baptism, but don't worry – accidents (sins) happen. Better sign up for the extended warranty (confession and penance), and while you're at it, maybe throw in some accessories (indulgences) to guarantee peak performance in the afterlife. The only difference is, Apple never claimed your eternal destiny depended on the upgrade plan.

Now, some might say, "But John, surely they believed they were helping people." And maybe some did. I'm not here to demonize every priest who ever donned a collar. Many of them sincerely thought they were saving souls. But the institution as a whole? It knew exactly what it was doing. Fear was profitable. Guilt kept the coffers full. And the bigger the institution grew, the more it needed that revenue. Empires aren't built on voluntary Love offerings. They're built on systemic obligation.

Take tithing, for example. Ten percent of your income straight to the Church. Not optional. Not negotiable. And why would people hand over that much of their livelihood? Because if you're guilty from birth and the Church holds the keys to heaven, you don't argue with the doorman. You pay the cover charge. Better broke on earth than damned in eternity, right?

The political power followed naturally. Kings and emperors bent the knee because the Church controlled not just people's wallets, but their consciences. A ruler who defied Rome could be excommunicated, which meant his people were told they'd go to hell if they obeyed him. That's not just spiritual authority – that's political extortion. And it all rested on the foundation of original sin.

Let's pause and contrast this with Jeshua's actual message (and yes, I'll repeat it yet again because repetition here is medicine): Jeshua said the Kingdom of Heaven is within you. He said Love fulfills the law. He said forgiveness is free. None of those teachings can be monetized.

You can't build a multimillion-dollar cathedral on "You're already whole." But "You're guilty, and only we can fix you"? That's a billion- dollar idea.

I sometimes imagine Jeshua walking into St. Peter's Basilica, looking up at the gilded ceilings, the priceless art, the sheer opulence, and saying, "So let me get this straight. You built this with money you got by convincing people they were broken? And you did it in my name? Guys, I washed feet. How did you get this from me washing feet?"

The irony is painful, but it's also liberating once you see it. Because the moment you realize original sin was the ultimate sales pitch, you stop buying. You take your wallet, your conscience, and your soul back. You realize that Love can't be sold, presence can't be taxed, forgiveness can't be monopolized.

And here's the truth institutions don't want you to know: once people stop feeling guilty for being human, they stop needing permission to live. They stop tithing out of fear and start giving out of Love. They stop confessing to intermediaries and start confessing directly to themselves and God. They stop looking upward at thrones and start looking inward at their own divinity.

That shift terrifies institutions. Because free people can't be controlled. And so the myth of original sin continues to be preached, not because it's true but because it's useful.

So, let's state it clearly, one more time for the folks in the back: original sin was never about God's disappointment. It was about the

Church's profit. And until we name that truth, the cycle of guilt and gold keeps spinning.

The Cost of Believing You're Broken

By now, we've seen how original sin was born from Augustine's tortured psychology, how it became institutional gold, and how Jeshua's real message was buried under it all. But here's where the rubber meets the road: the personal cost. Because this doctrine doesn't just sit in theology books or church sermons. It burrows deep into human hearts and rewires lives. And the cost of believing you're broken is staggering.

Let's start with identity. From the moment you're told you're guilty at birth, your sense of self is shaped by that lie. Instead of waking up to life as a miracle, you wake up as a problem. You carry an invisible label: *unworthy.* And once that label sticks, it colors everything. Your decisions, your relationships, your ambitions – all of it gets filtered through the belief that you are defective.

I've met people who could not look in the mirror without hearing the echo of those early teachings. They didn't see a face. They saw failure. They saw disappointment. They saw sin. And that belief led them to sabotage themselves over and over. "Why try? I'm broken anyway." "Why dream? I don't deserve it." "Why love myself? I'm not worthy." That's the inner soundtrack of original sin.

And it doesn't stop at self-image. It seeps into how you treat your body. If you've been told that even your natural impulses – hunger, desire, curiosity – are suspect, then you start distrusting the very vessel you live in. Food becomes a battlefield of fasting and guilt.

Sexuality becomes a source of shame instead of intimacy. Joy becomes suspicious, as if laughter is one step away from damnation. Instead of embracing your humanity, you wage war against it.

I sometimes wonder what heaven must look like if the doctrine of original sin were literally true. A bunch of saints sitting around, sipping holy water, saying, "Man, I'm so glad we spent our entire earthly lives feeling miserable. Totally worth it." Meanwhile, Jeshua is in the corner muttering, "I told you to Love one another. Where did you get all this misery from?"

But here's the painful part: people live entire lives like this. They stay in toxic relationships because they think suffering is holy. They let abuse continue because they believe they deserve punishment. They never pursue their gifts because they think ambition is pride. Original sin doesn't just break theology — it breaks people.

And the damage is generational. Parents pass it to children, not always through explicit words, but through subtle cues. A child who sees their parents living under guilt absorbs it like secondhand smoke. It becomes the family atmosphere: don't trust yourself, don't enjoy too much, don't step out of line. Before you know it, three or four generations are chained to the same lie, wondering why joy feels so foreign.

Now let's talk about society. A culture built on the belief that people are broken will inevitably create systems of control. Laws become punitive instead of restorative. Leaders govern by fear instead of trust.

Communities organize around suspicion instead of Love. If you think people are inherently depraved, then of course you'll design institutions to keep them in line. The doctrine of original sin doesn't just haunt individuals — it shapes civilizations.

And all of this — every ounce of suffering, shame, and smallness — comes from believing a story. A story about two people, a tree, and a piece of fruit. A story that was twisted, institutionalized, and handed down as fact. A story that could have been left as myth but instead became a chain.

Here's where I circle back to Jeshua, because repetition here is salvation: Jeshua never told you that you were broken. He told you that you were beLoved. He never said you were unworthy. He said you were the light of the world. He never condemned you for being human. He celebrated humanity as the vessel of divinity. The cost of believing otherwise is nothing less than your life wasted under lies.

So let's name it clearly. The cost of believing you're broken is:

- A fractured self-image.
- Distrust of your own body and desires.
- Generational chains of guilt.
- Societal systems built on control.
- The theft of joy.

- The silencing of your true voice.

And here's the kicker: the longer you carry it, the heavier it gets. What begins as a theological idea grows into a psychological weight, then into a cultural norm, until eventually people can't even imagine life without it. That's the real danger. When lies become so normalized that truth feels radical.

But the good news — and there is always good news — is that this cost doesn't have to be paid forever. The bill can be torn up. The label can be peeled off. The lie can be exposed. And once you see the cost clearly, you have the power to stop paying it.

That's where we're headed next.

Practices for Reclaiming Innocence

By now, you're thinking that it's one thing to intellectually reject original sin. You can nod your head, laugh at Augustine's hang-ups, agree that the Church profited from guilt. But knowing isn't enough. Centuries of programming don't unravel just because you read a chapter. To really reclaim innocence, you need practices. Simple, daily ways to unlearn the lie and live the truth.

The first practice is **rewriting the story.** Take out a note pad and write your own creation myth. Not one where you're guilty for fruit you never ate, but one where you are born from Love. Picture God saying, "You are my beLoved child, and in you I am well pleased." Write it until it feels true, because it *is* true. Stories shape us — so tell yourself a better one.

The second practice is **visualization.** Sit quietly and picture yourself as a newborn. See the innocence in your own face. See the purity in your own eyes. Then imagine a priest rushing toward you with a bucket of water, shouting about sin. And laugh. Laugh at the absurdity. Laugh until the chains loosen. Because humor is holy medicine, and laughter is one of the fastest ways to dissolve guilt.

The third practice is **declaration.** Simple words can rewire a lifetime of lies. Say this often: *I was born whole. I live whole. I am enough."* Say it when guilt whispers. Say it when shame knocks. Say it until the words stop feeling foreign and start feeling like home.

The fourth practice is what I call **sitting in Love.** Forget doctrine, forget ritual, forget Augustine. Just sit quietly, exhale, and feel Love. Let it expand in your chest. Let it flow outward. Don't try to deserve it. Don't try to earn it. Just feel it. That's innocence in action. That's original blessing reclaiming its place.

And finally, **practice confession** to yourself. Not to a priest. To yourself. Sit down and admit where you've believed lies. Admit where you've carried guilt that wasn't yours. Admit where you've let shame make decisions for you. And then forgive yourself. Out loud. That's what Jeshua would have wanted – not obedience to a system, but liberation of the soul.

These practices aren't complicated. That's the point. Guilt thrives on complication. Innocence thrives on simplicity. And when you practice them, you'll start to notice the shift: lighter shoulders, freer laughter, a quieter mind. That's what it feels like to remember the truth.

We've traveled far in this chapter. We saw how the story of a fruit in a garden became the foundation of a doctrine. We saw how Augustine's struggles became humanity's burden. We saw how guilt was institutionalized and monetized. We contrasted it with Jeshua's actual message of Love and presence. We named the staggering cost of believing you're broken. And we offered practices to reclaim innocence.

Here's the truth worth repeating until it sinks deep: you were never guilty for being born. You were never broken at your core. You were never defective in the eyes of God. That was a story told to control you. A story that profited institutions but stole joy from individuals.

Jeshua's message was always the opposite. You are light. You are Loved. You are whole. The Kingdom is within you. No doctrine, no priest, no ritual required. Just you and the Divine, already united.

Chapter 1 taught us to recognize the weight of doctrine. Chapter 2 exposed the heaviest brick in that bag: original sin. And now, having set it down, we stand lighter, freer, ready to step into the chapters ahead. Because the story isn't about being broken – it's about remembering the wholeness we never lost.

Chapter 8: Escaping the Shadow of Guilt

Naming the Shadow

By the time you've grown up Catholic (or under any guilt-heavy religion), guilt doesn't just feel like something you carry, it feels like part of who you are. It's the shadow that follows you into every decision, every relationship, every quiet moment. Even after you've consciously rejected the doctrine of original sin, the residue lingers. You know the theology is nonsense, but the psychology? That takes longer to wash off.

That's why the first step in escaping guilt's grip is naming it for what it is: a shadow, not your essence.

Let's go back for a moment. We traced how Augustine's tortured relationship with his own humanity metastasized into a doctrine that made everyone else guilty, too. We saw how the Church institutionalized guilt, monetized it, and weaponized it. And we explored the staggering cost of believing you were broken from birth. But here's the tricky part: just because you intellectually reject a lie doesn't mean you've fully uprooted it. Lies have a way of embedding themselves deep, especially when they're reinforced by family, community, and culture.

So here's the work: you've got to shine a light on guilt and call it out. You have to notice when guilt is speaking, and when truth is speaking. And often, the only way you can tell the difference is by how it feels.

Guilt feels heavy. It constricts your chest. It whispers in that nagging tone: "Don't do that, who do you think you are? You should feel bad." Truth feels light. It expands your chest. It whispers in a gentle, affirming way: "Yes, you can. You are enough. You are Loved." One voice shrinks you. The other liberates you. Both can sound convincing, but only one is real.

When I first started confronting my own guilt, I was shocked at how sneaky it was. It wasn't just about big "sins" like missing Mass or breaking commandments. It showed up in ordinary moments.

Enjoying a lazy afternoon? "You're wasting time." Laughing too loud at a joke? "That's frivolous." Saying no to someone's request? "You're selfish." That's how guilt works: it creeps into every corner, convincing you that being fully human is somehow a crime.

This is why I call it a distortion. It doesn't create anything new – it just distorts what's already there. Stand in sunlight, and you're radiant.

Step into guilt, and suddenly you doubt the very light you're casting. But here's the liberating truth: shadows only exist when there's light. The fact that guilt hounds you means there's already light in you. You wouldn't have a shadow if you weren't already radiant.

Now let's loop back to Jeshua, because he understood shadows better than anyone. His whole ministry was about naming illusions and lifting burdens. "You are the light of the world," he said. Not "You are worms, groveling in guilt." Light of the world. But what does guilt do? It convinces you to hide that light under a basket. It says, "Don't shine too bright. Don't love too boldly. Don't laugh too freely. Stay small, stay ashamed." And Jeshua says, "Nonsense. Let your light shine."

Other great teachers echo this same wisdom. Buddha warned against clinging to unhelpful beliefs. Lao Tzu reminded us that when you realize nothing is lacking, the whole world belongs to you. Muhammad emphasized God's nearness, closer than your own jugular. None of them said, "You're guilty for being alive." The shadow of guilt is the exception, not the rule, in spiritual wisdom.

I sometimes imagine guilt as that annoying neighbor who always has something to say. You mow your lawn? "Too short." You leave it? "Too long." You wave? "Too fake." You ignore them? "Too rude." You can't win, because the neighbor isn't interested in truth – they're interested in nagging. That's guilt. And the only way to deal with it isn't to keep arguing. It's to realize you don't have to live by their commentary. You can close the blinds, turn up the music, and dance anyway.

But here's the hard part: many people mistake guilt for God's voice. They think that heavy, constricting whisper is divine disapproval.

That's the deepest wound of original sin – confusing institutional programming with spiritual truth. Jeshua warned about this when he confronted the Pharisees, who piled burdens on people but didn't lift a finger to help. He made it clear: God doesn't speak in condemnation. Love doesn't shame. Presence doesn't punish.

So what does it look like to name the shadow in your life? It looks like catching guilt in the act. When you feel that old heaviness creeping in, pause. Ask yourself, "Is this voice shrinking me or expanding me? Is it condemning me or inviting me?" Nine times out of ten, if it's condemning, it's the shadow. If it's inviting, it's truth.

For example:

- You rest instead of working overtime. Distortion says: "Lazy." Truth says: "You deserve rest."
- You follow joy instead of obligation. Distortion says: "Irresponsible." Truth says: "Joy is holy."
- You say no to something that drains you. Distortion says: "Selfish." Truth says: "Boundaries are Love."

The more you practice noticing, the clearer it becomes. The distortion loses its grip once you call it by name.

Here's the empowering repetition: You are not guilty for being human. You never were. That's the lie of original sin. The distortion may whisper otherwise, but every breath of Love, every laugh, every moment of joy proves it wrong.

Naming the shadow doesn't make it vanish overnight. But it robs it of its power. Once you see guilt for what it is – a leftover story, not a divine decree – you can step out of its shade and back into the sunlight of your true self.

And that's the first step in escaping the shadow of guilt.

The Chains of Fear

If guilt is the shadow, then fear is the chain that keeps you from stepping out of it. Guilt tells you, "You're wrong," and fear hisses, "And if you don't obey, you'll pay." The two are inseparable. Original sin would never have worked as a doctrine if it were just about feeling bad. What made it stick was the terrifying promise of punishment – eternal, unending, unimaginably painful punishment.

Hell. Fire. Brimstone. The whole Dante's Inferno package deal. And let's be honest: what better way to scare people into compliance than to dangle eternal torture over their heads? Fear became the enforcement mechanism of guilt. Guilt whispered, "You're broken," and fear shouted, "And if you don't get fixed,

God's going to barbecue you forever." Talk about a one-two punch.

As a kid, I absorbed this like secondhand smoke. Priests didn't even have to preach fire and brimstone every week – the fear was already baked into the atmosphere. Miss Mass on Sunday? Mortal sin. Mortal sin equals hell. Even if you were sick, even if you were exhausted, even if your parents forgot to drive you – didn't matter. Hell. One wrong step and the eternal flames were waiting. That's a heavy load for a child to carry. I used to wonder if God had a giant chalkboard in heaven, marking down every misstep in big, permanent strokes. "Talked back to Mom – strike one. Didn't finish the rosary – strike two. Thought about kissing that girl in class – strike three, eternal damnation."

And let's not forget purgatory. Because apparently hell wasn't scary enough, so they invented an in-between holding tank of suffering. It's the cosmic DMV, where you sit in eternal fluorescent lighting until your paperwork clears. And of course, the Church had a solution for that too: indulgences, Masses for the dead, prayers, donations. Fear made sure the line for indulgences was always full.

The psychology of fear is fascinating. When you live in fear, your brain goes into survival mode. Fight, flight, freeze. But in religion, fear rarely produces fight. You don't punch back at God. Flight isn't an option either – where would you run? Freeze becomes the default. You shrink, you obey, you try not to make waves. And that's exactly what institutions want: a population frozen in compliance.

Back to Jeshua...did he ever use fear as a motivator? Not once. He spoke of Love, of presence, of forgiveness. Even when he used strong language – like warning about "weeping and gnashing of teeth" – he was pointing to the natural consequences of living in fear and separation, not a divine torture chamber. He was describing what it feels like to live disconnected from Love, not what God plans to do with a giant cosmic blowtorch.

But Augustine and his successors? They leaned hard into fear. Because fear sells. Fear keeps people in line. Fear makes sure they show up, pay up, and shut up. And once fear is mixed with guilt, you have a psychological cocktail that can keep entire populations subdued for centuries.

Now here's the thing: fear doesn't just live in church pews. Once it's installed, it shows up everywhere. Fear of failure. Fear of rejection. Fear of being "not enough." Those aren't random anxieties – they're echoes of that primal programming that said, "You are guilty, and the punishment is waiting." Even outside religion, people drag the chains of fear through careers, marriages, parenting. They never trust themselves fully because they're haunted by the suspicion that they'll screw it up – and the consequences will be dire.

If God really wanted us to live in fear of eternal punishment, He could've just created an IRS that never closes. Eternal audits, endless forms, penalties that never end. That's what hell would look like for most of us. Instead, we were given life, laughter, beauty, sunsets, and bacon. Yet somehow, religion convinced us the main course was torment.

Here's the deeper tragedy: fear shrinks Love. When you're afraid, you can't Love freely. You can't laugh fully. You can't create boldly. Fear makes you cautious, hesitant, always looking over your shoulder. And Love – real Love – doesn't thrive in that environment. Jeshua's entire teaching was about casting out fear. "Perfect Love casts out fear," said the author of 1 John. But the Church flipped it. They used fear to cast out Love.

So how do you break these chains? Yoda said, "Named must your fears be before banish them you can." You start by noticing them. Ask yourself: where is fear running my life? Is it in my spirituality? My relationships? My work? Do I avoid joy because I fear it's frivolous? Do I avoid risks because I fear rejection? Do I avoid trusting myself because I fear being wrong? Every one of those fears is an echo of the original programming. And the first step in breaking a chain is realizing you're wearing one.

Then, you call it what it is: a lie. Not divine truth. Not God's voice. A lie told by people who profited from your fear. A lie reinforced by repetition until it felt like reality. A lie that loses its grip the moment you laugh at it. Because here's the secret: fear can't survive laughter. Fear needs solemnity, seriousness, reverence. But the moment you chuckle and say, "Really? Eternal flames over missing Mass? That's ridiculous," the chain weakens. Humor is bolt cutters for fear.

And again, repetition matters: Jeshua never taught fear. He taught Love. He never said, "Be afraid of hell." He said, "Fear not, for I am with you." He never said, "Tremble before God's wrath." He said, "Come to me, all who are weary, and I will give you rest." If you hear fear, it's not Jeshua's voice.

So let's name it clearly: the chains of fear are man-made. They were forged in the fires of Augustine's guilt and the Church's hunger for control. They are not your inheritance. Your inheritance is Love, joy, freedom. And every time you choose Love over fear, you snap another link in the chain.

That's how you begin to escape the shadow of guilt.

Reclaiming the Inner Child

Jeshua said something radical that still gets overlooked: *Unless you become like little children, you cannot enter the Kingdom of Heaven."* Notice what he didn't say. He didn't say, "Unless you memorize doctrine." He didn't say, "Unless you confess every week." He didn't say, "Unless you carry the weight of guilt for Adam and Eve." No, he pointed to children. Innocent. Joyful. Free. The exact opposite of what the doctrine of original sin teaches.

This is where we start finding the cure for guilt and fear: by reclaiming the part of us that remembers what innocence feels like. Because here's the truth – innocence isn't something you lost. It's something you were convinced to forget. And the only way back isn't through penance, but through presence. It's about peeling away the layers of guilt until the childlike heart underneath can breathe again.

Let's talk about children for a moment. Watch a toddler in action. They don't worry about whether God approves of their laughter. They don't second-guess whether they're "worthy" of running in the yard. They don't calculate how their joy looks to the neighbors. They simply *are.*

They laugh, they cry, they dance, they fall, they get back up. No guilt. No shame. Just presence. That's innocence in action. That's what Jeshua was pointing to.

So why did the Church turn children into sinners? Why invent the idea that a baby is born guilty? Because innocence is uncontrollable. A child's freedom threatens institutions that run on obedience. If people lived with that same spontaneity, that same trust, that same joy – you couldn't scare them into confession booths or tithe boxes. You couldn't herd them with fear of hell. They'd be too busy living in the Kingdom that's already within them.

Imagine telling a baby they're guilty of original sin. "Sorry, little one, I know you just got here, but you're already on probation. Try not to coo too loud, or God might get mad." The absurdity of it reveals the lie.

Children don't carry sin. They carry life.

The problem is, by the time we reach adulthood, we've been layered over with so much guilt and fear that we forget what that freedom feels like. The inner child gets buried under "shoulds" and "should nots." Should be serious. Shouldn't be too joyful. Should be obedient. Shouldn't ask too many questions. The innocence is still there, but it's trapped.

This is why reclaiming the inner child isn't just a cute psychological exercise – it's a spiritual revolution. Every time you laugh freely, you defy guilt. Every time you create for the joy of creating, you snap a chain of fear. Every time you let yourself rest, play, sing, or dance without apology, you're living Jeshua's message more than a thousand rosaries ever could.

Here's the deeper truth: your inner child never stopped trusting. It never stopped believing in Love. It never stopped shining. It just got locked in a basement by doctrines that convinced you joy was suspicious. Reclaiming that child means unlocking the door, letting them out, and saying, "Go ahead, laugh again. Run again. Love again."

Practical example: Try remembering a moment from your own childhood where you felt pure joy. Maybe it was riding a bike, catching fireflies, or eating ice cream on a summer day. Close your eyes and really recall it. Feel it in your body. That joy wasn't sinful. That laughter wasn't guilty. That was your natural state – and it still is. You didn't lose it. You just stopped giving it permission.

Jeshua understood this. That's why he gathered children around him, blessing them when everyone else dismissed them. He wasn't being sentimental – he was pointing out a spiritual truth. Children live in the present. They trust. They Love without calculation. They embody what the Kingdom looks like. And if we want to escape the shadow of guilt, we have to remember that way of being.

Now, this doesn't mean becoming childish. Jeshua wasn't telling us to throw tantrums in grocery stores. He was pointing to *childlikeness* – openness, wonder, presence.

Childishness avoids responsibility. Childlikeness embraces life with trust. The Church confused the two, branding childlikeness as naïve and replacing it with rigid adulthood. But rigidity isn't maturity – it's fear dressed up in robes.

Let's repeat the contrast, because it's crucial.

- Original sin says: You're born guilty.
- Jeshua says: Be like children.
- Original sin says: Fear your humanity.
- Jeshua says: Trust your humanity.
- Original sin says: Obey the hierarchy.
- Jeshua says: The Kingdom is already within you.

The difference couldn't be more stark.

So how do we reclaim the inner child practically? By practicing presence and play. Laugh without reason. Dance without choreography. Sing off-key. Rest without guilt. These aren't trivial acts, they're spiritual practices. Every moment of joy is an act of rebellion against guilt. Every burst of laughter is a sermon louder than any priest's homily. Every time you trust your inner child, you proclaim the truth Jeshua lived: you are already whole.

And here's the final point: reclaiming the inner child heals more than yourself. It heals the people around you. Joy is contagious. Innocence is magnetic. When you live from that place, you remind others of their own buried child. You give them permission to breathe, to laugh, to Love. In a world haunted by guilt and fear, nothing is more revolutionary than a free human being who dares to be as unselfconscious as a child.

So let's name it clearly: reclaiming the inner child is not regression. It's progression. It's the next step after tearing down guilt and breaking fear. It's what Jeshua invited us into all along. Innocence isn't something you need to regain from God. It's something you need to remember in yourself.

That's the heart of escaping the shadow of guilt. And that's why we start here.

Love as the Antidote

By now we've named the shadow of guilt, we've rattled the chains of fear, and we've brought the inner child back into the sunlight. But here's the turning point – the force that dissolves all of it: Love. Not the Hallmark card kind. Not the sentimental, flowers-and-roses variety. I'm talking about the deep, unconditional current of Love that Jeshua lived and breathed. Love as an antidote to guilt. Love as a cure for fear. Love as the original medicine for the human soul.

Let's be honest: guilt and fear have no natural predators – except Love. Logic can poke holes in doctrine, history can expose Augustine's hang-ups, humor can make the absurd laughable, but only Love changes the heart. Only Love lifts the burden. Only Love convinces the nervous system that it's safe to breathe again. You can't reason your way out of guilt's grip completely. You can't argue fear into silence. But the moment Love enters, guilt and fear scatter like cockroaches when the light turns on.

And Jeshua knew it. His entire teaching can be summed up in one line: *"Love one another."* That wasn't a suggestion for better manners. That was the operating system for the Kingdom. Because Love dissolves shame. Love unravels lies. Love tells the truth louder than guilt ever can.

Now let's revisit how guilt works, because repetition sharpens clarity.

Guilt whispers, "You are not enough." Love answers, "You are beLoved."

Fear says, "You're in danger." Love responds, "You're safe."

Guilt says, "You must pay." Love says, "There's nothing owed."

Every line of doctrine that has been used to keep humanity in chains can be undone by a single act of Love.

Now about the woman caught in adultery: The law said she should be stoned. The crowd stood ready, rocks in hand, fueled by guilt and fear. Jeshua stepped in and said, "Let the one without sin throw the first stone." The crowd melted away. And to the woman he said, "Neither do I condemn you." That's Love as antidote. Not permission for more mistakes, but freedom from condemnation. Love stopped the punishment, Love dissolved the guilt, Love opened the path forward.

Or think of Zacchaeus, the tax collector. Everyone despised him. He was guilty in the eyes of the community. Jeshua didn't lecture him. He didn't shame him. He simply said, "I'm coming to your house today." That one act of Love transformed Zacchaeus. He gave back what he had stolen, not because he was terrified of hell, but because Love had opened his heart. That's how transformation works. Fear coerces compliance. Love inspires change.

Now, here's the part most institutions miss: Love can't be controlled. You can't regulate it. You can't turn it into a checklist. You can't monetize it. And that's why the doctrine of original sin had to bury it. Love makes priests unnecessary. Love makes confession booths redundant. Love makes fear-based obedience laughable. If you know you're already Loved unconditionally, the whole system collapses.

But here's the challenge: Love feels dangerous when you've been conditioned by guilt. Think about it. If you've been told all your life that you're broken, then unconditional Love feels... suspicious. "Surely I have to earn this. Surely there's a catch. Surely God Loves me, but only if I behave." That's the programming talking. Love without condition feels too good to be true. But here's the irony: it's the only thing that actually *is* true.

Imagine going to confession and saying, "Bless me, Father, for I have Loved myself and others today. I laughed without guilt, rested without shame, and forgave myself without penance." The priest would probably faint. Because Love makes the whole apparatus obsolete.

And once you get a taste of it, you realize how silly the old system was.

Love as the antidote also changes how we deal with ourselves. Guilt beats us up for every mistake. Love embraces the mistake as part of learning. Fear warns us not to try. Love encourages us to leap. Guilt says, "You're not holy enough." Love says, "Holiness is just being fully alive." That's why Jeshua healed so freely – he wasn't checking doctrinal credentials. He was responding in Love. And the moment Love touched people, they were transformed.

Here's the practical side: how do you practice Love as the antidote? Start by turning it inward. For many of us, self-Love is the hardest Love of all. We've been told it's pride, arrogance, selfishness. But self-Love is the root. If you can't Love yourself, guilt will always find a way back in. Every morning, look in the mirror and say, "I am Loved. I am enough. I am innocent." Not because you've earned it, but because it's the truth.

Then extend it outward. Not through obligation, not through "should," but through presence. Smile at someone without needing them to smile back. Forgive someone without waiting for an apology. Give freely without keeping score. These aren't pious acts to rack up heavenly points. They're ways to live in alignment with the truth that Love is who you are.

And here's where we circle back again, because the drumbeat must continue: Jeshua never used guilt as medicine. He used Love. He never motivated with fear. He motivated with compassion. He never told people they were broken. He told them they were beLoved. If there's one antidote to the doctrine of original sin, it's Love. Radical, unconditional, uncontainable Love.

So let's name it clearly. Guilt lies. Fear chains. Love heals. And every time you choose Love, you dismantle centuries of programming. Every time you Love yourself without condition, you undo Augustine's hang- up. Every time you Love someone else without judgment, you overturn the tables of religious control.

Love is the antidote. And once you taste it, you'll never settle for guilt again.

The Courage to Live Free

By now, the pattern should be clear: guilt was the shadow, fear was the chain, and Love is the antidote. But here's the twist – knowing all that is one thing. *Living* it is another. It takes courage to actually walk free after years (or decades) of conditioning. Freedom sounds wonderful in theory, but in practice it's terrifying, because the old chains, heavy as they were, also felt familiar. And the familiar, no matter how miserable, can feel safer than the unknown.

Let me put it this way: imagine a prisoner who's been in a cell for 40 years. One day, the door swings open. No guards. No locks. Just freedom. You'd think they'd run for the hills, right? But often, they hesitate. Because outside the cell, there's no schedule, no routine, no predictable rules. There's responsibility. There's choice. There's the terrifying possibility of living on your own terms. That's what it's like leaving behind the doctrine of original sin. The door is open, but walking through it requires courage.

When I first began disentangling myself from Catholic guilt, I remember feeling almost... rebellious. Like I was sneaking out at night, breaking curfew, doing something illegal. Resting without guilt felt like a crime. Laughing without shame felt scandalous. Trusting myself felt downright heretical. And that's when I realized how deep the programming ran. Freedom required more than awareness. It required courage.

Why courage? Because guilt and fear don't just evaporate. They push back. They whisper, "Are you sure? What if you're wrong? What if God is angry?" Those echoes of old sermons don't vanish overnight. They haunt you like ghosts, trying to lure you back into the cell. And the only way forward is to meet them with courage. Not bravado. Not denial.

But the steady, quiet courage that says, "I hear you — and I'm walking anyway."

Now, here's the irony: courage itself is a form of Love. Because every act of courage is rooted in choosing Love over fear. Courage to rest is Love for your body. Courage to laugh is Love for your joy. Courage to trust yourself is Love for your divinity. Courage isn't about slaying dragons or storming castles. It's about choosing Love in the face of fear, again and again, until the old voices lose their grip.

And let's not romanticize it — courage is messy. Some days you'll feel bold, other days you'll crawl. Some days you'll laugh at guilt, other days guilt will sucker-punch you in the gut. That's normal. Courage isn't perfection. Courage is persistence. It's showing up one more time than fear knocks you down.

Let's bring Jeshua back into this (and yes, I'll keep repeating him because his words cut through centuries of lies). Jeshua didn't promise a life free of struggle. He promised a life free of condemnation. "Fear not," he said, "for I am with you." Notice that: not "for the institution is with you," but *I am with you.* The courage to live free comes from remembering that presence. Not the presence of doctrine, but the presence of Love that never leaves.

And Jeshua modeled courage himself. Think about it. He stood against the most powerful religious institution of his time. He called out hypocrisy. He broke Sabbath rules to heal people. He ate with outcasts. He Loved the unlovable. And he did it knowing it could cost him everything. That's courage. Not because he Loved suffering, but because he Loved freedom. He knew the Kingdom couldn't be built on fear. It had to be built on Love, and that required someone to stand up and say, "Enough."

Here's where courage gets practical. It looks like saying no when guilt says yes. It looks like resting when fear says work harder. It looks like choosing joy when doctrine says mourn. It looks like trusting your intuition when authority says you can't. These may sound small, but they're acts of spiritual revolution. Every time you do them, you chip away at centuries of programming.

The first time I skipped confession after realizing the system was bogus, I half expected a thunderbolt. I walked outside, looked up at the sky, and thought, "Alright, God, this is your chance." Nothing. No lightning. No ground opening up. Just silence – and maybe a chuckle from the heavens. That's when I knew: the danger was never real.

The chains were smoke. Courage just meant daring to test them.

The biggest lie guilt tells is that freedom is dangerous. That if you stop obeying, you'll fall apart. But the opposite is true. Freedom is the soil where your soul finally grows. Yes, it takes courage to plant your roots in that soil. Yes, it feels risky. But once you do, you'll wonder how you ever mistook the cage for a sanctuary.

And courage isn't just for yourself. When you live free, you give others permission to do the same. People see your laughter, your peace, your lightness, and something stirs in them. They think, "Maybe I could be free too." That ripple effect is unstoppable. Courage breeds courage. Freedom spreads like wildfire.

So let's repeat the heartbeat of this section: The door is open. The chains are broken. But walking into freedom requires courage.

Courage to Love yourself when guilt says you can't. Courage to trust life when fear says you shouldn't. Courage to live as Jeshua taught – in presence, in Love, in joy.

And the more you walk, the lighter it gets. The shadow of guilt grows dimmer. The chains of fear rust away. And Love – the true core of your being – becomes the atmosphere you breathe.

That's the courage to live free.

Practices of Freedom

Awareness is the spark. Courage is the engine. But practices? Practices are the fuel that keep you moving forward on the path of freedom. You can reject guilt intellectually, laugh at fear spiritually, and embrace Love emotionally – but without daily grounding, the old programming has a way of sneaking back in. Practices are how you retrain your nervous system, your mind, and your soul to live in the reality Jeshua actually pointed to: Love, presence, and freedom.

And let's be clear: these practices aren't complicated. Religion loves complication. It loves robes, rituals, rules, and requirements. But freedom thrives on simplicity. Jeshua's whole way was simple: sit, Love, forgive, be present. You don't need incense, stained glass, or holy water on tap. You just need to practice truth until it feels more natural than lies.

So let's lay out some practices of freedom – tools you can use to dismantle guilt, dissolve fear, and embody Love.

1. **Write it: Naming and Releasing Guilt**

Start with a pen and paper. Write down every rule, doctrine, or belief that still makes you feel heavy. "I must go to Mass every week." "I should pray this way." "I am sinful by nature." Whatever echoes of guilt you still hear, put them on the page. Naming them takes away their power.

Then, beside each one, write the truth. "The Kingdom of Heaven is within me." "Love is my true prayer." "I was born whole." This isn't just an exercise in words – it's reprogramming. You're training your mind to recognize guilt as a shadow and replace it with light.

2. **See it: Returning the Backpack**

Remember the metaphor from an earlier chapter – doctrine as a heavy backpack of guilt bricks? Here's a practice: Close your eyes, imagine yourself carrying that bag. Feel the weight on your shoulders. Then picture yourself walking up to the institution that handed it to you, whether the Church, the priest, Augustine himself if you like, and set it down. Say out loud, "This was never mine." Then walk away lighter. Do this as often as needed until the image of you burden-free becomes more natural than the image of you weighed down.

3. **Declare it: Replacing the Tape**

Guilt is like a bad cassette tape playing the same lies on repeat: "Not enough, not worthy, not holy." Declarations are how you record over that tape. Try these:

- *"I was born whole."*
- *"Love is my true nature."*
- *"The Kingdom of Heaven is within me."*
- *"I am free from guilt, fear, and shame."*

Say them in the morning, say them when guilt whispers, say them until your nervous system relaxes into them. Create a pattern interrupt of belief as a declaration. Negate any thought that is in conflict with your declaration until your declaration is your truth. Science says a new habit is formed somewhere between 21 and 60 days of continual action.

4. **Sitting in Love: Presence Without Performance**

Forget structured prayer for a moment. Forget checklists. Try this: sit quietly, exhale fully, relax your body, and just feel Love. Let it expand in your chest. Let it radiate outward. No words, no rules, no "doing it right." Just sitting in Love. This is one of the simplest – and most powerful – practices of freedom. It's what Jeshua meant when he said, "the Father and I are one." Not rules, but relationships.

5. **Confess it: Forgiveness Without Intermediaries**

Confession was never about telling a priest your sins. At its core, it was about releasing guilt. You don't need a booth or a collar for that. Try this: Sit down with yourself and admit where you've believed lies. Admit where you've carried guilt that wasn't yours. Admit where you let fear dictate your choices. Then, forgive yourself out loud. Not because you've earned it, but because Love demands it. That's freedom.

Play: Practicing Innocence

Play is spiritual warfare against guilt. It's how you reclaim the inner child. Dance in your kitchen. Sing in the shower. Paint something terrible. Build a sandcastle. Wrestle with your dog. Play reminds you that joy isn't sinful – it's sacred. Every laugh is an act of rebellion against Augustine's hang-ups. Every silly moment is proof you've remembered who you are.

1. **Service: Love in Action**

Freedom isn't just about you — it's about what flows through you. When you serve from Love, without obligation, you embody Jeshua's message. Cook a meal for a neighbor. Listen deeply to a friend. Smile at a stranger. Service without guilt is joy. It's not about earning points for heaven. It's about expanding heaven here and now.

2. **Humor: Laughing at the Lie**

Never underestimate the power of humor. Fear hates laughter. Guilt despises joy. Every time you chuckle at the absurdity of being condemned for eating bacon on Friday, you loosen the chains. Every time you tell a joke about confession lines or indulgence sales, you reclaim your power. Humor isn't disrespect. It's holy resistance. It says, "Your lie is ridiculous, and I refuse to bow to it." Remember in a laugh are the two key elements of every big spiritual experience. You are completely present and completely fearless.

3. **Daily Reflection: Love or Fear?**

At the end of each day, ask yourself one question: Did I act more from Love or from fear today? No judgment. No guilt. Just noticing. The more you notice, the more you'll naturally choose Love. And the more you choose Love, the freer you become.

These practices aren't about creating new obligations. They're about cultivating freedom until it becomes natural. Religion made spirituality heavy. Jeshua made it light. These practices are your way of remembering that lightness.

And yes, I'll repeat it for the drumbeat of this book: You are not guilty. You are not broken. You don't need saving from yourself. You need remembering of yourself. And practices of freedom are how you do that day by day, step by step, until the shadow fades, the chains fall, and Love is the air you breathe.

Stepping Into the Light

We've spent this chapter naming the shadow, rattling the chains, reclaiming innocence, and practicing freedom. Now comes the part Jeshua always pointed to — stepping into the light. Because escaping guilt isn't just about rejecting lies. It's about embracing truth so fully that the lies no longer have any power over you. It's about moving from survival mode to creation mode, from fear to joy, from bondage to freedom.

Let's pause and remember the journey so far. We recognized the crushing weight of doctrine. We exposed the heaviest brick in that burden: original sin. Here, we've traced how guilt became a shadow, how fear became a chain, how innocence was buried, how Love heals, how courage sustains, and how practices keep us grounded. That repetition matters, because the old voices will keep repeating themselves too. Doctrine doesn't go quietly. Guilt doesn't resign politely. Fear doesn't wave a white flag. They linger. And so you counter them with your own repetition: You are whole. You are Loved. You are free.

Stepping into the light begins with permission. Permission to be who you already are without apology. Permission to laugh without worrying if heaven is keeping score. Permission to rest without guilt, to create without fear, to Love without condition. It's not about becoming perfect. It's about becoming real. And reality, at its core, is already holy.

Jeshua used to say, *"You are the light of the world."* He didn't mean someday, after enough rituals or sacrifices. He meant now. Already. The only thing left is to stop hiding it under a basket of guilt and fear. Stepping into the light is uncovering what was never lost.

So what does it look like in practice? It looks like simple, human things, because that's where divinity shows up. You step into the light when you look someone in the eye and see their humanity without judgment. You step into the light when you forgive yourself for mistakes and keep moving forward. You step into the light when you allow joy to be sacred, when you allow laughter to be prayer, when you allow Love to be your doctrine.

The light is not somewhere else. It's not waiting in a cathedral or a monastery. It's here, now, within you. That's why guilt had to be invented in the first place – to distract you from the obvious truth that you were always enough. The shadow existed only to make you doubt the sun that never stopped shining.

I sometimes imagine God watching humanity trudge around under guilt, shaking His head and saying, "I gave them sunsets, music, laughter, and chocolate – and they think I'm mad about bacon on Friday? Somebody needs to tell them the light switch was never off."

Stepping into the light doesn't mean you'll never hear the old voices again. You will. They'll whisper. They'll try to pull you back. But the difference is, you'll know they're shadows. You'll recognize them as echoes of Augustine's neuroses and institutional power plays, not divine decrees. And the moment you see them for what they are, they lose their grip.

This is why practices matter – not to earn Love, but to remember Love. This is why courage matters – not to prove yourself, but to live yourself. This is why Love matters – not as an obligation, but as oxygen. Every time you choose presence over guilt, joy over fear, Love over shame, you step further into the light.

And once you're in the light, something beautiful happens: you become a light for others. Jeshua didn't say, "You *might* be the light of the world if you behave." He said, "You *are* the light of the world." That means your freedom illuminates others' paths. Your laughter gives permission. Your joy spreads. Your courage inspires. The shadow loses its reach when even one person dares to shine.

So let's name the closing truth of this chapter clearly: You were never guilty at birth. You were never condemned by default. You were never meant to live under chains of fear. Those were inventions, not truths. The truth is that you are innocent. You are Loved. You are light. And stepping into that light is the only doctrine that matters.

We've escaped the shadow of guilt. In the next chapter, we'll take the next step: exploring how to live in wholeness – not just breaking free from lies, but building a life rooted in truth, joy, and divine presence.

Because escaping is only the beginning. Creating is where the adventure truly begins.

Chapter 9: Living in Wholeness

Wholeness as Your Birthright

When you strip away centuries of guilt, when you set down the heavy backpack of doctrine, when you step out of the shadow of fear, what's left? Wholeness. Not a goal to achieve, not a reward for obedience, not a future prize after enough penance. Wholeness as the truth of who you already are.

The tragedy of religion's obsession with sin is that it blinds you to this reality. If you were told from birth that you're broken, then of course you'll spend your life trying to fix yourself. But here's the cosmic joke: you were never broken in the first place. You were whole all along.

Jeshua wasn't trying to fix sinners — he was trying to wake people up to their wholeness.

Let's linger here because (again) repetition matters: wholeness is not something you earn. Wholeness is not something granted by priests or revoked by bishops. Wholeness is not something waiting at the end of a long road of suffering. It is your birthright. You were born with it, you'll die with it, and nothing in between can take it away. The only thing that can obscure it is the lie that you're broken.

Think about how babies enter the world. They don't come out ashamed. They don't look around for a priest to declare them worthy. They arrive screaming, breathing, alive — whole. Their wholeness is obvious. It's only later, through indoctrination, that they're taught to doubt it. Jeshua's teaching was essentially this: go back to what you knew as a child. Stop doubting your wholeness. Stop believing the lie.

This is why he said, "The Kingdom of Heaven is within you." Not will be, not might be, not after forty confessions. *Is.* Right now. Already whole.

Imagine the Creator of the Universe going through the trouble of crafting galaxies, stars, oceans, laughter, music, only to say, "Oops, humans came out defective. Better spend eternity punishing them." It's absurd. No loving creator would build a masterpiece and then stamp it "factory reject." The absurdity is your clue that the doctrine was human invention, not divine truth.

So what does it mean to claim wholeness as your birthright? It means living differently. It means moving from survival to creation. It means your choices aren't about earning worth but expressing worth. You don't meditate to become worthy – you meditate to remember your worth. You don't Love to get points with God – you Love because you *are* Love. Every act becomes an expression of wholeness, not an attempt to fill a void.

And here's the beauty: when you know you're whole, the pressure lifts. You don't have to prove anything. You don't have to fear mistakes. You don't have to hustle for divine approval. You can rest. You can breathe. You can create. Wholeness is the great exhale after centuries of holding your breath under guilt.

But let's be real: embracing wholeness feels risky at first. It feels like rebellion, because the voices of guilt will whisper, "Careful. Don't get too free. Don't get too joyful. Don't forget the rules." That's why we keep repeating it: wholeness is your birthright. It can't be taken, only forgotten. And remembering it is the heart of living in freedom.

So here's the invitation of this section: Stop striving to be fixed. Start living as if you were already whole – because you are. And once you claim that birthright, everything else changes.

The Illusion of Separation

If wholeness is your birthright, then what's the enemy of wholeness? Not sin, not temptation, not even death. The real enemy is the illusion of separation. That whisper in the back of your mind that says, "God is over there, and you're over here. The Divine is distant, and you're cut off. Maybe, if you try hard enough, you can earn your way back." That illusion is the oldest trick in the religious playbook, and it has robbed more people of joy than any actual wrongdoing ever could.

Think about how religions describe God. He's "up there" in the sky, enthroned above the clouds. Or He's locked in the "Holy of Holies," hidden behind curtains in the Temple. Or He's mediated by priests, bishops, or popes – always someone else's hands on the controls. And what does that picture do? It convinces you that you're on the outside, looking in. You're not in the circle. You're estranged. You're lost. And you'd better play by the rules if you ever want to get back in.

But Jeshua shattered that illusion every chance he got. *The Kingdom of Heaven is within you."* Not far away. Not behind temple walls. *Within you.* He ate meals with outcasts, touched lepers, spoke to women others avoided. His actions were a living sermon: *there is no separation.* The Divine is here, now, in you, in me, in all of us.

So why do we still buy the illusion? Because separation is profitable. If God is distant, then you need middlemen. You need rituals, sacraments, tithes, indulgences, holy relics, holy water — the whole spiritual supply chain. If the Kingdom is within you, the Church can't sell it. If the Kingdom is far away, the Church can set up toll booths on the road and charge you at every stop.

I sometimes picture the Church as a cosmic cable company. "Sure, God's presence is out there, but you'll need our package to access it. Basic plan includes Sunday Mass and baptism. For confession and indulgences, upgrade to Premium. Oh, and heaven? That's part of our Eternal Plus package — limited-time offer!" It's absurd, but that's exactly how separation has been marketed.

Here's the truth: you can't be separate from God. It's metaphysically impossible. How could you be? If God is the source of life, the breath in your lungs, the spark in your being, then how could you ever be apart from that? You can *believe* you're separate, sure. You can *feel* like you're separate. But that's illusion, not reality. Like a wave believing it's not part of the ocean. Like a ray of light believing it's cut off from the sun. The belief is possible. The reality isn't.

This illusion of separation is what feeds guilt and fear. Guilt says, "You've messed up, so you're even further away now." Fear says, "If you don't close the gap, punishment awaits." And Love — real Love — says, "What gap? You were never apart. You were never lost. You are home." Jeshua's parable of the prodigal son isn't about fixing separation. It's about realizing separation was never real to begin with. The father wasn't distant. He was watching, waiting, ready to run.

And let's not miss this: other great teachers dismantled the illusion too. Buddha said, "Look within; you are the Buddha." Lao Tzu said, "When you realize there is nothing lacking, the whole world belongs to you." Muhammad said, "God is closer than your jugular vein." The universal voice of wisdom always says the same thing: you're not separate. You never were.

The illusion is sticky, though, because it feels real. When you've been told since birth that you're cut off, you start interpreting life through that lens. You pray and feel nothing? Proof of separation. You make a mistake? Proof of separation. You feel unworthy? Proof of separation. But notice the pattern – it's all interpretation. The silence in prayer is not absence. The mistake is not exile. The unworthiness is not reality. They're shadows cast by the lie, not light from the truth.

So how do you undo the illusion? By practicing presence. Every time you drop into this moment – your breath, your heartbeat, your awareness – you find God already there. Not distant. Not conditional. Present. You break the illusion not by striving to get "closer" but by realizing you were never far.

Let's repeat this clearly, because repetition drives it home: the greatest lie religion ever told was that you are separate from God. The greatest truth Jeshua ever revealed was that you are one with God already. And once you see the illusion for what it is, separation collapses like mist in sunlight.

So here's the invitation of this section: stop living as if you're on the outside. Stop bargaining your way back into a circle you never left. Step into the reality Jeshua declared: *I and the Father are one... and you will do greater works than these."* That's wholeness. That's freedom. That's the light breaking through the illusion.

Healing the Split Within

If the illusion of separation is the grand lie that disconnects us from God, then its evil twin is the split it creates inside of us. It's not just that we believe we're cut off from the Divine – we also start living as if we're cut off from ourselves. That inner fracture is one of the deepest wounds of original sin and healing it is essential to living in wholeness.

Let me explain. The doctrine of guilt creates a civil war inside your soul. On one side is your humanity: your desires, your instincts, your laughter, your creativity, your hunger, your sexuality, your individuality. On the other side is the religious programming: the voice of guilt, the rules, the fear, the voice that says, "Don't trust yourself. Your humanity is the problem." The result? You live split down the middle, suspicious of your own heart, doubting your own mind, distrusting your own body.

I lived this split for years. Part of me wanted to be joyful, spontaneous, creative. Another part of me whispered, "Careful, that's not holy." Part of me longed for intimacy and connection. Another voice warned, "Danger – temptation." Part of me wanted to breathe free. Another voice hissed, "Better not, or God will get you." That's the split: a constant tug-of-war inside. No wonder so many religious people are anxious, depressed, and burned out. You can't live whole when half of you is at war with the other half.

Imagine buying a new car and being told, "Now, don't use the engine too much – it's dangerous. Don't trust the brakes either. And those wheels? Probably sinful. Just sit in the driveway and pray about it." That's what religion did with humanity. It gave us bodies, minds, and desires, and then told us not to trust any of them. It's like handing someone a guitar and then saying, "Whatever you do, don't touch the strings."

The irony is that Jeshua consistently healed the split, while the Church deepened it. Jeshua touched lepers, restoring not just their health but their dignity. He spoke to women, honoring them when society dismissed them. He forgave sinners, reuniting them with themselves before reuniting them with the community. He didn't teach people to distrust their humanity – he taught them to trust that the Divine could shine through it. His life was one long sermon: *you are not two halves in conflict; you are one whole in Love.*

But how do you heal that split today, after centuries of programming? The first step is awareness. Start noticing when the war flares up inside you. Notice when you feel guilty for resting. Notice when you feel ashamed for desiring. Notice when you feel unworthy for being yourself. Don't judge it. Just name it: "*Ah, that's the old split talking.*" Naming the fracture is the beginning of healing it.

The second step is integration. That means letting your humanity and your divinity sit at the same table. When you feel desire, don't label it as sinful. Ask: "How can this desire be an expression of Love?" When you feel joy, don't dismiss it as frivolous. Say: "*This joy is sacred.*" When you feel tired, don't accuse yourself of laziness. Whisper: "*Rest is holy.*" Every time you integrate instead of divide, the split closes a little more.

The third step is compassion. Be gentle with yourself when the old voices flare up. Healing the split doesn't happen overnight. Centuries of guilt don't dissolve in a weekend retreat. You'll stumble. You'll catch yourself falling back into shame. That's normal. The practice is not perfection. The practice is kindness. When guilt hisses, "You blew it," compassion answers, "*No, I'm learning.*" That shift is healing in action.

Now, let's circle back to the bigger truth because repetition reinforces freedom: you were never actually split. The illusion of separation convinced you there was a war inside, but the war was manufactured. Your humanity and your divinity were never enemies. They were always partners. Your laughter is divine. Your creativity is divine. Your Love is divine. Your humanity is not the obstacle to God – it's the expression of God.

Other spiritual traditions understood this too. In the Bhagavad Gita, Krishna says, "*I am the taste in water... the light of the sun and moon... the intelligence of the intelligent.*" That's integration – God in the ordinary. In Zen, enlightenment is said to be as simple as chopping wood and carrying water – not escaping humanity, but inhabiting it fully. Jeshua stood in the same lineage: God is here, now, in you, through you, as you.

So what does healing the split within look like day to day? It looks like eating with gratitude instead of guilt. It looks like enjoying intimacy as sacred instead of sinful. It looks like laughing loudly without apology. It looks like letting your body move, rest, create, and Love – not as obstacles to holiness, but as holiness itself. Every act of wholeness heals the fracture.

Here's the drumbeat:

Guilt fractures, Love unites. Fear divides, presence integrates. Wholeness isn't something you manufacture. It's something you uncover once the lies are stripped away. You were never two halves. You were always one.

So let's name the invitation of this section clearly: stop fighting yourself. Stop distrusting your humanity. Stop living like you're split in two. Step into the truth Jeshua embodied – that the human and the divine are not separate. They are one. And when you live from that place, the shadow of guilt finally loses its power.

That's healing the split within.

Embodying Divine Humanity

It's one thing to talk about healing the split within, to say that our humanity and divinity aren't enemies. It's another thing to live it out in the flesh-and-blood world of bills, arguments, Monday mornings, and burnt toast. "Divine humanity" sounds lofty, almost like a New Age bumper sticker. But Jeshua didn't preach bumper stickers. He embodied divine humanity in daily life – in dusty sandals, around dinner tables, with laughter, tears, and dirty hands from healing the untouchable.

The genius of Jeshua's way wasn't that he floated above human experience. It was that he dove straight into it. Hungry? He ate. Tired? He rested. Happy? He celebrated. Surrounded by outcasts? He pulled up a chair. And yet in all of it, he revealed the presence of the Divine. He wasn't divine *despite* being human. He was divine *because* he was fully human. That's the model: not to escape our humanity, but to embody it as the very vessel of divinity.

Now here's where things get sticky. Religion has spent centuries teaching that holiness means escaping humanity. Monks in cloisters, saints starving themselves, priests denying their own desires. The holier you were, the less human you were supposed to appear. But that's the exact opposite of Jeshua's message. Holiness isn't less humanity. Holiness is *full* humanity, lit up by Love.

Let's pause here and name the pattern again, because repetition breaks the spell:

- Religion says: suppress your humanity. Jeshua says: express your humanity.
- Religion says: flee the world. Jeshua says: embody God in the world.
- Religion says: you are fallen. Jeshua says: you are the light of the world.

The difference couldn't be starker.

So what does it mean to embody divine humanity in your own life? Let's get practical.

1. **In Your Body:** Instead of distrusting your body, honor it. Feed it well, rest it, move it, enjoy it. Your body isn't a problem to be punished, it's a temple to be celebrated. Every breath is holy. Every laugh is sacred. Every embrace is

divine. Treat your body as the place where heaven and earth meet, because that's exactly what it is.

2. **In Your Emotions:** Stop labeling some emotions as "holy" and others as "sinful." Anger can reveal injustice. Sadness can deepen compassion. Joy can expand gratitude. Even fear can teach you where you need Love. Embodying divine humanity means welcoming your emotions as messengers, not enemies.
3. **In Your Work:** Whatever you do – whether it's teaching, parenting, building, creating, cooking – do it with presence and Love. Jeshua himself was a carpenter. His divinity showed up in wood shavings and sweat, not just in miracles. Your daily work can be just as holy as any ritual, if you bring your whole self into it.
4. **In Your Relationships:** See others as both human and divine. When your partner annoys you, remember they're also the light of the world. When a coworker frustrates you, remember the Kingdom is within them too. It doesn't mean excusing bad behavior. It means refusing to reduce anyone to just their flaws. Divine humanity means holding both truths: the messy and the magnificent.
5. **In Your Failures:** Here's the big one. Religion says failure proves your brokenness. Jeshua says failure is just another doorway into Love. Embodying divine humanity means learning, forgiving, and growing, not wallowing in shame. The cross itself wasn't a symbol of defeat; it was proof that even in suffering, Love has the last word.

Imagine trying to explain to Augustine that sex, laughter, and a good glass of wine could all be holy. His head might've exploded. But Jeshua had no problem turning water into wine at a wedding. His first miracle wasn't raising the dead or parting seas; it was keeping the party going. That tells you everything about divine humanity – joy is not just permitted, it's celebrated.

And let's be honest: embodying divine humanity takes practice, because the old programming runs deep. You'll catch yourself apologizing for resting, shaming yourself for desire, suppressing your joy. That's okay. Every time you notice, you get another chance to choose differently. To embody Love instead of guilt. To embody presence instead of fear. To embody divinity in humanity.

Here's the kicker: when you live this way, people notice. They may not have words for it, but they feel it. Your peace radiates. Your joy invites. Your presence heals. That's what Jeshua meant when he said, *Let your light shine before others, so they may see your good works and glorify your Father in heaven."* Not good works as in rule-following. Good works as in living fully, freely, and lovingly as yourself.

Other traditions echo the same message. Rumi, the Sufi mystic, said, "*Stop acting so small. You are the universe in ecstatic motion.*" The Upanishads declared, "*You are That*" (the divine spark within).

Embodying divine humanity is simply living as if those truths were actually real — because they are.

So let's name it clearly, because clarity sets us free: you are not meant to escape your humanity. You are meant to embody it as the vessel of divinity. Every smile, every breath, every act of kindness is God expressing through you. That's not arrogance. That's reality.

And once you start living this way, the shadow of guilt has no place to land. Fear has no chain to grip. Because Love — embodied in humanity — is too bright to be overshadowed.

That's what it means to embody divine humanity. And it's the heart of living in wholeness.

The Power of Presence

If there's one theme Jeshua hammered over and over — one key that unlocks wholeness, freedom, and divine humanity — it's presence. *Take no thought for tomorrow." "Do not worry about your life." "Sufficient for the day is its own trouble."* Again and again, he pointed people back to the now. Why? Because the present moment is the only place guilt and fear lose their grip. Presence is the power source of wholeness.

Think about it. Where does guilt live? In the past. In memories of what you did or didn't do. Where does fear live? In the future. In anxieties about what might happen, what God might do, what punishment might come. But where does life live? In the present. Right here. Right now. Which means wholeness can't be experienced in the "someday" of doctrine or the "if only" of guilt.

Wholeness can only be lived now, in this breath, in this heartbeat, in this moment.

This is why religion has always been so invested in pulling people out of presence. "Repent for what you've done!" (Past). "Fear for your eternal soul!" (Future). Rarely do you hear, "Be here, now, and know that God is already with you." That doesn't sell indulgences. That doesn't build cathedrals. That doesn't keep confession booths busy. But it does awaken freedom. And awakened people are hard to control.

If churches actually taught presence, the sermons would be hilariously short. "Good morning, everyone. God is here, now. Exhale. Love each other. See you next week." But you can't pass the collection plate after two minutes, so instead we got centuries of fear-driven monologues.

Presence is powerful because it cuts through illusion. When you actually sit in this moment – not in the story about the moment, but in the moment itself – you realize nothing is lacking. You're breathing.

You're alive. You're whole. In presence, guilt's accusations about the past evaporate, because the past is gone. In presence, fear's warnings about the future dissolve, because the future hasn't arrived. Presence leaves only truth: you are here, and here is enough.

Jeshua knew this. That's why he constantly pulled people back to now.

"*Don't worry about tomorrow.*" Why? Because tomorrow isn't real yet.

"*Look at the birds of the air.*" Why? Because they embody presence. They're not worrying about next week's worm supply.

They're alive, now. And if the Divine provides for them, won't the Divine also provide for you? Jeshua wasn't offering poetic nature lessons. He was teaching the mechanics of presence.

Other teachers across other traditions understood the same. Buddha's entire path is about mindfulness – awareness of the present moment. Lao Tzu wrote, "*If you are depressed you are living in the past. If you are anxious you are living in the future. If you are at peace you are living in the present.*" These aren't just platitudes.

They're maps. Maps that all point to the same destination: wholeness is here, now.

So how do we practice presence in daily life? Start simple. Notice your breath. Right now. Feel the air moving in and out. That's presence. Taste your food instead of rushing. That's presence. Look someone in the eye and really see them. That's presence.

These little practices are revolutionary, because they anchor you in the only place wholeness can be experienced. And yes, your mind will wander. Guilt will drag you backward. Fear will yank you forward. That's okay. The practice isn't to never wander. The practice is to notice when you've wandered, and return. Every return strengthens the muscle of presence. Every return brings you back to the truth Jeshua already declared: the Kingdom is within you.

Let's repeat this because the old programming needs to be overwritten: Guilt lives in the past. Fear lives in the future. Wholeness lives in the present. The more you dwell here, the freer you become.

Presence also has another gift: it reveals the Divine in the ordinary. When you're truly here, a sip of water becomes holy. A child's laugh becomes scripture. A sunset becomes liturgy. You don't need stained glass to see God. You just need open eyes, here and now. Jeshua's miracles were really lessons in presence: healing wasn't magic, it was showing people what happens when Love meets the moment fully.

Imagine telling a first-century fisherman, "Two thousand years from now, people will argue about whether Jesus was fully God or fully human." The fisherman would probably shrug and say, "He was fully here. Isn't that enough?" Exactly. Presence was the real miracle.

So here's the invitation: practice presence as often as you can. Not as a duty, but as a joy. Sit in stillness. Notice beauty. Laugh fully. Love deeply. Every act of presence is an act of wholeness. Because presence doesn't just heal you. It heals the world. A *present* person listens better. Loves better. Serves better. Creates better.

Presence is contagious. When you live fully here and now, you give others permission to drop their guilt about yesterday and their fear about tomorrow. You invite them into the only place God can ever be found: now.

So let's name it clearly: the power of presence is the power of wholeness. It is the antidote to guilt, the chain-breaker of fear, the doorway into divine humanity. And every time you practice it, you live Jeshua's message more fully than any doctrine ever could.

That's the power of presence.

Practices of Wholeness

Wholeness isn't an abstract theory. It's not a pretty idea you put on a shelf next to your copy of the Catechism and dust off once a year.

Wholeness is lived. It's breathed. It's practiced. If the doctrine of original sin trained us into fragmentation, fear, and guilt through repeated rituals, then we reclaim our wholeness through repeated practices that restore truth, Love, and presence.

These practices aren't about earning anything. Let me say that again (because centuries of programming make it hard to hear): *you are not practicing to earn Love or prove worth.* You are practicing to remember the wholeness that's already yours. Think of these as daily reminders, little course corrections, gentle nudges that bring you back to center when guilt or fear tries to drag you off-track.

Here are some practices of wholeness – simple, doable, transformative.

1. **Claiming Wholeness at Sunrise:** Before the world rushes in with emails, obligations, and old programming, begin your day by claiming wholeness. Sit quietly, breathe deeply, and affirm: *"I am whole. I am Loved. I am light."* Don't recite it mechanically – feel it. Let the words land in your chest. Imagine yourself stepping into the day already full, not scrambling to earn approval. This one practice sets the tone for everything that follows.
2. **The Sacred Pause:** Throughout the day, stop for just 30 seconds. Close your eyes, take a breath, and notice: *Am I in the past, the future, or the present?* If you catch yourself in guilt (past) or fear (future), gently return to now. That pause is holy. It's a reset button, a reminder that wholeness only lives here. Jeshua's invitation to "take no thought for tomorrow" becomes real every time you hit pause.
3. **Gratitude as Daily Liturgy:** Forget rosaries of repetitive guilt. Build rosaries of gratitude instead. At the end of each day,

list three things you're grateful for. They can be big – health, family, breakthroughs – or small – a good cup of coffee, a laugh with a friend, the way sunlight hit the trees. Gratitude is wholeness in action, because it roots you in abundance instead of lack. It rewires your brain to see blessing where guilt once saw failure.

4. **The Body as Temple Practice:** Treat your body like the sacred space it is. Move it, rest it, feed it, enjoy it. Stretch in the morning. Take a walk in the afternoon. Rest without apology. Eat without guilt. Drink water like it's holy water. When you treat your body with Love, you reject centuries of programming that called it dirty, shameful, or dangerous. Your body isn't the enemy of wholeness – it's the expression of it.
5. **The Mirror Blessing:** This one feels silly at first, but it's powerful. Stand in front of a mirror. Look yourself in the eye. And say out loud: *"I Love you. You are whole."* Religion taught us to look up at statues for blessing. Jeshua taught us to look within. The mirror blessing reclaims that truth. It heals the split inside by declaring that your reflection isn't defective – it's divine.
6. **Acts of Joy:** Schedule joy. Yes, literally. Write it in your planner if you have to. Play music and dance in your kitchen. Watch a funny movie. Draw badly on purpose. Blow bubbles with your kids or grandkids. Joy is not trivial – it's holy rebellion. Every laugh is a sermon against guilt. Every smile is a hymn against fear. Acts of joy remind you that wholeness isn't serious. It's playful.
7. **Forgiveness Rituals:** Not the Church's forgiveness – your own. Take a piece of paper and write down the guilt you've been carrying. Then burn it, shred it, or flush it. Say out loud: *"I release this. I am forgiven. I am whole."* Jeshua said, "Neither do I condemn you." Take him at his word. Let it sink in. Forgiveness is the medicine that heals the wounds guilt left behind.
8. **Love in Action:** Practice wholeness by extending it outward. Smile at a stranger. Listen fully to a friend. Offer help without obligation. Buy a coffee for the person behind you in line. These aren't random acts of kindness, they're living

sacraments. Every act of Love you offer reaffirms that you are whole and so is the world around you. Jeshua said, "Love one another." Not as a command, but as a description of how wholeness flows when it's lived.

9. **Nightly Exhale:** End your day by letting go. Sit quietly before bed and say: "Whatever I did today, it was enough. Whatever I didn't do today, it can wait. I am whole, and I rest in Love." That exhale breaks the cycle of guilt that religion tried to program into every night: tally your sins, panic about hell, beg for mercy. Instead, you end in peace, grounded in wholeness.

Can you imagine if the Church had replaced confession booths with bubble machines, gratitude journals, and mirror blessings? People would've walked out lighter, freer, and probably a lot more fun at dinner parties. But then again, cathedrals don't get built on bubble machines. And that's why it's up to us now to reclaim these simple practices.

The beauty of these practices is that they're not obligations. They're invitations. They don't weigh you down. They lighten you. They don't remind you of your brokenness. They remind you of your wholeness. They don't trap you in guilt. They free you into joy.

And here's the drumbeat worth repeating: Jeshua's Way was never about rituals of fear. It was about practices of Love. Living wholeness isn't about obeying rules. It's about embodying truth. These practices are just tools to help you remember what you already are: whole, Loved, divine.

That's the practice of wholeness.

Living as Light

We've covered a lot of ground in this chapter. We've claimed wholeness as our birthright, exposed the illusion of separation, healed the inner split, embraced divine humanity, rediscovered the power of presence, and practiced daily wholeness. Now it's time to put it all together and step fully into the role Jeshua said was already ours: *"You are the light of the world."*

Let's stop and really hear that. Jeshua didn't say, "One day, after you've been purified and perfected, maybe you'll shine a little." He said, *"You are the light of the world."* Present tense. Already shining. The tragedy is that guilt and fear convinced us to hide that light under a basket, to dim ourselves for the comfort of institutions, to believe our glow was suspect. But the truth has never changed: you are light.

Living in wholeness means living as that light – boldly, unapologetically, joyfully.

What does it mean to live as light? It means showing up authentically. It means being yourself fully, without shrinking to fit doctrines or inflating to earn approval. Light doesn't ask permission to shine. It just does. When you live your truth with Love, you don't need to preach, argue, or defend. You simply shine, and others see by your light.

Living as light also means being visible. Religion has trained us to hide. Hide your questions. Hide your desires. Hide your joy. Hide your doubts. But light hidden is no light at all. Jeshua said, *"A city on a hill cannot be hidden."* Living in wholeness means refusing to hide. Speak your truth. Share your Love. Laugh out loud. The world doesn't need more shadows of guilt – it needs people radiant with presence.

Now, let's circle back to the rhythm of repetition, because it drives this book like a drumbeat:

- Guilt says, "*You're broken.*" Wholeness says, "*You're light.*"
- Fear says, "*Stay small.*" Love says, "*Shine boldly.*"
- Doctrine says, "*Hide behind us.*" Jeshua says, "*You are already the light of the world.*"

Living as light isn't about perfection. Light doesn't shine because it's flawless. It shines because it *is.* A candle doesn't apologize for dripping wax. The sun doesn't apologize for setting. They simply shine when it's their time. Likewise, you don't need to wait until you have everything figured out to shine. Your cracks don't disqualify you – they're where the light pours through.

Imagine confession lines if people believed they were light. "Bless me, Father, for I shined too brightly this week. People kept asking me for hope and joy. I'm afraid I might've inspired someone." The whole system would collapse. And maybe that's the point. Jeshua never wanted confession booths. He wanted cities on hills.

Living as light also means reflecting Love into the dark corners of the world. Not by force. Not by fear. But by presence. A single candle doesn't fight the darkness – it simply shines, and darkness cannot withstand it. When you embody Love in your daily life – kindness to a stranger, compassion for yourself, forgiveness for someone who wronged you – you're not just talking about wholeness. You're living it. And living it is contagious.

Other voices confirm this same truth. Rumi said, *Don t get lost in your pain, know that one day your pain will become your cure."* The Bhagavad Gita reminds us, *Among lights, I am the radiant sun."* The Gospel of John opens with, *The light shines in the darkness, and the darkness has not overcome it."* Everywhere wisdom speaks, it speaks of light. Because light is the essence of wholeness.

So how do you sustain living as light? By continuing the practices. By staying in presence. By laughing often. By choosing Love. By forgiving quickly. By remembering daily: *I am whole. I am Loved. I am light.*

Living as light is not a one-time choice. It's a rhythm. A way of being. A habit of shining.

And here's the beautiful truth: light multiplies. One flame can ignite a thousand candles without diminishing itself. Your wholeness doesn't just free you – it frees others. Your laughter doesn't just heal you – it heals those who hear it. Your presence doesn't just ground you – it grounds the people around you. Living as light is not selfish. It's the most generous thing you can do.

So let's name it clearly as we close this chapter: Living in wholeness is not about becoming something new. It's about remembering what you've always been – light. The illusion of separation has been exposed. The shadow of guilt has lost its grip. The chains of fear are broken. The split within is healed. What remains is you – radiant, whole, beLoved, shining.

That's living as light. And from here, the journey only deepens. Because if this chapter is about living whole, the next chapter will be about creating from wholeness – building a life and a world that reflect the Love, presence, and light you've reclaimed.

Chapter 10: Creating from Wholeness

Creation as a Divine Act

When you finally lay down the burden of guilt, when you reject the illusion of separation, when you step into the light of wholeness, something shifts. You're no longer just surviving. You're no longer hustling to earn worth or begging for forgiveness. You're free. And freedom always leads to creativity. The next step in this journey isn't just about *being* whole. It's about *creating* from wholeness. Because creation, at its heart, is a divine act.

Look back to the very first lines of scripture: *"In the beginning, God created..."* The first thing the Divine ever does is create. Not punish, not judge, not condemn. Create. Light, sky, earth, oceans, laughter, music, Love – all of it springs from creation. Which means every time you create, you're participating in that same divine flow. You're not imitating God from a distance; you're embodying God from within.

This is why Jeshua was always pointing people back to their own creative power. *The Kingdom of Heaven is within you." "You will do even greater works than I." "Ask and it will be given, seek and you will find."* He wasn't telling people to grovel; He was telling them to create. To co-labor with the Divine in shaping life. That's what prayer was meant to be: not begging, but aligning. Not pleading, but participating.

But here's the tragedy: the doctrine of original sin flipped the whole script. Instead of being creators, we were cast as criminals. Instead of being co-laborers, we were reduced to dependents. Instead of being children of God, we were labeled unworthy beggars. And creativity – the very essence of divine humanity – was shamed as pride or arrogance. "Who are you to create?" the Church asked. The real question is: "Who are you *not* to?"

I sometimes imagine the Creator watching us hesitate to create. God's up there saying, "I made galaxies, sunsets, and giraffes – and you're afraid to paint a picture because you might mess it up? Have you seen the platypus? I was experimenting! Go ahead and try!"

That's the truth: creation isn't about perfection. It's about participation. When you create from wholeness, you're not trying to prove anything. You're not trying to earn anything. You're expressing the truth that's already within you. Whether it's painting, cooking, writing, building, singing, gardening, inventing – it all flows from the same source.

Creativity is Love made visible.

And here's the crucial piece: creating from wholeness feels different from creating from guilt. Creating from guilt says, "I need to prove my worth." It's anxious, heavy, competitive. It's art as performance.

Creating from wholeness says, "I am already worthy, so let me express it." It's light, joyful, free. It's art as overflow. The difference is night and day.

This is why so much "religious art" through history was simultaneously beautiful and suffocating. Cathedrals, paintings, hymns – many of them breathtaking. But many of them also carried an undertone of fear, obligation, and guilt. "We'd better make this perfect, or God will be angry." That's creation from fear, not from Love. True creation, Jeshua-style creation, comes from the inner knowing: "*I and the Father are one. Therefore, what I create is already holy.*"

So how do you start creating from wholeness?

First, you give yourself permission. Permission to try. Permission to fail. Permission to make a mess. Remember: the Divine made mosquitoes. Clearly, perfection wasn't the requirement. Creation is about flow, not flawlessness.

Second, you follow joy. Pay attention to what lights you up. Maybe it's music. Maybe it's writing. Maybe it's cooking a meal and watching people smile as they eat. Wherever joy sparks, creation flows.

Jeshua's miracles weren't just about fixing problems. They were acts of joy. Water into wine. Feeding crowds. Healing bodies. Each one was a creation of joy where fear once reigned.

Third, you release comparison. Your creation doesn't have to look like anyone else's. A daisy doesn't compete with a rose. The ocean doesn't envy the mountains. Why should your painting, song, or story compare to anyone else's? Wholeness means your unique creation is sacred simply because it's yours.

Fourth, you share. Creation isn't meant to be hoarded. A song unsung, a painting unseen, a kindness unexpressed – it withers. But when you share, you multiply light. Your creativity becomes someone else's healing, someone else's inspiration, someone else's permission to shine. That's why Jeshua said, *"No one lights a lamp and hides it under a basket."* Creation from wholeness demands visibility.

Let's repeat the truth, because it needs to sink deep: You are not guilty. You are not broken. You are whole. And because you are whole, you are a creator. Every choice, every thought, every action is creation. You are shaping reality with your presence. The only question is whether you'll create from fear or from Love, from guilt or from wholeness.

Other traditions echo the same call. In Hinduism, the concept of *Lila* – divine play – reminds us that creation itself is playful, joyous, not rigid. In Taoism, creation is flow, the effortless unfolding of the Tao. In modern psychology, creativity is linked to healing and integration.

Everywhere wisdom speaks, it affirms: creation is life expressing itself through you.

So let's name it clearly as we open this chapter: creation is not optional. It's not a hobby for the gifted. It's the essence of your divine humanity. To live whole is to create. To Love is to create. To forgive is to create. To laugh is to create. Every moment, you are shaping the world. The question is: will you create from the shadow of guilt, or from the light of wholeness?

That's why Jeshua's message still matters. He didn't just preach wholeness. He lived creation. His life was a masterpiece of Love expressed in time and space. And his invitation was never, "Worship me for doing it." His invitation was, "*Follow me in doing it yourself.*"

That's the heart of this chapter. Creation as a divine act. Creation as the next step after wholeness. Creation as the way you and I bring heaven to earth, not someday, but now.

Co-Creation with the Divine

If creation is a divine act, then here's the next revelation: you're not doing it alone. You never were. Every act of creation is a partnership with the Source that animates all life. Call it God, call it Love, call it Spirit, call it the Breath – whatever name you use, it's the same reality. You are not a disconnected artist scratching on the margins of the universe. You are a co-creator with the Divine itself.

Now, that word *co-creation* gets tossed around a lot in New Age circles, usually accompanied by sparkly graphics of galaxies and yoga poses. But let's strip away the glitter and get real. Co-creation doesn't mean you're a magician waving your wand to manifest Lamborghinis out of thin air (though if you pull that off, let me know). It means your life is constantly in dialogue with the Source. Every thought, every action, every intention is part of a conversation. You create, and the universe responds. The universe nudges, and you respond. Together, you and the Divine weave the fabric of reality.

This isn't a new idea. Jeshua taught it plainly. *"Ask, and it will be given you."* That's not a vending machine promise. That's a co-creation principle. You ask by aligning your heart. The Divine responds by opening doors, drawing connections, stirring people and opportunities into motion. Jeshua also said, *"The Father and I are one."* That wasn't metaphysical bragging. It was a model. He was showing us how co-creation works when you live in alignment – not begging from a distant God, but creating with a present God.

Think about the miracles. When Jeshua fed the five thousand, did bread and fish rain down from the sky? No. He took what was already there, blessed it, and multiplied it. That's co-creation. Human hands offering, divine presence amplifying. When he healed, he didn't say, "Behold, I alone did this." He often said, *"Your faith has made you well."* Co-creation. Human openness, divine response. Every miracle was a partnership.

Imagine Jeshua trying to explain co-creation to a group of modern Christians who believe God does everything while humans do nothing. "So, you know how I said you'll do greater works than me? That wasn't a metaphor. I meant it. Get off your pew and start co-creating already."

The illusion of separation tries to tell us we're powerless. "God is up there, you're down here, and your only job is to beg for mercy." But wholeness says, "God is within you. You and the Divine are dance partners." You don't drag God onto the floor. You don't control the rhythm. You listen, you move, you respond. And in that dance, beauty unfolds.

So how do we practice co-creation? Here are some anchors:

1. **Set Intentions with Love.** Every day, ask yourself: what do I want to create today? Not from fear, not from guilt, but from Love. Maybe it's a peaceful home, a joyful interaction, a project that inspires. Intentions are like invitations to the Divine: "Here's what I'm dancing into reality today."
2. **Stay Present to the Nudges.** Co-creation isn't one-sided. God delivers through the path of least resistance. The key is to recognize what it is. The Divine nudges you. A thought arises. A synchronicity appears. A person calls. A door opens. Pay attention. The dance floor shifts constantly. Your job isn't to force it, but to follow the rhythm.
3. **Act Boldly.** Creation isn't passive. You can't just sit and wish. Jeshua didn't tell the disciples, "Manifest fish in your minds." He told them, "Pass out the bread." They had to act, and in acting, the miracle unfolded. Co-creation means doing your part with courage and trust.
4. **Release Control.** This is the hardest part. Co-creation isn't about micromanaging outcomes. You don't dictate the "how" and "when." You align with Love, you act, and then you trust the bigger flow. The harvest rarely looks exactly like the seed you planted, but it's always aligned with the Love that planted it.

This is why prayer, in Jeshua's sense, is so radically different from the prayers many of us grew up with. Prayer wasn't groveling. It wasn't bargaining. It was aligning. It was saying, "Here's what I long for. Here's what I'm ready to create. Partner with me." And then trusting the dance.

Other traditions echo this beautifully. In Hinduism, karma yoga is the path of selfless action, offering your work as co-creation with the Divine. In Taoism, *wu wei* is effortless action, flowing with the Tao instead of forcing against it. Even modern psychology speaks of "flow state" – those moments when your creativity feels guided, effortless, beyond your ego. All of these are just different languages for co- creation.

Now, here's the drumbeat worth repeating: You are not powerless. You are not cut off. You are not waiting for God to swoop in while you cower in fear. You are a co-creator, already dancing with the Divine, whether you realize it or not. The question isn't *if* you're co-creating. It's *how*. Are you co-creating from fear or from Love? From guilt or from wholeness? From shadow or from light?

If you've ever prayed, "God, give me patience!" and then found yourself in traffic the next morning, congratulations – you've experienced co-creation. You asked, the universe responded, just not in the way you expected. God gives you what you focus on. The Bhagavad Gita says, "*Thought by thought you forged your destiny, therefore to keep your mind upon the positive rather than the negative is considered the austerity of the mind.*" The idea of needing "patience" is the belief in something you need patience from. So that is what is given.

So let's name the invitation of this section clearly: Start living as a conscious co-creator. Set intentions from Love. Act boldly. Listen to the nudges. Trust the flow. When you do, you'll discover what Jeshua promised: that you can and will do greater works. Not because you're replacing God, but because you're finally remembering you're never separate from God.

That's co-creation with the Divine.

Imagination as Sacred Power

If creation is a divine act and co-creation is our partnership with the Source, then imagination is the sacred workshop where all of it begins. Before there's a painting, there's an image in the mind. Before there's a book, there's a story whispered in the heart. Before there's a cathedral or a comedy show or even a YouTube channel about reclaiming spirituality – there's imagination. Without it, nothing gets built. With it, even the impossible becomes possible. Even Albert Einstein said, "*The imagination is the preview of life's coming attractions.*"

And yet, for centuries, imagination has been treated with suspicion. Religion, especially in its guilt-heavy forms, has often cast imagination as dangerous. "Idle thoughts are sinful." "Keep your mind on holy things." "Don't indulge in fantasies." As if imagination were a playground for the devil instead of a gift from God. But here's the radical truth: imagination is one of the most sacred powers we possess. It is not a distraction from holiness – it is the very canvas where holiness is made visible.

Think about how powerful imagination is. Augustine imagined that all humanity was doomed because he couldn't make peace with his own desires. That single act of imagination gave us the doctrine of original sin, which haunted billions for centuries. If imagination hijacked by guilt could create such a damaging narrative, how much more powerful is imagination rooted in Love, wholeness, and truth?

Jeshua and Imaginative Teaching

Jeshua understood this power. That's why he taught in parables. *"The Kingdom of Heaven is like..."* he said again and again. Like a mustard seed. Like yeast in dough. Like treasure hidden in a field. These weren't dry definitions from a catechism. They were imaginative doorways. They gave people a way to picture, to feel, to taste what he was talking about. He knew that once the imagination was lit up, the heart would follow.

And he didn't stop with abstract parables. He used everyday images: a lost coin, a rebellious son, a farmer sowing seeds. He grounded the cosmic truth of Love and presence in images people could hold in their minds. Jeshua wasn't against imagination – he was a master of it. He planted pictures so vivid they've lasted 2,000 years.

Imagine Jeshua in our time. "The Kingdom of Heaven is like a Wi-Fi signal. You don't always see it, but it's everywhere, and when you connect, you suddenly have access to infinite possibilities." Half the crowd would nod in wonder, and the other half would argue about whether Comcast is demonic. That's the power of imagination – it speaks in the language of the moment.

Imagination Shapes Reality

Science now backs up what Jeshua embodied. Athletes use visualization to improve performance, and the brain reacts almost the same way as if the body had actually done the task. Patients who imagine healing processes often show measurable recovery.

Imagination isn't fluff – it literally rewires the brain and body. It is rehearsal for reality.

Which means this: when religion fills your imagination with hellfire, wrath, and shame, it shapes your reality into fear and smallness. But when you fill your imagination with Love, wholeness, and possibility, your life bends toward freedom. The canvas of imagination will always be painted on. The only question is: are you letting fear hold the brush, or Love?

Reclaiming Imagination as Sacred

So how do we reclaim imagination as a tool for wholeness instead of a weapon of guilt?

1. **Rewrite the Stories.** Take the old imagery of judgment and reframe it. Instead of picturing a wrathful God in the sky tallying your sins, imagine the Divine as a loving parent cheering you on at every step. Instead of hellfire, imagine the radiance of Love burning away illusions. Instead of a courtroom, imagine a feast where you're always welcome. Rewrite the mental stage until Love becomes the backdrop.
2. **Visualize Your Wholeness.** Every day, spend a few minutes picturing yourself whole. See your body radiant with health, your mind at peace, your heart open. Feel it. This isn't "faking it." This is aligning with the truth Jeshua already declared: *"You are the light of the world."*
3. **Dream Boldly.** Ask yourself: if guilt and fear weren't running the show, what would I dare to imagine for my life? Maybe it's writing that book, starting that business, creating that song, or simply living with joy. Dream it. Because what you dare to imagine becomes what you dare to live.
4. **Make Vision Altars.** Surround yourself with symbols of the life you're co-creating. Pictures, words, objects that remind you of Love, presence, and possibility. Let your environment feed your imagination instead of fear.

From Fear to Creative Flow

I remember growing up terrified of my imagination. Every "impure thought" was a sin. Every daydream was "idle." I learned to police my mind like it was a criminal neighborhood. And the more I did, the smaller my world became. It wasn't until I stopped seeing imagination as dangerous and started seeing it as divine that my creativity — and my freedom — exploded. Suddenly, ideas flowed. Videos came alive. Books took shape. Imagination, once suppressed, became my greatest ally.

Imagine if God had been as uptight as Augustine about imagination. The moment He thought up the giraffe, He would've said, "Too weird, too unholy, let's scrap it." Instead, we got giraffes, platypuses, and octopuses – proof that imagination is not only sacred, it's playful.

Tradition and Imagination

And this isn't unique to Jeshua. In Hinduism, meditation often uses visualizations of gods and goddesses, not as superstition, but as ways of embodying divine qualities. In Tibetan Buddhism, practitioners imagine themselves as compassionate deities to awaken those qualities within. In Sufism, Rumi's poetry paints images so vivid they still ignite hearts centuries later. Across traditions, imagination is recognized as sacred power.

The Drumbeat Truth

So let's repeat the drumbeat:

- Imagination isn't childish. It's divine.
- Imagination isn't dangerous. Fear-filled imagination is – but Love-filled imagination heals.
- Imagination isn't distraction. It's participation in creation itself.

Every cathedral, every song, every invention, every act of compassion was imagined before it was lived. Your imagination is the doorway through which heaven enters earth.

Living the Invitation

Here's the invitation: reclaim imagination. Let it be filled with Love, wholeness, and light. Use it not to punish yourself with fearful fantasies but to build lives of freedom, joy, and presence. Jeshua said the Kingdom is like a mustard seed – tiny at first, but it grows into a tree where all can rest. Imagination is the seed. Wholeness is the tree. Love is the fruit.

That's imagination as sacred power.

Creativity in Daily Life

When people hear the word *creativity,* they often picture artists in berets painting masterpieces, novelists pounding away at typewriters in candlelit attics, or musicians composing symphonies by moonlight. And sure, those are creative acts. But if we only confine creativity to grand artistic pursuits, we miss the real miracle: creativity shows up in daily life. Every choice, every problem solved, every meal cooked, every joke told is an act of creation. When you live in wholeness, creativity isn't just a rare event. It's the air you breathe.

One of the most tragic consequences of guilt-based religion is that it made creativity suspicious. "Don't color outside the lines." "Don't think for yourself." "Stick to tradition." Creativity became dangerous, even heretical. But Jeshua's way flipped that script. He lived as if every moment could be infused with divine creativity.

Healing the sick? Creative. Forgiving enemies? Creative. Turning water into wine at a wedding feast? Definitely creative – and let's be honest, a little mischievous too. Jeshua's life was a masterclass in creative living.

Imagine Jeshua today at a church potluck. The organizers run out of mac and cheese, and Jeshua says, "Don't worry, we'll multiply the lasagna." Suddenly, the whole buffet table is full again, and everyone's arguing about whether that counts as an official miracle or just good catering. That's creativity in daily life: responding to needs with imagination and Love.

The Myth of "Big-C" Creativity

A lot of people dismiss themselves with the line, "I'm just not creative." They think creativity belongs to painters, writers, or YouTubers. But that's like saying, "I'm just not alive." Creativity isn't something you either have or don't. It's the essence of being human. Every time you improvise, adapt, solve a problem, or bring joy into a situation, you're being creative.

Cooking dinner? Creativity. Parenting a child through a meltdown? Creativity. Figuring out how to pay bills when money's tight? Creativity. Making someone laugh when the room feels heavy? Creativity. You don't have to publish a novel to be creative. You just have to live.

Creativity as Wholeness in Action

Here's why creativity is so sacred: it's wholeness in action. Guilt shrinks you. Fear paralyzes you. But wholeness expresses itself. When you know you're whole, you stop playing small. You let your ideas flow. You try things. You risk failure because you know failure doesn't define you. Creativity is simply the overflow of wholeness spilling into the world.

Think about children again. They're endlessly creative. Give a kid a cardboard box, and it's instantly a spaceship, a castle, a submarine. No shame. No self-consciousness. Just flow. That's divine creativity at work – natural, joyful, unforced. When you reclaim your inner child (as we discussed earlier), you reclaim that daily creativity.

Everyday Examples

Let's get practical. What does creativity in daily life look like?

- **In the Kitchen:** Instead of treating meals as chores, treat them as art. Throw in new spices. Experiment with colors. Make it playful. Creativity turns survival into celebration.
- **In Relationships:** When tension arises, instead of defaulting to the same arguments, get creative. Try humor. Try listening differently. Try writing your feelings instead of speaking them. Creativity builds bridges.
- **At Work:** Even if your job isn't "artistic," creativity still applies. Problem-solving, brainstorming, finding new ways to serve clients – all creativity. Your wholeness shows up every time you innovate.
- **In Spiritual Practice:** Instead of rote prayers, write your own. Instead of forced rituals, invent new ones. Maybe your prayer is a walk in nature. Maybe your ritual is singing in the shower. Creativity keeps spirituality alive and authentic.
- **In Service:** Find creative ways to Love people. Write a silly note. Leave a gift anonymously. Turn an errand into an adventure with someone you Love. Creativity in service multiplies joy.

Breaking the Old Programming

Of course, the old programming whispers: "Don't be silly. Don't risk embarrassment. Don't get it wrong." That's guilt trying to shut down creativity. But here's the truth: there is no "wrong" way to create when you're rooted in Love. Sure, your painting may not end up in the Louvre. But if it makes you smile, if it reminds you of your wholeness, if it adds one drop of joy to the world – it's holy.

When I first started to paint. I ended up with something that looked like a toddler's finger painting after a sugar binge. But you know what? I laughed. And that laughter was worth more than any polished masterpiece. The only thing I "created" that day was joy, and that was enough.

Creativity as Resistance

Here's a radical thought: daily creativity is resistance against the forces of guilt and fear. Every time you create with Love, you defy the system that told you to stay small. You declare: "I am not broken. I am not afraid. I am whole, and I am shaping life with joy." That's why creativity is so powerful – it's not just personal, it's political, spiritual, revolutionary.

Jeshua embodied this. Healing on the Sabbath wasn't just compassion – it was creative resistance. Eating with sinners wasn't just kindness – it was creative defiance. Forgiving enemies wasn't just generosity – it was creative rebellion against the culture of retaliation. Creativity in daily life isn't fluffy. It's the most practical form of Love in action.

Here are some ways to cultivate creativity in daily life:

1. **Ask New Questions.** Instead of "What's wrong?" ask, "What's possible?" Instead of "Why me?" ask, "What can I create here?" Questions open doors.
2. **Change One Thing.** Sit in a different chair. Take a new route. Rearrange a room. Small changes spark fresh perspectives.
3. **Play Daily.** Do something pointless on purpose. Doodle. Sing off- key. Tell bad jokes. Play disarms guilt and reopens the flow of imagination.
4. **Share Your Creations.** Don't hoard your poems, doodles, or ideas. Share them. The act of sharing multiplies light.
5. **Bless the Ordinary.** Next time you wash dishes, imagine you're baptizing them. Next time you mow the lawn, imagine you're painting with grass. Creativity is often just seeing ordinary tasks through sacred eyes.

The Drumbeat Truth

So let's repeat: creativity isn't reserved for artists. Creativity is daily. Creativity is how wholeness expresses itself. Creativity is how Love takes form. Every meal, every laugh, every problem solved, every act of kindness is creation. And when you do it from wholeness instead of guilt, the entire atmosphere changes.

Living as light isn't about grand gestures. It's about daily creativity. Jeshua didn't just perform "big" miracles – he embodied presence in the ordinary. And that's the invitation for us. To see every moment as an opportunity to create, to play, to Love, to shine.

That's creativity in daily life.

The Courage to Dream Big

Up to now, we've talked about everyday creativity, the kind that shows up in meals, conversations, problem-solving, and laughter. But there's another layer to creativity, one that frightens people even more than painting a bad picture or singing off-key: dreaming big. Not the kind of "big" that strokes the ego, but the kind of "big" that scares the old programming half to death. The kind of "big" that whispers: *What if my life could be more than survival? What if I could create something that changes me – and maybe even changes the world?*

Dreaming big takes courage. Because when you've been told your whole life that you're broken, unworthy, guilty, and small, the idea of dreaming big feels dangerous. Who are you to imagine that much? Who are you to create boldly? Who are you to think you can shine that brightly?

The old programming hisses: Stay small. Don't get ahead of yourself. Don't risk disappointment. Don't offend God with your ambition. But here's the truth: dreaming big isn't arrogance. It's obedience to your wholeness. It's listening to the inner voice that knows you were born with divine possibility pulsing in your veins. It's saying yes to the seeds Jeshua planted when he said, *"You will do even greater works than these."*

If God really wanted us to play small, He wouldn't have made the universe so ridiculously big. Galaxies upon galaxies, billions of stars, black holes, nebulae that look like cosmic lava lamps – and yet Saints wanted us to believe the main storyline was "humanity is a worm." If creation is that extravagant, maybe our dreams are supposed to be bigger than, "I hope I make it through life without angering God too much."

Why We Fear Big Dreams

Let's be honest: big dreams terrify us. They expose us to risk. They make failure a possibility. They invite criticism. And they threaten the little cages built by doctrine and fear. That's why most people stay in the "safe zone" of guilt-driven obedience. It's predictable. It doesn't risk embarrassment. It doesn't attract attention. But it also doesn't awaken the soul.

Religion helped cement that fear by labeling big dreams as prideful. Build a business? Pride. Write a book? Pride. Change the world? Definitely pride.

Unless, of course, you were building a cathedral for the Church – then suddenly it was holy ambition. Funny how that worked. The truth is, dreaming big outside of institutional approval was always threatening, because it put power back in your hands.

But Jeshua? He was a big dreamer. He dreamed of a world where the poor were lifted, the sick were healed, the outcasts were included, the violent were disarmed, and the whole thing ran on Love instead of fear. That wasn't small. That wasn't cautious. That was a dream so big it shook the Roman Empire. And he invited us to dream just as big.

Big Dreams as Acts of Love

Here's the crucial shift: big dreams aren't about ego. They're about Love. The question isn't, "How can I make myself great?" The question is, "What dream would let Love flow most fully through me into the world?" For one person, that might mean writing a book. For another, raising children with Love. For another, inventing technology. For another, building community. Big doesn't always mean visible. Big means aligned with Love's expansive flow.

Practical Steps to Dream Big

So how do you cultivate the courage to dream big?

1. **Listen to Desire Without Shame.** Desire is the seed of dreaming. For centuries, religion taught us to fear desire, as if every longing was sinful. But not all desires are selfish. Many desires are divine sparks. The desire to create, to

serve, to explore, to expand — those are holy. Sit with your desires and ask: "What Love is trying to be born through me?"

2. **Name the Old Voices.** When you dream big, the voices of fear and guilt will get loud. "Who are you to try that?" "What if you fail?" "You'll look foolish." Don't fight those voices. Name them. "Ah, that's guilt talking. That's fear echoing." Once you name them, you take away their power.
3. **Imagine Boldly.** Use the sacred power of imagination we talked about earlier. Picture the dream. Feel it as if it's real. Let it expand in your heart until it feels less like fantasy and more like destiny.
4. **Take Small Steps.** Big dreams don't happen all at once. They unfold step by step. Start small, but start. Write the first page. Make the first phone call. Take the first risk. Each step builds courage.
5. **Surround Yourself with Light.** Find people who believe in dreaming. Spend less time with those who feed fear. Jeshua didn't build his movement with cautious rule-followers. He gathered people who dared to imagine a different world.

Humor and Dreams

I remember the first time I seriously dreamed about creating something that mattered, a project that felt bigger than me. My first thought wasn't inspiration, it was, "Well, that's ridiculous." My second thought was, "Who do you think you are?" My third thought was, "Maybe I'll just take a nap." That's the thing about dreaming big — it often comes with a nap's worth of resistance. But if you push past the nap, you might actually change your life.

Other Traditions on Big Dreams

Dreaming big isn't unique to Christianity. In Buddhism, the Bodhisattva vow is a dream so big it spans lifetimes: to awaken not just for yourself but for all beings. In Hinduism, the Bhagavad Gita invites us into *dharma:* living our highest calling, no matter the cost. In Sufism, Rumi wrote, *"You were born with wings. Why prefer to crawl through life?"* All of them echo Jeshua's invitation: live big, Love big, dream big.

The Drumbeat Truth

So let's repeat it clearly, because the repetition helps it sink deeper than the fear:

- Smallness is not holiness.
- Playing safe is not faith.
- Dreaming big isn't arrogance – it's alignment.
- Your wholeness demands expression, not repression.

You are whole. You are Love. You are light. And light was never meant to be hidden under a basket.

So here's the invitation: dare to dream big. Not for ego, not for approval, but for Love. Let your wholeness overflow into visions that stretch you, challenge you, and maybe even scare you. That's the sign you're on the right track. Because guilt will always keep you small. Fear will always shrink your world. But Love – Love always expands.

That's the courage to dream big.

Manifesting Through Action

Dreaming big is powerful, but here's the danger: if you stop at dreaming, your vision stays locked inside your head like an unwritten book or an unopened gift. Imagination sparks the fire, but action carries the flame. Manifestation isn't magic – it's Love plus imagination plus action. And if wholeness has taught us anything, it's that your life is too sacred to leave your dreams gathering dust.

Religion often told us to wait.

"Pray and be patient."

"Wait for God's timing.

"Don't act until you're absolutely certain this is God's will."

Which usually translated into: "Stay passive, stay small, don't risk rocking the boat."

But Jeshua never modeled passivity. He acted. He didn't wait until it was convenient to heal on the Sabbath – he healed. He didn't wait until Rome approved his message – he preached. He didn't wait for permission to Love outsiders – he Loved them. Action was his language of faith.

Why Action Feels Risky

The problem is that guilt and fear make action terrifying. What if I fail? What if I'm wrong? What if God disapproves? What if people laugh? Those "what ifs" keep most dreams in permanent storage. Action feels dangerous because it makes your dream real. Once you act, it's out there. You can't hide behind "someday" anymore.

I once had a brilliant idea that I carried in my head for months. In my mind, it was perfect – revolutionary, life-changing. Then I finally tried it. Let's just say it crashed faster than a Windows 95 computer trying to run TikTok. But here's the thing – even though it failed, I learned more in that one messy attempt than in months of daydreaming. And the next attempt? Way better. That's the secret: failure in action is more fruitful than perfection in theory.

Jeshua on Manifestation

Jeshua's teachings were full of action. "Ask, seek, knock." Notice the verbs – not "wish, hope, sit quietly." Ask. Seek. Knock. All three require movement. When he fed the crowds, he told the disciples to *pass out the bread.* He didn't just zap everyone full with divine energy. He made them act. When he healed people, he often told them to *do something*: "*Take up your mat and walk.*" "*Go and show yourself to the priest.*" "*Stretch out your hand.*" Manifestation wasn't just about divine power – it was about human action aligned with divine flow. Using the full capacity of your thoughts, words, and deeds.

Manifestation Misunderstood

Now, let's clear up a misconception. A lot of modern spiritual circles talk about manifestation like it's a cosmic vending machine: visualize a Ferrari, and poof! The universe delivers. That's not creation, that's shopping with the Divine like it's Amazon Prime. Real manifestation is deeper. It's not about greed. It's about aligning your heart with Love, imagining boldly, and then acting courageously to bring it into form.

So yes, you might manifest abundance, but not to hoard it – to create, to share, to bless. Yes, you might manifest opportunities, but not to prove yourself – to expand Love's presence in the world.

Manifestation through action is about embodying wholeness, not inflating ego.

Practical Steps to Manifest Through Action

1. **Break the Dream into Steps.** Big dreams can feel overwhelming. Write them down and break them into bite-sized steps. If your dream is to write a book, your first step isn't "publish worldwide." It's "write a paragraph." Action begins small.
2. **Set Timelines Without Fear.** Not rigid deadlines that punish you, but gentle timelines that keep you moving. "I'll draft the outline this week." "I'll talk to one person about my idea this month." Timelines turn dreams into commitments.
3. **Practice Consistency.** Action isn't about grand bursts of energy. It's about steady movement. Ten minutes a day on your dream is better than waiting for a mythical free weekend that never comes.
4. **Celebrate Progress.** Every step counts. Every paragraph written, every conversation had, every experiment tried – celebrate it. Gratitude fuels momentum.
5. **Fail Forward.** When something flops, don't retreat. Ask, "What did I learn? How can I improve?" Failure isn't the opposite of manifestation – it's part of it.

Jeshua's own path included rejection and crucifixion. Yet even that was transformed into resurrection. Nothing is wasted when you act from Love.

The Cost of Inaction

Here's the hard truth: inaction is also a choice. It manifests something too: stagnation, frustration, regret. We often think waiting is safe, but it's not. Waiting robs the world of your light. Waiting denies Love the chance to flow through you. Waiting feeds guilt's lie that you're powerless. Action is the antidote.

Imagine if Jeshua had said, "You know what, guys? I think I'll hold off on this whole Kingdom of Heaven thing until the timing feels more aligned. Maybe in a couple of centuries when people are more open-minded." Christianity would still be a group chat of 12 fishermen arguing about lunch. Action matters.

Other Traditions on Action

Buddhism speaks of *right action* – living in alignment with compassion. Hinduism emphasizes *karma yoga* – selfless action as worship. Jeshua put water in the jugs before there was wine.

Everywhere, wisdom traditions affirm that dreams become reality not through passive wishing, but through courageous, aligned action.

The Drumbeat Truth

So let's repeat:

- Imagination sparks. Action grounds.
- Dreams inspire. Action manifests.
- Wholeness isn't just an inner state – it's expressed through what you *do.*

You are not guilty. You are not powerless. You are whole. And because you are whole, you act. Not out of fear. Not out of desperation. But out of Love overflowing into the world.

Manifesting through action is simply Love moving its feet, hands, and voice through you. It's how heaven shows up on earth. It's how wholeness takes shape in time and space. And every time you act, no matter how small, you're not just creating for yourself. You're expanding light for the world.

So don't just dream big. Act big. And when you stumble, act again. Because every act of Love is a miracle in motion.

That's manifesting through action.

Creating a World of Love

By now we've journeyed through the stages of creativity: discovering creation as a divine act, realizing we are co-creators with the Source, reclaiming imagination as sacred power, expressing creativity in daily life, daring to dream big, and manifesting those dreams through action. Each piece has been leading to this: the truth that your creativity doesn't just transform *you* – it transforms the world.

Wholeness isn't a private luxury. It's a collective revolution. The point of creating from wholeness is nothing less than creating a world of Love.

The Personal and the Global

At first glance, that might sound too big. After all, how can one person create a world of Love? But remember: every act of creation ripples outward. A laugh lightens the burden of another. A kind word shifts someone's day. A book changes a generation's thinking. A movement begins because one person dared to act differently. Jeshua himself didn't overthrow Rome with armies – he did it by planting seeds of Love so contagious they're still growing two millennia later.

The world of Love doesn't appear all at once. It's not handed down from heaven like a ready-made package. It's built moment by moment, act by act, dream by dream. When you choose Love over fear, forgiveness over revenge, presence over distraction, creation over passivity, you are literally shaping the world. And when millions do the same, culture shifts.

Jeshua's World of Love

Jeshua's entire mission was about this. He imagined a kingdom not built on domination but on compassion. Not on fear but on Love. Not on hierarchy but on equality. In his world of Love, the last were first, the poor were blessed, the outcasts were welcomed, the broken were healed. That wasn't a future dream. It was a present invitation. He said, *"The Kingdom of God is at hand."* Not someday. Now. And then he embodied it in action – eating with sinners, forgiving enemies, healing the untouchable. He created a microcosm of Love in his daily life, and it rippled outward into history.

Imagine Jeshua at a modern political rally. Instead of promising tax cuts or military power, he steps up to the mic and says, *"Blessed are the peacemakers. Blessed are the poor. Love your enemies."* Half the crowd would cheer, half would boo, and Twitter would explode with hashtags like #LoveIsSocialism. But that's the thing: Love is always revolutionary.

The Obstacles to a World of Love

Of course, guilt and fear don't go quietly. They whisper that Love is naïve. That compassion is weakness. That forgiveness is foolish. Institutions profit from fear, so they'll always sow division. Empires thrive on control, so they'll always resist Love's leveling force. But here's the truth: Love outlasts them all. Empires crumble. Doctrines shift. Fear burns out. Love endures. Every time.

The challenge is that building a world of Love requires persistence. It's not a one-day project. It's a lifelong practice. You'll meet resistance, cynicism, mockery. But that's where courage comes in. You keep showing up. You keep creating. You keep embodying wholeness until Love becomes not just your personal reality, but a collective one.

Practical Ways to Create a World of Love

1. **Start Local.** You don't have to fix the whole planet in one swoop. Start with your circle. Bring Love into your family, your workplace, your community. Small ripples expand into big waves.
2. **Use Your Gifts.** What lights you up? Writing, teaching, cooking, building, listening? Use it. Your unique creativity is your contribution to the world of Love. Don't downplay it because it seems small. A cup of water offered in Love is world-changing.
3. **Challenge Systems of Fear.** Whenever you see institutions spreading fear or shame, speak up. Whether it's a workplace culture of control, a religious leader guilt-tripping a congregation, or a political system scapegoating the vulnerable, resist it with truth and Love.
4. **Build Communities of Wholeness.** Wholeness grows best in community. Gather with others who are committed to Love. Create spaces where people can breathe freely, laugh deeply, and dream boldly. Jeshua didn't go it alone. He built community. So should we.
5. **Live the Example.** Nothing is more persuasive than a life lived in Love. When you embody joy, forgiveness, peace, and courage, others notice. They may not understand it, but they'll be drawn to it. Your life becomes an invitation.

Humor and Hope

Imagine if, instead of guilt-laden sermons, churches worldwide had comedy nights where the whole point was to laugh, Love, and enjoy each other's company. Attendance would skyrocket.

Donations would probably triple. And best of all, people would walk out lighter, freer, and more likely to create a world of Love in their neighborhoods.

Maybe Jeshua's first miracle at the wedding wasn't about wine at all; maybe it was about saying, "*Don't forget: joy builds the kingdom.*"

Other Voices on a World of Love

This dream isn't unique to Jeshua. Buddha dreamed of a compassionate society where suffering was eased by mindfulness and kindness. Muhammad spoke of justice and mercy as central to community. The prophets of Israel cried for swords to be beaten into plowshares. Modern voices like Gandhi, Martin Luther King Jr., and Mother Teresa all dreamed and acted toward a world of Love. Different traditions, same heartbeat.

The Drumbeat Truth

Let's repeat the truths that carry us forward:

- You are whole.
- Because you are whole, you create.
- Because you create, you shape the world.
- And when you create from Love, the world bends toward Love.

That's how empires fall and communities heal. That's how guilt loses its grip and joy takes its place. That's how heaven comes to earth – not through fear, but through creation rooted in wholeness.

The Invitation

Here's the invitation: don't stop with personal healing. Don't stop with private creativity. Let your wholeness spill into the world. Let your laughter shake the walls of fear. Let your forgiveness dismantle chains of hate. Let your joy be contagious. Let your dreams turn into action that blesses others.

Because the endgame of all this isn't just you living free. It's humanity living free. It's not just your shadow of guilt dissolving. It's the collective shadow lifting. It's not just you stepping into the light. It's the world awakening to its light.

That's the ultimate act of creation: a world of Love. And it begins, as always, here and now, with you.

Chapter 11: Living the Way of Love

Love as the Core of the Way

We've dismantled the weight of doctrine, exposed the invention of original sin, stepped out of the shadow of guilt, reclaimed our wholeness, and begun to create from that wholeness. But if there's one word that captures the essence of Jeshua's entire teaching, one thread that ties everything together, it's this: **Love.**

Not duty. Not guilt. Not fear. Love. That was the core of Jeshua's Way. Strip away the centuries of dogma, the layers of ritual, the theological gymnastics – what remains is disarmingly simple: Love God, Love yourself, Love others. Everything else is commentary.

Love is Misunderstood

The problem is, "Love" is one of the most overused and misunderstood words in human history. It's been turned into a slogan, watered down into sentimentality, and weaponized into obligation. How many sermons have ended with "Love one another," immediately followed by a laundry list of conditions, rules, and exclusions? "Of course we Love people, but only if they repent." "We Love the sinner but hate the sin." "We Love our neighbors, but only the ones in our denomination." That's not Love. That's legalism in disguise.

Jeshua's Love was far more radical. It had no conditions, no boundaries, no fine print. He Loved the outcast, the foreigner, the enemy. He Loved the people religion said were unworthy. He Loved without fear that he'd be tainted by association. He Loved not as performance, but as presence.

Imagine Jeshua showing up at a modern church potluck. He sits down with the divorced woman, the gay teenager, the guy with tattoos and piercings, and the alcoholic uncle who everyone else avoids. Half the congregation whispers, "How scandalous!" Jeshua just laughs and passes the mashed potatoes. That's Love – not the sanitized version, but the raw, inclusive, messy kind.

Love as Wholeness Expressed

Here's why Love is central: Love is what wholeness looks like in motion. Wholeness without Love is just theory. But when you live as if you're whole, Love naturally flows outward. You forgive, not because you "should," but because holding grudges feels unnatural when you know you're whole. You serve, not to earn points, but because Love wants to overflow. You laugh, not to prove joy, but because joy is Love's native tongue.

That's why Jeshua said the greatest commandments were about Love. Love God. Love neighbor. Love yourself. He boiled down centuries of religious law into a single principle: wholeness expressed through Love.

The Cost of Love

Of course, Love isn't cheap. It's not easy. Real Love costs you your fear, your pride, your need to control. Loving enemies costs you your comfort. Loving yourself costs you your shame. Loving without condition costs you the approval of those who thrive on judgment.

Jeshua was crucified not because he hated, but because he Loved too freely. Love threatened the systems of fear, so they tried to silence it.

But here's the truth: Love is stronger than death. That's the point of resurrection — not a magic trick, but the cosmic announcement that Love cannot be killed. Empires fall, doctrines fade, fear burns out, but Love endures.

Practicing Love Daily

So how do we live Love in practical terms?

1. **Begin Within:** Self-Love is not selfish. It's the foundation. When you treat yourself with compassion, you break the cycle of shame and guilt. Talk to yourself kindly. Rest without apology. Forgive your mistakes.
2. **Extend Outward:** Look for opportunities to Love in small ways: a smile, a listening ear, a kind word, a simple act of service. Love doesn't need to be grand to be holy.
3. **Stretch Further:** Practice loving beyond your comfort zone. Who triggers you? Who feels undeserving? Who's the "enemy" in your story? Love doesn't mean excusing harm, but it does mean refusing to dehumanize.
4. **Create Systems of Love:** Love isn't just personal — it's structural. Advocate for justice. Build communities where

people are valued. Love must move from private virtue to public practice.

Other Voices on Love

This isn't just Jeshua's message. Buddha taught compassion for all beings. The Bhagavad Gita speaks of devotion (bhakti) as the highest path. The Quran says, "*God is Love.*" Modern voices echo it too – Martin Luther King, Jr., said, *Love is the only force capable of transforming an enemy into a friend."* Everywhere wisdom speaks, Love is the heartbeat.

Humor and Humanity

If churches actually took Jeshua's command to "Love your neighbor" literally, church parking lots would be full of potlucks with rival denominations, karaoke nights with atheists, and football games where everyone shared the nachos. Instead, we had centuries of schisms and arguments about doctrine. Love got buried under paperwork. But Love doesn't care about paperwork. It cares about people.

The Drumbeat Truth

So let's repeat, because this truth is the foundation of everything that follows:

- Love is not optional. It's the essence of the Way.
- Love is not conditional. It includes everyone, no exceptions.
- Love is not weak. It's the most powerful force in the universe.
- Love is not abstract. It's practical, embodied, daily.

The Enduring Way

This is why Jeshua's Way has endured while empires have crumbled. Not because of complex theology or rigid rituals, but because Love is eternal. When you live in Love, you live in alignment with the deepest truth of the universe. And when enough of us do that together, we don't just heal ourselves – we create a world of Love.

That's the core of the Way. That's why everything we've explored so far leads here. Wholeness, freedom, creativity – all of it finds its meaning when expressed as Love.

Love Beyond Doctrine

Love is the heartbeat of Jeshua's Way. Let us take this a step further: Love is not bound by doctrine. In fact, Love often has to break through doctrine just to breathe. Doctrine builds fences. Love tears them down. Doctrine says, "In, out, right, wrong, worthy, unworthy." Love says, "All belong. All are worthy. All are Loved."

Doctrine as a Cage

Doctrine is essentially humanity's attempt to manage mystery. Someone has an experience of God – profound, liberating, beyond words. But then the institution comes along and says, "We need to regulate this. We need rules. We need a manual." And just like that, the living water of Love gets poured into jars of dogma. Over time, those jars start to crack. The water leaks. What once was alive turns stagnant.

The Catholic Church, where I spent much of my youth, is a perfect example. Doctrine after doctrine layered on top of Jeshua's simple message until it became unrecognizable. Original sin. Mortal sin versus venial sin. Transubstantiation. Purgatory. Limbo. The Immaculate Conception. Papal infallibility. Each one another brick in the wall, another hoop to jump through, another burden to carry. None of them central to Jeshua's Way, all of them distractions from Love.

Doctrine is like a cosmic Terms of Service agreement. "By clicking 'accept,' you agree to abide by the following 237 conditions. Violations may result in eternal damnation." And unlike Apple, you can't scroll to the bottom and click "I agree" without reading. The Church insists you memorize it all.

Jeshua's Radical Simplicity

Contrast that with Jeshua. He was constantly pushing against doctrinal boundaries. Healing on the Sabbath? Against the rules. Touching lepers? Against the rules. Talking to women in public? Against the rules. Forgiving sins without temple rituals? Definitely against the rules. Jeshua's whole ministry was one long confrontation with doctrine. Not because he hated his tradition, but because he Loved too much to let doctrine suffocate compassion.

When asked to summarize the law, Jeshua didn't rattle off a list of 613 commandments. He said, *Love God with all your heart. Love your neighbor as yourself. On these hang all the law and the prophets."* In other words, "Love is the doctrine. The rest is commentary." That was scandalous then, and it's still scandalous now.

Love Without Boundaries

Here's the radical truth: Love doesn't need doctrine to justify it. Love is self-validating. When you forgive, when you serve, when you include, when you uplift, you don't need a theological treatise to back it up. The act itself proves its divinity. Love beyond doctrine doesn't ask, "What does the catechism say?" It asks, "What does compassion require?"

Of course, that makes institutions nervous. Because if Love is the only measure, then you don't need bishops, councils, or papal decrees.

You don't need confessions or indulgences. You don't need a religious bureaucracy. You just need Love. And that threatens the entire enterprise built on controlling access to God.

Imagine if churches replaced catechism classes with Love labs. Instead of memorizing doctrine, kids would practice random acts of kindness, write letters of forgiveness, and invent new ways to serve their neighbors. The Vatican would collapse within a decade – but the Kingdom of Heaven would flourish.

Love Over Rules

Imagine sitting in confession, rattling off your list of sins – some real, most imaginary – when the priest interrupted and said, "You know, God already Loves you. You don't need to torture yourself like this." That would be a crack in the wall. For a split second, doctrine lost its grip, and Love broke through. You would leave lighter, not because of the ritual, but because someone dared to point you back to Love.

Practical Ways to Live Love Beyond Doctrine

So how do we actually live this?

1. **Prioritize Compassion Over Rules.** When rules and Love clash, choose Love. Every time. If a doctrine tells you to

exclude, shame, or punish, ask yourself: "Does this align with Love?" If not, let it go.

2. **See People, Not Labels.** Doctrines love labels: sinner, saint, heretic, believer, outsider. Love ignores labels. It looks into eyes and sees humanity. Practice seeing people beyond their categories.
3. **Trust Inner Guidance.** Doctrines are external. Love flows from within. When you feel a nudge toward kindness, trust it. That's the Spirit's law written on your heart, not on stone tablets.
4. **Build Communities Around Love.** Create groups, circles, families, workplaces where the guiding principle is Love, not dogma. Celebrate creativity, compassion, and presence. Let Love be the organizing force.

Wisdom Beyond Christianity

This truth isn't unique to Jeshua. Buddha taught that attachment to rules and rituals can be a trap. The Tao Te Ching says, "*The more prohibitions there are, the poorer the people become.*" Rumi declared, "*Out beyond ideas of wrongdoing and rightdoing, there is a field. I'll meet you there.*" Love beyond doctrine is that field.

The Drumbeat Truth

Let's drive it home with repetition:

- Doctrine divides. Love unites.
- Doctrine complicates. Love simplifies.
- Doctrine excludes. Love includes.
- Doctrine demands. Love gives.

Love beyond doctrine is not lawless. It's law fulfilled. Jeshua didn't abolish the law – he fulfilled it by embodying Love. That's the Way.

Dare to live Love beyond doctrine. Let compassion be your catechism. Let kindness be your creed. Let humanity be your theology. When in doubt, choose Love. Always.

That's how we begin to live the Way of Love.

Love of Self and Others

If Jeshua's Way could be reduced to a single formula, it might be this: *Love God, Love your neighbor, Love yourself.* But here's the part religion often misses: those three Loves are not separate commands. They're one reality. You can't Love God without loving people. You can't Love people without loving yourself. And you can't Love yourself without recognizing the Divine presence within you. They're not three hoops to jump through — they're one circle of Love.

The Problem with Skipping Self-Love

The Church has spent centuries preaching "Love your neighbor," but almost never "Love yourself." In fact, self-Love was often painted as pride, vanity, or selfishness. "Deny yourself" was interpreted as "despise yourself." The result? Whole generations of people trying to Love others while hating themselves. That doesn't work. You can't pour from an empty cup. You can't share Love you refuse to give yourself.

Imagine trying to bake cookies for your neighbor while refusing to eat anything yourself. By day three, you'd collapse in the kitchen, surrounded by crumbs, muttering, "But at least the doctrine says I'm selfless!" That's how ridiculous it is to think self-hatred is holy.

Jeshua never taught self-hatred. He taught wholeness. And wholeness includes you. When he said, *Love your neighbor as yourself,"* the assumption was that you *do* Love yourself. That you nourish your body, forgive your mistakes, honor your humanity. Self-Love was the baseline. Without it, the whole formula collapses.

Loving Yourself as a Sacred Act

So what does self-Love look like in Jeshua's Way? It's not ego-inflation. It's not arrogance. It's recognizing your worth as a child of the Divine. It's saying, "*I am not broken. I am whole. I am Loved.*" And then living as if that were true.

Self-Love means caring for your body not as an enemy but as a temple. It means resting without guilt. It means feeding yourself with good things, physically and spiritually. It means forgiving your failures, because Love keeps no record of wrongs. It means speaking kindly to yourself instead of repeating the insults of guilt.

Self-Love is sacred because it affirms what God already affirmed when He breathed life into you: *"It is very good."*

The Overflow into Others

And here's the beauty: when you Love yourself, it doesn't stop with you. It overflows. Forgiven people forgive. Joyful people spread joy. Whole people create wholeness. When you treat yourself with compassion, you find it easier to extend compassion to others. When you stop beating yourself up, you stop beating up the people around you.

Jeshua understood this. That's why he tied self-Love and neighbor-Love together. They're not two commands but two sides of the same coin. You Love your neighbor in the same way you Love yourself. If your self-Love is harsh, your neighbor-Love will be too. If your self-Love is compassionate, your neighbor-Love will follow suit.

The Trap of Self-Neglect

Religion often romanticizes self-neglect. The saints who starved themselves, whipped their backs, or lived in misery were held up as examples. But what did that teach ordinary people? That the more you despised yourself, the holier you were. That's not holiness. That's trauma dressed in robes.

Jeshua ate with joy, drank wine at weddings, rested when tired, and Loved himself enough to withdraw for solitude when necessary. He modeled healthy self-Love. He didn't burn himself out. He embodied balance. If the Son of Man needed naps, maybe we can too.

Picture Jeshua on a modern self-care Instagram page. "Today's reminder: take naps, drink water, forgive yourself, and don't argue with Pharisees on Twitter." He'd have millions of followers – and probably just as many trolls.

Loving Others Practically

Once you've reclaimed self-Love, loving others becomes natural. And loving others is more than vague sentiment – it's practical, embodied.

- **Listening deeply.** Giving someone your full attention is an act of Love.
- **Showing kindness.** Small acts (holding a door, offering a smile) ripple outward.

- **Offering forgiveness.** Not holding grudges frees both you and the other.
- **Seeking justice.** Love isn't passive. It challenges systems that harm people.
- **Sharing joy.** Laughing with others is one of the simplest and most healing acts of Love.

Notice that all of these mirror what you practice with yourself. Listening to your own needs helps you listen to others. Forgiving yourself helps you forgive others. Bringing joy to yourself helps you share joy with others. The pattern repeats outward.

Other Traditions on Self and Neighbor

This unity of self-Love and neighbor-Love shows up everywhere. Buddha said, *You yourself, as much as anybody in the entire universe, deserve your Love and affection."* The Quran says, *None of you truly believes until he Loves for his brother what he Loves for himself."* The Talmud echoes, *What is hateful to you, do not do to your neighbor."* Everywhere wisdom speaks, it links Love of self and others.

Practices to Cultivate Both

1. **Mirror Work.** Look in the mirror and tell yourself daily: "I Love you. I forgive you. I am whole." This builds the muscle of self-Love.
2. **Gratitude Journals.** Write down things you Love about yourself and things you Love about others. Gratitude expands Love both ways.
3. **Compassionate Dialogue.** When you catch yourself judging someone harshly, ask: "Do I treat myself the same way?" Then shift both inner and outer speech to compassion.
4. **Acts of Service.** Do something kind for yourself each day (rest, play, nourishment), and something kind for someone else. Balance creates flow.

The Drumbeat Truth

Let's hammer this home:

- Self-Love is not selfish. It's sacred.
- Neighbor-Love is not optional. It's essential.

- The two are inseparable. To deny one is to diminish the other.
- Together, they form the living circle of Jeshua's Way.

Stop hating yourself in the name of holiness. Stop neglecting yourself in the name of service. Stop dividing what Jeshua united. Love yourself. Love others. And in doing so, Love God. It's all one circle, one flow, one reality.

That's Love of self and others – the heart of the Way in action.

Love of Enemies

If there's one teaching of Jeshua that makes people squirm, it's this one: *Love your enemies, do good to those who hate you, bless those who curse you, pray for those who mistreat you."* Let's be honest – it sounds insane. Loving your friends? Easy. Loving your family? Possible (on good days). Loving your neighbor? With some patience.

But loving your enemies? That feels like crossing into the twilight zone.

And yet, this is where Jeshua's Way breaks completely from fear-based religion. Most religions, especially in their institutional forms, draw lines between "us" and "them." Love your people, but hate your enemies. Bless your tribe, but curse the outsiders. Jeshua torched that whole framework. He said Love doesn't stop at the border. Love doesn't stop at the sanctuary door. Love doesn't even stop when people actively hate you. Love keeps going.

Why Enemy Love Is So Radical

Enemy Love is radical because it dismantles the cycle of fear and retaliation. Fear says, "Protect yourself by striking first." Ego says, "Get even." Guilt says, "They're bad, so punish them." But Love says, "Even here, even now, this person remains human. They are not beyond compassion."

Imagine what that meant in Jeshua's time. His people lived under Roman occupation: soldiers everywhere, taxes that crushed the poor, crucifixions on the roadside. The Pharisees wanted purity through rigid rules. The Zealots wanted violent revolt. Jeshua said, "Love your enemies." It wasn't a sweet sentiment. It was a revolutionary act. Refusing to hate Rome was more dangerous than raising a sword. It undercut the entire system of violence.

Picture Jeshua at a Roman checkpoint. A soldier snarls, "Carry my pack a mile!" Jeshua says, "*Sure – I'll take it two.*" The soldier stares, confused, thinking, "Did this guy just volunteer for overtime?" That's the power of enemy Love. It flips the script so thoroughly that the oppressor doesn't know how to respond.

Why It Feels Impossible

Let's admit it – this teaching feels impossible. Loving enemies goes against every instinct. When you've been hurt, betrayed, lied to, or oppressed, Love feels like weakness. The old programming screams, "If I Love them, they'll just keep hurting me. If I forgive, they'll get away with it."

But Jeshua never said enemy Love meant being a doormat. He didn't say, "Let people abuse you forever." He didn't say, "Stay in toxic relationships." He said, "*Do not return hate with hate. Do not let violence define you. Do not let fear shrink your humanity.*" Loving enemies isn't about excusing harm – it's about refusing to let harm turn you into a mirror image of your oppressor.

Enemy Love in Practice

So how do we actually live this out?

1. **Humanize them.** See your enemy as human first. They have fears, wounds, and stories. They are not just "villain." This doesn't excuse harm, but it breaks the illusion that they are monsters beyond redemption.
2. **Refuse retaliation.** When attacked, resist the urge to strike back in kind. Responding with hate keeps the cycle alive. Breaking the cycle requires a different energy.
3. **Pray or wish them well.** Not easy, but transformative. When you bless someone who hurt you, you shift the energy. You stop feeding their darkness with your darkness.
4. **Set boundaries in Love.** Loving enemies doesn't mean letting them destroy you. Sometimes Love means walking away. Sometimes Love means holding them accountable. But the spirit behind it is healing, not vengeance.

5. **Let Love transform you.** Even if your enemy never changes, your heart changes. You stop carrying the poison of hatred. You stop letting bitterness rot you from within.

I once carried a deep grudge against someone who betrayed my trust. For years, I replayed the hurt. I imagined confrontations, victories, clever comebacks. All it did was keep me trapped in anger. The day I decided to let it go, to Love them from afar, to wish them healing, I felt lighter. They didn't change, but I did. That's the gift of enemy Love: it liberates you first.

Other Traditions on Enemy Love

This teaching isn't unique to Jeshua, though he expressed it most boldly. Buddha taught compassion even for those who harm you. Gandhi embodied nonviolence, insisting that even oppressors must be confronted with Love. Martin Luther King Jr. preached that *"hate cannot drive out hate; only Love can do that."* Across cultures, the wisdom is clear: enemy Love is the only force strong enough to break cycles of violence.

Humor and Humanity

Imagine a world where drivers actually practiced enemy Love on the highway. Someone cuts you off, and instead of honking, you say, "*Bless you, friend, may you reach your destination safely.*" Road rage would disappear overnight. Insurance companies would go out of business. Jeshua would be proud.

The Drumbeat Truth

Let's repeat it, because this truth is too radical to sink in all at once:

- Loving enemies is not weakness. It is the highest strength.
- Loving enemies doesn't excuse harm. It transforms response.
- Loving enemies doesn't guarantee they'll change. It guarantees *you* will.
- Loving enemies is not optional in Jeshua's Way. It is the heart of it.

The Ultimate Test

Enemy Love is the ultimate test of wholeness. It takes everything we've learned – presence, imagination, courage, forgiveness – and applies it where it's hardest. And that's why it's the most powerful.

Anyone can Love their friends. Anyone can Love their family (again, with effort). But to Love your enemies – that's divine. That's when you truly embody the Way of Love.

Think of your enemies. The people who hurt you. The ones who trigger your anger. The ones you'd rather curse than bless. And dare to Love them. Not perfectly. Not all at once. But in some small way, today. Because that's where the Kingdom of Love truly breaks into the world.

That's Love of enemies – Jeshua's most radical call, and our most transformative practice.

Love in Action

Talking about Love is easy. We can debate it, define it, even sing about it. But unless Love becomes action, it remains an idea – nice, poetic, and utterly useless. Jeshua didn't come to give us a Hallmark card; he came to show us a Way. And the Way was not abstract. It was concrete, embodied, lived out in sweat, laughter, tears, bread, wine, and healing touch. Love in action is what turned a radical idea into a living movement.

Why Action Matters

Religion has always been tempted to stop at words. Long creeds, endless sermons, theological treatises – mountains of talk. But Jeshua was not a philosopher spinning theories. He was a carpenter-turned-healer who *did* things. He touched lepers. He ate with outcasts. He washed feet. He fed the hungry. He forgave enemies. Each act was Love made visible.

This is why the early church spread: not because of its doctrine, but because of its action. Pagans in the Roman Empire noted that Christians cared for the sick, rescued abandoned infants, and shared food with the poor. It was Love in action, not Love in theory, that caught people's attention.

Imagine if Jeshua had acted like a modern-day theologian. Someone asks, "What must I do to inherit eternal life?" Instead of telling the story of the Good Samaritan, he pulls out a 400-page doctrinal manual and says, "First, let's define justification." The crowds would've vanished by chapter two.

The Pitfall of Words Without Action

Words without action breed hypocrisy. Saying, "I Love everyone" but refusing to actually Love anyone is empty. It's like promising to bake cookies but never turning on the oven. The world doesn't need more theories of Love. It needs more acts of Love.

And here's the thing: guilt-based religion often substitutes words for action. Confess the creed, repeat the prayers, recite the doctrine – and never actually Love your neighbor. Jeshua flipped it: "If you Love me, feed my sheep." Action first. Words second.

What Does Love in Action Look Like?

It doesn't have to be dramatic. You don't have to walk on water. Love in action shows up in the small and ordinary.

- Feeding someone who's hungry.
- Listening without judgment.
- Helping a neighbor with a chore.
- Forgiving when you could retaliate.
- Showing up for someone in crisis.

These acts may seem small, but in the logic of Love, they're massive. Jeshua said giving a cup of water mattered. A cup of water! That's Love in action.

Love as Daily Practice

Love in action is not a one-time grand gesture. It's a daily rhythm. Each morning, you ask: "How can I embody Love today?" Each night, you reflect: "Where did I live Love? Where can I grow?" It's a practice, like breathing.

1. **In Family.** Love looks like patience with your kids, kindness with your partner, forgiveness when tensions rise.
2. **In Work.** Love looks like integrity, generosity, and serving colleagues rather than competing with them.
3. **In Community.** Love looks like volunteering, advocating, and caring for those who are often ignored.
4. **In Strangers.** Love looks like smiles, generosity, and small acts of kindness that ripple outward.

Picture Jeshua in a modern grocery store. He sees a stressed-out mom juggling kids and groceries, and instead of quoting Isaiah, he says, "Here, let me bag those for you." That's Love in action. And it probably says more about God than 90% of sermons.

The Courage to Act

Let's be honest – Love in action takes courage. It's easier to talk about Love than to risk living it. Action requires vulnerability. It requires energy. It sometimes requires standing up against injustice, even when it costs you. Jeshua didn't just say "Love your enemies." He acted it out, forgiving his executioners even as they nailed him to wood. That's not safe. That's not easy. But it's Love in its purest form.

Practical Practices

How can we practice Love in action?

1. **Daily Intention.** Start each day by choosing one concrete act of Love you'll do. Small or big, just commit.
2. **Love Lists.** Keep a running list of needs you notice around you. Look for opportunities to meet one each week.
3. **Secret Acts.** Practice Love anonymously. Leave a gift. Pay for someone's meal. Encourage without credit. Secret Love deepens sincerity.
4. **Active Forgiveness.** Take a step toward reconciling with someone, not just in your mind but with an action – a call, a note, a gesture.
5. **Embodied Presence.** Sometimes Love is simply showing up. Be physically present where people need support.

Other Traditions on Love in Action

The Bhagavad Gita calls it *karma yoga:* Love expressed in selfless action. Buddhism calls it *compassion in practice:* reducing suffering through daily deeds. Islam emphasizes charity as a pillar of faith.

Everywhere, wisdom traditions insist: Love is meaningless unless embodied.

The Drumbeat Truth

So let's repeat until it sinks:

- Love in words is easy. Love in action is transformative.
- Love in theory is safe. Love in action is risky – and real.
- Love in private is good. Love in public is world-changing. You are not called to talk about Love. You are called to live it.

At the end of the day, Jeshua won't ask if we memorized doctrine. He'll ask if we Loved. Did we feed the hungry? Did we forgive enemies? Did we lift the fallen? Did we embody compassion? That's Love in action. That's the Way.

Stop talking about Love as if it's optional. Start living it as if it's your nature. Because it is. Wholeness without Love in action is incomplete. But Love embodied? That changes everything.

That's Love in action.

The Transformative Power of Love

We've talked about Love as the core of Jeshua's Way, Love beyond doctrine, Love of self and others, Love of enemies, and Love in action. But now we need to step back and look at the bigger picture: Love doesn't just make us feel good. It transforms us. It transforms relationships. It transforms communities. And ultimately, it transforms history. Love is not just an emotion; it's a force. When lived fully, it reshapes everything it touches.

How Love Transforms the Individual

Let's start with the personal. Love transforms you first. Think about the times you've truly felt Loved – not tolerated, not conditionally accepted, but Loved for who you are. What happened? You relaxed. You breathed easier. You stopped pretending. You dared to dream again. Love has this uncanny way of dismantling fear at the root. Fear makes you shrink. Love makes you expand.

This is why Jeshua's encounters with people were so transformative. The woman at the well went from outcast to evangelist after one conversation. Zacchaeus the tax collector gave half his wealth to the poor after one dinner. Why? Because they were

Loved. Not judged, not lectured, not threatened. Loved. That Love woke them up to who they truly were.

Imagine if Jeshua had tried the church's usual method. He sees Zacchaeus up in the tree and says, "Hey, sinner! You've broken seventeen laws and you'll burn forever unless you fix it." Zacchaeus probably would've climbed higher into the branches and stayed there. Instead, Jeshua said, "*I'm coming to your house for dinner.*" That's Love in action – and it transformed Zacchaeus.

How Love Transforms Relationships

Love doesn't just change individuals. It changes relationships. When you respond to others with Love instead of fear, something shifts.

Arguments de-escalate. Trust builds. Forgiveness becomes possible. Love doesn't guarantee every relationship will survive, but it guarantees that when it does, it will be healthier.

Think about marriages or friendships. Without Love, they become transactions: "What can I get from you?" With Love, they become sanctuaries: "*How can we grow together*?" Love turns competition into collaboration, suspicion into trust, bitterness into healing.

How Love Transforms Communities

But Love doesn't stop at individuals and relationships. It expands into communities. Imagine a neighborhood where people actually Loved their neighbors – sharing resources, helping each other, forgiving offenses. Crime would plummet. Isolation would disappear. Joy would rise. Communities built on fear build walls. Communities built on Love build tables.

This is why the early Christian movement was so magnetic. People looked at the communities Jeshua's followers built and said, "See how they Love one another." That Love was transformative. It drew people in. Not because the theology was airtight, but because the Love was undeniable.

Picture a modern neighborhood transformed by Love. Instead of fighting over HOA rules about lawn height, neighbors host potlucks and share lawnmowers. Instead of complaining about barking dogs, they babysit each other's pets. Instead of stealing Amazon packages, they deliver them to each other's doors. It sounds like a miracle. And it is, because Love transforms ordinary streets into sacred spaces.

How Love Transforms Systems

Now let's go even bigger. Love transforms systems. Fear-based systems thrive on control, punishment, and division. Love dismantles them. Think about slavery. It was Love — the conviction that every human is equal, worthy, divine — that fueled abolition movements.

Think about segregation. It was Love — nonviolent, courageous, resilient — that fueled the civil rights movement. Every great social shift toward justice has been powered by Love refusing to bow to fear.

This is why Jeshua's teaching was so dangerous. He wasn't just telling individuals to be nice. He was challenging systems of oppression with the force of Love. When he touched lepers, he defied purity laws. When he healed on the Sabbath, he defied religious control. When he forgave enemies, he defied political violence. Love wasn't a Hallmark card. It was a revolution.

The Inner Alchemy of Love

On a mystical level, Love transforms because it is alchemical. It takes fear and turns it into courage. It takes guilt and turns it into forgiveness. It takes shame and turns it into dignity. It takes death and turns it into resurrection. Love doesn't ignore pain — it transmutes it.

Jeshua on the cross is the ultimate example: violence was transformed into forgiveness, despair into hope, death into life.

Practices for Transformative Love

So how do we tap into this power in our daily lives?

1. **Practice Radical Forgiveness.** Not cheap forgiveness, but deep release. Transform resentment into compassion.
2. **Embody Presence.** Love transforms most when you are fully here with someone — listening, seeing, honoring.
3. **Serve Where It Hurts.** Love in easy places is fine. Love in hard places is transformative. Go where need is great.
4. **Refuse Dehumanization.** Whenever fear paints someone as less than human, resist. See their wholeness.

5. **Create Love Systems.** Organize communities, businesses, or families around Love – fairness, compassion, and creativity.

Other Traditions on Transformative Love

The Bhagavad Gita says devotion (bhakti) transforms even the most broken soul. Buddhism teaches meta-meditation – radiating loving-kindness until it transforms perception and relationship. Sufism is drenched in the transformative poetry of Rumi: *Through Love all that is bitter will be sweet; through Love all that is copper will be gold."* Everywhere wisdom speaks, Love is the great transformer.

The Drumbeat Truth

Let's repeat the truths we must not forget:

- Love transforms fear into courage.
- Love transforms guilt into forgiveness.
- Love transforms strangers into family.
- Love transforms the world, one act at a time.

This isn't theory. It's history. It's experience. It's the heart of Jeshua's Way.

So don't settle for Love as a warm feeling. Don't water it down into sentimentality. Dare to live the transformative power of Love. Let it change you first, then your relationships, then your community, then the world. That's how the Kingdom of Heaven breaks in – not through fear, not through doctrine, not through force, but through Love transforming everything it touches.

That's the transformative power of Love.

Living as Love

We've explored Love as the heartbeat of Jeshua's Way, as something that breaks beyond doctrine, as a circle that embraces self and others, as a force even toward enemies, as action in daily life, and as transformation for individuals and systems. Now comes the deepest invitation of all: to *live as Love itself.* Not just to practice Love occasionally, not just to admire it as an ideal, but to let it become your very identity.

Love as Identity

Most of us think of Love as something we *do* — a verb, an action. And yes, Love is action. But Jeshua pointed us to something even more radical: Love as *being. "God is Love,"* said John in his gospel and letters. If God is Love and the Kingdom of God is within you, then Love is not just what you do. It is who you *are.*

Living as Love means you stop seeing Love as a choice you make when you're in the mood. Instead, it becomes the default posture of your existence. Just as the sun doesn't decide whether to shine, Love doesn't decide whether to Love. It simply radiates, because that's its nature. To live as Love is to realize that your deepest identity is not fear, not guilt, not even personality — it's Love.

Imagine if the sun acted like us. "You know what, Earth? I don't feel like shining today. I'm tired. You've taken me for granted." Life would collapse. Luckily, the sun doesn't take things personally. It just shines. That's living as Love.

Why Living as Love Feels Hard

Of course, the idea sounds beautiful. The reality feels brutal. Living as Love requires dismantling lifetimes of programming. We were taught to live as guilt. To live as fear. To live as survival. Love got layered over with suspicion, cynicism, and self-protection. So when we talk about "living as Love," something in us resists. "That's too idealistic. Too naïve. Too impractical."

But here's the paradox: living as fear is what's naïve. Fear has been tried for millennia. It hasn't worked. Wars, oppression, injustice — none of it has created peace. Living as Love may sound risky, but it's the only path that actually transforms.

What Living as Love Looks Like

What does this look like in real life?

- **In Daily Encounters.** Living as Love means every person you meet is treated as holy ground. The cashier, the co-worker, the neighbor — each interaction becomes a chance to embody kindness.
- **In Conflict.** Living as Love means you respond to hostility not with retaliation but with grounded

compassion. You hold firm boundaries, but you refuse to dehumanize.

- **In Service.** Living as Love means you use your gifts not just for your own gain but to uplift others. Your creativity, your resources, your time — all become channels of blessing.
- **In Presence.** Living as Love means you bring your full self into the moment. You listen deeply. You notice beauty. You savor joy. That presence itself is Love.
- **In Vision.** Living as Love means you dream not just for yourself but for the flourishing of all. Your goals align with collective wholeness.

Epiphany

When I finally began to grasp this, I realized how much of my life had been lived as guilt instead of Love. Every decision ran through the filter of "Am I good enough? Am I right enough? Am I holy enough?" It was exhausting. But the day I started asking, "*What does Love look like here*?" everything changed. Conversations softened. Work felt lighter. Even my mistakes became opportunities to learn instead of excuses to hate myself. That's the shift — from performing to embodying.

Practices to Live as Love

How do we cultivate this identity?

1. **Morning Alignment.** Begin each day by affirming: *"I am Love."* Not "I will try to Love." *I am Love.* Let it shape how you move through the day.
2. **The Love Filter.** In every situation, ask: "*What does Love look like here?*" Use it as your compass.
3. **Radical Presence.** Slow down. Pay attention. Love thrives in the present moment. Fear lives in the future or past.
4. **Embody Love Physically.** Smile. Touch with kindness. Move with gentleness. Let your body express Love as much as your words do.
5. **Expand the Circle.** Each week, find someone outside your usual circle to extend Love to — a stranger, an "enemy," someone forgotten. Stretch the boundaries of your heart.

6. **Evening Reflection.** End each day asking, "*Where did I live as Love? Where can I grow tomorrow?*" Celebrate the wins. Forgive the misses. Keep learning.

Other Voices

This isn't just Jeshua's idea. Rumi wrote, *Your task is not to seek for Love, but merely to seek and find all the barriers within yourself that you have built against it.*"The Bhagavad Gita teaches that the highest yogi is one who "*regards every being as the same, whether friend or enemy, because he sees with Love.*" Buddhism emphasizes *bodhicitta* – awakening the heart for the benefit of all beings. Everywhere, the wisest teachers agree: Love isn't just something you do. It's what you *are*.

If we all lived as Love, customer service calls would be unrecognizable. Instead of 45 minutes on hold and a rep saying, "Sorry, nothing I can do," you'd hear, "I can feel your frustration, and I Love you. Let's fix this together." World peace might actually start with tech support.

The Transformation of Living as Love

When you live as Love, you stop needing external validation. Guilt-driven religion kept us running on approval – from priests, from communities, from God. But living as Love means you already are the approval. You already radiate the divine presence. You stop chasing worth. You start embodying it.

And when enough of us live as Love, systems shift. Violence loses power. Division crumbles. Fear fades. Living as Love is not naïve optimism. It's the most practical revolution.

The Drumbeat Truth

Let's repeat it until it becomes mantra:

- Love is not what you do occasionally. It is who you *are*.
- Living as Love is not weakness. It is strength in its purest form.
- Living as Love is not idealism. It is the only practical hope for transformation.
- You are not guilt. You are not fear. You are Love.

Dibble Dabble

Stop dabbling in Love. Stop treating it as an extracurricular activity. Make it your core identity. Let Love shape your thoughts, your words, your actions, your very presence. Jeshua didn't just preach Love. He lived as Love. And he invited us to do the same.

That's the culmination of this chapter. To live not just for Love, not just with Love, but as Love. That's the Way.

Chapter 12: Freedom from Fear: the Grip of Fear

If guilt was the Church's favorite tool to control you, fear was its partner in crime. They work together like a bad comedy duo: guilt whispers, *"You're broken,"* and fear adds, *"And if you don't fix it, you'll burn forever."* Together, they keep people small, obedient, and dependent on an institution instead of trusting their own inner light.

Fear is powerful because it operates at the core of human survival. Biologically, fear is meant to protect us. Fight or flight kicks in when a bear charges or when you almost step into traffic. But religion hijacked that system. Instead of fear helping you survive, it got weaponized to keep you enslaved. You weren't afraid of bears or cars – you were afraid of God. You were afraid of hell. You were afraid of eternity. You were afraid of yourself.

Fear in My Own Story

I know this grip well. As a young Catholic boy, I was told that one wrong move could condemn me forever. Miss Mass on Sunday? Mortal sin. Eat before Communion? Mortal sin. Fail to confess every detail? Mortal sin. The logic was terrifying: one mistake could erase all the "grace points" I'd built up, and if I died that day, too bad – eternal fire. I lived with constant background panic, like a cosmic parole officer was tracking my every move.

I remember being told that chewing gum before Communion was a sin. So there I was, nine years old, spitting gum into my hand like it was radioactive, terrified I'd burn in hell for a stick of Juicy Fruit. That's not spirituality – that's trauma.

The Structure of Fear

Fear thrives in structures of control. And religion built elaborate ones:

- **Hellfire Preaching.** Eternal damnation was the ultimate scare tactic. Nothing motivates like the threat of infinite pain.
- **Punitive God.** God was portrayed less like a loving parent and more like an angry judge. One slip-up, and you're toast.

- **Rigid Rules.** Fear flourishes in systems where the rules are impossible to keep. No one can succeed, so everyone stays anxious.
- **Intermediaries of Fear.** Priests and bishops became the "fear managers," doling out forgiveness like rationed bread.

The result? People lived small, terrified lives. They confused obedience with holiness. They confused submission with Love.

The Cost of Fear

Here's the tragedy: fear doesn't produce Love. It produces compliance. People might obey under fear, but they don't flourish. Fear narrows your world. It makes you defensive, suspicious, rigid. It shrinks imagination. It suffocates joy. Fear trains you to look over your shoulder instead of lifting your eyes.

And worst of all, fear disconnects you from God. When God is the thing you fear, how can you Love? Jeshua knew this, which is why he constantly said, *"Do not be afraid."* Those were not throwaway words. They were the antidote to centuries of fear-based control.

Jeshua and Fearlessness

Jeshua embodied freedom from fear. He touched lepers without hesitation. He confronted religious leaders without flinching. He stood before Pilate, silent, refusing to grovel. Even on the cross, he forgave instead of cursing. That's not because he was superhuman. It's because he was rooted in Love so deeply that fear lost its grip.

Imagine Jeshua at a modern-day airport. Everyone else is panicking about delays, lost luggage, and security lines. Jeshua just sits calmly, blessing the TSA agent and multiplying the sandwiches in the food court. That's what freedom from fear looks like: presence in chaos.

Other Traditions on Fear

Across traditions, wise teachers point out the same truth: fear is the enemy of freedom. The Bhagavad Gita says the yogi is free from fear because he sees himself as one with the Divine. Buddhism teaches that fear arises from attachment and dissolves in mindfulness. The Quran repeats, *"Fear not, for I am with you."* Everywhere wisdom speaks, it echoes Jeshua: Love drives out fear.

Practices to Name the Grip

So how do we begin loosening fear's grip?

1. **Name It.** Fear thrives in the shadows. Write down your fears. Speak them aloud. Naming fear robs it of some of its power.
2. **Trace Its Source.** Is this fear biological (a real danger) or theological (a programmed threat)? Most religious fear collapses when you trace it to its manmade roots.
3. **Breathe Into Presence.** Fear lives in imagined futures. Breath anchors you in now. Each exhale says, "I am safe here."
4. **Replace the Image.** If you were taught to picture God as a punisher, re-imagine God as loving presence. Visualization rewires fear.
5. **Repeat Love's Mantra.** Jeshua's words *"Do not be afraid"* become your daily declaration.

The Drumbeat Truth

Let's drive it home:

- Fear is not holy. It's control.
- Fear is not Love. It's the opposite.
- Fear does not connect you to God. It pushes you away.
- Freedom from fear is the beginning of Love.

Recognize the grip of fear. See how it has shaped you, how it has shrunk you, how it has lied to you. And then begin loosening its hold, one breath, one truth, one act of courage at a time. Jeshua's Way is not a path of fear. It is a path of freedom. That's the first step: naming the grip of fear.

Fear as a Tool of Control

If fear were just a personal quirk, like being afraid of clowns or elevators, it wouldn't deserve a whole chapter. But fear in religion isn't random – it's systematic. For centuries, institutions have weaponized fear as their most reliable tool of control. Doctrine may build walls, guilt may lay foundations, but fear is the iron bars that keep people from leaving.

How Fear Got Institutionalized

Early on, Jeshua's Way was about Love, empowerment, and freedom. People gathered in homes, shared meals, and lived as equals. But as the movement grew, leaders realized Love wasn't as efficient a management tool as fear. Love inspires freedom. Fear enforces obedience. Guess which one bureaucrats prefer?

And so, slowly but surely, fear got baked into the system:

- **Hell.** The ultimate fear tactic. Nothing motivates like eternal torment.
- **Excommunication.** Step out of line? Lose your community, your livelihood, your salvation.
- **Inquisition.** Doubt or dissent? Torture until you comply.
- **Confession.** Miss a detail? Risk eternal punishment. Better confess everything – just in case.

Fear became the invisible leash. People didn't need chains; they carried the prison inside their minds.

Imagine if airlines adopted the same model. "Welcome aboard! Please obey all instructions. Noncompliance will result in eternal damnation." Suddenly, even middle seats wouldn't feel so bad.

The Psychology of Fear Control

Fear works because it hijacks the brain. When you're afraid, you stop thinking clearly. You default to survival mode. Institutions knew this instinctively: keep people afraid, and they'll cling to you for safety. The Church became both the arsonist and the firefighter – it lit the fires of fear, then offered itself as the only way out.

Psychologists call this the "double bind." Religion perfected it: *You re broken, but we can fix you. You re guilty, but we can forgive you. You re damned, but we can save you."* People trapped in fear loops don't question the system; they cling tighter to it.

Historical Examples

Let's not sugarcoat it – history is full of this manipulation.

- **The Dark Ages:** Preachers used hellfire sermons to keep peasants obedient. Illiterate and powerless, they had no defense against fear-soaked imagery.
- **The Crusades:** Fear of damnation was weaponized to recruit armies. "Take up the cross or risk your soul."

- **The Inquisition:** Fear kept entire populations in check. Speak against the Church, and you risked torture, prison, or death.
- **The Reformation Wars:** Both Catholics and Protestants wielded fear to secure allegiance. "Join us or face eternal consequences."

Fear wasn't a side effect. It was policy.

Jeshua vs. Fear Systems

Now contrast that with Jeshua. He told people not to fear. He invited them to see God as a Loving Father, "Abba," not punisher. He offered parables of Love, not threats of hell. His entire ministry was a rebellion against fear systems. That's why he was so dangerous. You can't control people who aren't afraid. Jeshua's fearlessness threatened both Rome and the Temple. Kill him, they thought, and fear will return. But even resurrection is the ultimate fear-buster – Love stronger than death.

Imagine Jeshua at a medieval cathedral during a hellfire sermon. The priest is painting vivid pictures of demons with pitchforks, and Jeshua interrupts: "*Actually, the Kingdom of Heaven is within you.*" The priest faints. The congregation gasps. The ushers escort Jeshua out for disrupting "the program."

The Modern Face of Fear

We like to think we've moved past all that, but fear-based religion is alive and well. Modern churches still use fear to control:

- "If you don't tithe, God won't bless you."
- "If you question the pastor, you're in rebellion."
- "If you don't believe this exact doctrine, you'll go to hell."
- "If you leave this church, you're leaving God."

Fear may sound more polished now, but the mechanism is the same. Keep people afraid, and they'll keep coming back.

The Cost of Fear-Based Control

The cost is devastating. Fear-driven religion produces anxious, guilt-ridden people who never feel safe. They can't trust their own hearts. They can't rest in Love. They live like spiritual refugees, always scrambling to avoid punishment. And the irony? Fear-driven religion kills real faith. People either burn out and leave altogether, or they stay trapped in shallow compliance. Either way, Love gets lost.

Practical Steps to See Through Fear Control

So how do we dismantle this tool of control in our own lives?

1. **Recognize the Pattern.** Notice when someone is using fear to motivate you. Ask: "Is this Love speaking or fear speaking?"
2. **Question the Source.** Trace fear claims back to their origins. Most doctrines of fear (like hell as eternal torture) were later inventions, not Jeshua's teaching.
3. **Compare with Love.** Jeshua's filter was always Love. If a teaching contradicts Love, it's not his Way.
4. **Reclaim Authority.** Stop outsourcing your safety to institutions. Trust the Kingdom within.
5. **Practice Fear Detox.** Meditate, journal, breathe, laugh. Fear loses grip when you flood your system with presence and joy.

Other Traditions

Fear as control isn't unique to Christianity. Every empire has used it. But wisdom traditions always offer the counter-narrative. The Tao Te Ching warns, *The more laws and prohibitions, the more thieves and bandits."* Buddha said, *An insincere and evil friend is more to be feared than a wild beast."* Even secular voices echo it – Franklin D. Roosevelt: *The only thing we have to fear is fear itself."* Everywhere, the wise dismantle fear's power.

The Drumbeat Truth

Let's nail it down with repetition:

- Fear is not a teacher. It's a jailer.
- Fear is not divine. It's a tool of control.
- Fear may keep you compliant, but it will never make you whole.
- Love, not fear, is the true foundation of Jeshua's Way.

See through the system. Recognize how fear has been used to control you. Name it. Call it out. Laugh at it if you can. And then walk free. Because the Kingdom of Heaven is not fear-based. It is

Love-based. And once you taste that freedom, no threat of hell or excommunication will ever hold you again.

That's fear as a tool of control – and why we must let it go.

Fear of Death

If fear is the foundation of control, then the fear of death is the cornerstone. Strip away all the doctrines, all the rituals, all the threats, and you'll find this lurking underneath: humanity's terror of mortality.

Death is the big unknown, the final curtain, the shadow that religion has leveraged more effectively than any other. "Do what we say," the Church implied, "and maybe, just maybe, you'll avoid the worst after death."

Death as the Ultimate Leverage

From the beginning, institutions realized that nothing motivates like mortality. Taxes are bad, punishments are scary, but death is inescapable. What better way to control people than to tie their eternal fate to obedience? Hell was invented, expanded, and preached with terrifying detail, precisely to keep people compliant.

Think about it: without fear of death, how many doctrines collapse? Eternal damnation? Useless. Purgatory? Irrelevant. Indulgences, Masses for the dead, prayers for souls in limbo – all designed to manage death anxiety. The entire machinery of fear-based religion leans on this primal terror.

Imagine if priests admitted, "We actually don't know what happens after death. But stick with us, and at least the potlucks are good." Membership would plummet. Instead, fear of death became the eternal sales pitch.

My Own Story of Death Fear

As a child, I was haunted by it. The thought of dying and waking up in flames terrified me. I'd lie in bed at night trying to confess every possible sin, terrified I'd miss one. The image of hell burned brighter than any image of heaven. And even heaven wasn't appealing – an eternity of harps and clouds sounded more like a punishment than a reward. Death became the boogeyman the Church waved in my face to keep me obedient.

It wasn't until much later — through my experiences of presence, through the message of Jeshua, through near-death stories and mystical glimpses — that I realized the fear of death is an illusion. Death isn't the end. It isn't punishment. It's a doorway.

Jeshua on Death

Jeshua confronted the fear of death head-on. His whole message was about life beyond death, not just in the afterlife, but here and now. *"I am the resurrection and the life,"* he said. Notice: not "someday in the future," but *I am now.*

When he raised Lazarus, he didn't just show power over death — he showed that death was not ultimate. When he faced his own crucifixion, he didn't resist. He walked into it with presence, forgiving even as he died. And when resurrection followed, it was the ultimate mic drop: death, the greatest weapon of fear, had lost its sting.

Other Voices on Death

All wisdom traditions wrestle with mortality. Buddhism teaches impermanence — that clinging to life is the root of suffering. The Bhagavad Gita has Krishna telling Arjuna, *For the soul there is neither birth nor death... it is eternal."* The Quran comforts: *Every soul will taste death, but only to return to God."* Everywhere, the great teachers whisper the same truth: death is not the enemy. Fear of death is.

Why We Fear Death

Psychologically, death represents the great unknown. Our brains are wired for survival. The thought of nonexistence triggers panic. Religion poured gasoline on that fire by filling the unknown with horror stories.

Eternal torment, endless darkness, separation from God — all designed to amplify fear.

But think about this: you've already experienced "death" countless times. Every night you sleep, you lose awareness. Every old identity you shed, every old season you leave behind, is a kind of death. And yet here you are, still alive, still growing. Death isn't annihilation. It's transformation.

Imagine death as the universe saying, "New phone, who dis?" You're not erased – you're upgraded. Religion made death the worst news. Jeshua made it the best.

Practices to Face Death Without Fear

So how do we actually loosen this primal grip?

1. **Contemplate Mortality.** Not morbidly, but honestly. Meditate on the fact that life is impermanent. It helps you cherish each moment.
2. **Reframe the Afterlife.** Instead of hellfire, picture death as a doorway into greater Love, as Jeshua and mystics across traditions described.
3. **Embrace Small Deaths.** Practice letting go: of grudges, of roles, of fears. Each release is a rehearsal for the big letting go.
4. **Cultivate Presence.** Fear of death lives in the future. Presence anchors you in the now, where death has no power.
5. **Listen to Witnesses.** Read near-death experiences, mystical visions, stories from those who've glimpsed beyond. They almost always describe Love, not terror.

The Drumbeat Truth

Let's repeat, because fear of death runs deep:

- Death is not the end. It is transformation.
- Death is not punishment. Fear invented that.
- Death is not to be dreaded. It is to be embraced with trust.
- Freedom from death fear is the doorway to truly living.

Stop letting fear of death shrink your life. Stop letting institutions manipulate your mortality. Begin to see death as Jeshua saw it – not as a threat, but as part of life's wholeness. When you lose fear of death, you lose fear itself. And when you lose fear, you are finally free to live.

That's freedom from the fear of death – and the beginning of eternal life here and now.

Fear of Judgment

If the fear of death is the cornerstone of religious control, then the fear of judgment is the paint and plaster that makes the prison look terrifyingly permanent. Death itself is one thing – inevitable, mysterious. But judgment? That's personal. That's the idea that when you die, your entire life is reviewed, scored, and weighed on cosmic scales. And depending on the outcome, you either win the jackpot of heaven or get thrown into hellfire like a defective product.

How Judgment Was Weaponized

The fear of judgment was never Jeshua's invention. In fact, it grew far more elaborate after his time. Early Christianity took some imagery from Hebrew scriptures, added Greek philosophical dualism, and sprinkled in Rome's love of legal systems. The result? A courtroom God.

In this model, God is the ultimate judge, Jeshua is your defense attorney (if you've signed up for the right membership plan), and the Church is the courthouse that controls access to the appeals process.

Suddenly, your life isn't a journey of Love; it's a trial waiting for sentencing. Every choice, every thought, every desire is entered into the record.

Fear made this system effective. Who wouldn't behave if they thought the Judge was taking notes on everything from chewing gum to sexual thoughts? People were terrified into compliance.

Picture God as the celestial auditor. "John Davis, on March 12th, age nine, you stole a grape from the grocery store. On April 8th, you muttered a swear word after stubbing your toe. Eternal damnation!" If God is really that petty, we're all doomed. Luckily, that's not Love – that's bureaucracy gone wild.

Jeshua's Actual Teaching

Here's what's wild: Jeshua didn't preach judgment as fear. He preached judgment as light. *The light has come into the world."* John's gospel says, *but people Loved darkness instead of light."* Judgment wasn't God's wrath; it was simply the truth being revealed. When light shines, you see clearly. That's not about punishment – it's about clarity.

When Jeshua told parables about judgment, they weren't designed to terrify people into obedience. They were invitations to live awake. The sheep and goats story, for example, wasn't about God gleefully sentencing half the population to hell. It was about how Love (feeding the hungry, clothing the naked, visiting the imprisoned) is the real measure of life. Judgment was never about religious rituals. It was about whether you lived Love.

My Own Fear of Judgment

Growing up, I was obsessed with judgment. I pictured a cosmic movie theater where my entire life would be replayed in front of everyone I knew. The thought horrified me. What if they saw every mistake, every doubt, every "impure thought"? I lived like someone constantly preparing for an impossible exam.

That fear paralyzed me. It made me cautious, rigid, unable to trust myself. But the more I leaned into Jeshua's teaching, the more I realized judgment wasn't about fear. It was about truth. And the truth is Love. If God is Love, then judgment is simply Love revealing where fear still hides.

Judgment as Awakening

Here's the reframe: judgment isn't condemnation. Judgment is awakening. It's the moment the illusions fall away and you see clearly. It's like light flooding into a dark room – yes, it can be uncomfortable at first, but it liberates. You realize the "sins" you carried weren't eternal crimes. They were wounds, confusions, and shadows. And Love shines them away.

Think of Jeshua with the woman caught in adultery. The crowd wanted judgment – stoning, punishment, shame. Jeshua turned the whole thing upside down: *Let the one without sin cast the first stone."* When they all walked away, he said, *Neither do I condemn you. Go and sin no more."* That's judgment transformed: not condemnation, but liberation.

Imagine if churches modeled that. Instead of "judgment day" sermons about hellfire, they'd host "judgment brunches" where everyone gets pancakes and forgiveness. Attendance would skyrocket, and guilt would plummet.

Why Fear of Judgment Persists

Still, the fear is sticky. Why? Because it works. People terrified of eternal condemnation will hand over their freedom for a shot at safety. Institutions know this. That's why judgment language fills sermons, catechisms, and theology books. Fear sells. Fear fills pews. Fear keeps donations flowing.

But the cost is devastating. People raised under fear of judgment live anxious, shame-soaked lives. They second-guess every decision.

They obsess over perfection. They hide their true selves for fear of exposure. And tragically, they miss the freedom Jeshua promised.

Practices to Break Free

So how do we step out of this fear?

1. **Redefine Judgment.** Stop picturing a courtroom. Picture light. Picture Love shining into every part of you – not to condemn, but to heal.
2. **Practice Self-Compassion.** When old guilt resurfaces, treat yourself kindly. If Love is the final word, practice it now.
3. **Read Jeshua's Parables Closely.** Notice how often he equates "judgment" with compassion, forgiveness, and inclusion rather than wrath.
4. **Replace Fear with Presence.** Fear of judgment is always future-oriented. Presence keeps you in the now, where Love lives.
5. **Trust Wholeness.** If the Kingdom of Heaven is within you, then judgment isn't about condemnation. It's about awakening to the wholeness already inside.

Other Traditions

The Bhagavad Gita reframes judgment as alignment with your true dharma, not punishment. Buddhism teaches karma as cause-and-effect, not eternal damnation. Sufism sings of judgment as the burning away of illusions in divine Love. Across traditions, the wisest voices agree: judgment is not terror. It's truth.

The Drumbeat Truth

Let's hammer this home:

- Judgment is not condemnation. It is illumination.
- Judgment is not wrath. It is Love revealing truth.
- Judgment is not to be feared. It is to be welcomed.

- Freedom from judgment frees you to live authentically now.

Let go of the courtroom God. Let go of the cosmic trial. Let go of the terror of eternal sentencing. Begin to see judgment as Jeshua saw it: the shining of Love into every corner, freeing you from shadows, awakening you to wholeness.

That's freedom from the fear of judgment — and it's the next step toward living unchained.

Fear of the Unknown

If death is the grand fear and judgment is the terrifying sequel, then the unknown is the fog that surrounds both. Humans don't just fear death itself; they fear *not knowing* what comes after. They don't just fear judgment; they fear the uncertainty of whether they've done "enough" to pass. The unknown is the blank screen onto which religion projects its scariest horror films.

Why the Unknown Scares Us

The human brain craves certainty. We want to know the rules, the outcomes, the schedule. It's why we check weather apps five times a day even though the forecast is wrong half the time. The unknown triggers anxiety because it strips us of control. And nothing feels more out of control than the big mysteries: What happens when we die? Is there a God? Does my life matter?

Religion stepped into this gap and said, "Don't worry — we have all the answers." Heaven, hell, purgatory, limbo, pearly gates, harps, fire, angels with clipboards. The unknown became scripted. Certainty was promised, but at a price: obedience, conformity, submission.

It's like going on a guided tour where the tour guide says, "Everything will be fine, as long as you never look left, never ask questions, and always tip me 10% of your income." That's not certainty. That's control disguised as guidance.

Jeshua and the Unknown

Here's what makes Jeshua radical: he didn't eliminate the unknown. He invited people to trust in the middle of it. *Do not worry about tomorrow,"* he said. *Each day has enough trouble of its own."* He wasn't promising detailed maps of the afterlife. He was teaching presence — the art of living here and now, even when the future is unclear.

When the disciples panicked during a storm at sea, Jeshua didn't hand them a weather report. He said, *"Peace, be still."* He didn't solve the unknown with information; he dissolved it with presence.

My Own Battles with the Unknown

I used to hate the unknown. As a kid, I wanted answers for everything. Where do we go when we die? How many sins are too many? What exactly does heaven look like? The Church had answers, but they only made the unknown scarier. Heaven sounded boring, hell sounded terrifying, purgatory sounded endless, and limbo sounded lonely.

It wasn't until I began practicing presence that the unknown stopped being an enemy. The truth is that life is always unknown. You don't know what tomorrow brings. You don't know if you'll live another decade or another hour. The unknown is the fabric of existence. Fighting it only breeds fear. Embracing it leads to freedom.

Other Voices on the Unknown

Buddha taught that clinging to certainty creates suffering. The Tao Te Ching insists the Tao cannot be fully named or known — it's mystery itself. The Bhagavad Gita tells Arjuna to act without knowing outcomes, trusting the divine flow. Everywhere, the wisest teachers point to the same truth: the unknown isn't a curse. It's the field where trust and Love grow.

Imagine if life came with a complete manual. You'd get a book at birth titled "Your Life: Spoilers Edition." Chapter 7 would tell you the exact date and cause of your death. Chapter 3 would warn you about the time you embarrass yourself at prom. Sure, you'd know everything — but where's the adventure? The unknown, scary as it is, is also what makes life meaningful.

Why Religion Exploited the Unknown

Institutions Love the unknown because it creates dependence. When people feel lost, they look for guides. Religion stepped in and said, "We'll tell you what's beyond the fog. Just don't ask too many questions." Over time, the Church painted the unknown with terrifying imagery to keep people obedient. Fire and brimstone sermons weren't about truth – they were about crowd control.

The irony? Nobody actually knows. Priests, popes, pastors – they've never died. Their authority rests not on knowledge, but on confidence. Fear fills in the gaps where certainty is impossible.

Practices for Living with the Unknown

So how do we reclaim peace in the fog?

1. **Breathe into Mystery.** Instead of resisting the unknown, welcome it. Inhale: "I don't know." Exhale: "And that's okay."
2. **Anchor in the Present.** Fear of the unknown lives in imaginary futures. Practice grounding yourself in what's real right now.
3. **Reframe Uncertainty.** See it not as a threat, but as possibility. The unknown is also where creativity, adventure, and growth live.
4. **Release the Need to Control.** Control is an illusion anyway. When you stop demanding certainty, fear loses its grip.
5. **Trust Love, Not Maps.** You don't need all the answers when you know the Presence that holds you is Love.

A Personal Shift

One day, after sitting in Love, I realized something: the unknown is where God lives. If the Kingdom of Heaven is within, then the unknown is not emptiness – it's fullness I haven't discovered yet. That realization shifted everything. Instead of fearing the fog, I started walking into it with curiosity. What gift might be hidden here? What Love might surprise me? The unknown stopped being an enemy and became a companion.

The Drumbeat Truth

Let's engrave this into memory:

- The unknown is not danger. It is possibility.
- The unknown is not emptiness. It is mystery.
- The unknown is not to be feared. It is to be trusted.

- Jeshua's Way is not about eliminating the unknown, but living free within it.

Stop letting the unknown scare you into obedience. Stop demanding certainty as the price for peace. Instead, embrace mystery as the sacred playground of Love. Jeshua didn't map out every answer. He invited us to trust. And trust, not certainty, is the foundation of freedom.

That's how we dissolve fear of the unknown — by walking into it hand in hand with Love.

Fear of Not Being Enough

If guilt was the seed planted in childhood and fear of death was the looming storm cloud on the horizon, then fear of not being enough is the daily drizzle that soaks everything in between. It's that persistent background hum whispering, "You're not holy enough. Not good enough. Not worthy enough. Not obedient enough. Not spiritual enough. Not enough, period."

How Religion Cultivated "Not Enough"

This fear is one of the most insidious tools of religious control, because it doesn't just attack your behavior — it attacks your identity. It convinces you that no matter what you do, it will never measure up.

Catholicism was especially effective at this. Mortal sin, venial sin, confession requirements, holy days of obligation — even when you tried your hardest, there was always some new rule you didn't know about, some new layer of holiness you hadn't achieved. Missed confession? Not enough. Didn't fast properly? Not enough. Didn't pray the rosary the right number of times? Not enough.

The result was a lifetime of striving without ever arriving. Like being on a treadmill that never stops — exhausting, endless, and designed to keep you dependent on the Church as the dangling carrot of "enoughness."

Imagine playing a video game where no matter how many levels you beat, the game just keeps saying, "Almost there, but not quite." That's what Catholic spirituality felt like — the world's most depressing Nintendo.

My Own Story of "Not Enough"

I carried this fear for years. I remember as a kid, kneeling in church, staring at the crucifix, and thinking, "I'll never be good enough for that." Every sin felt like another nail in the cross. Every failure confirmed the whisper that I wasn't worthy.

Even later, when I stepped away from Catholicism, the ghost of "not enough" followed me. It wasn't just about religion anymore – it seeped into relationships, work, creativity. No matter what I accomplished, the voice was still there: *Not enough.*

It wasn't until I began sitting in presence – what I now call "sitting in Love" – that the voice started losing power. In silence, I realized something profound: I didn't need to earn enoughness. I was already whole.

Jeshua's Answer to "Not Enough"

Jeshua never preached unworthiness. He never said, "You're not enough." He said the opposite: *You are the light of the world." "The Kingdom of Heaven is within you." "You will do greater works than these."* Those are not the words of a teacher trying to convince people of their inadequacy. They're the words of someone awakening people to their inherent divinity.

When Jeshua interacted with people society declared "not enough" (tax collectors, prostitutes, lepers) he didn't shame them. He lifted them. He ate with them. He healed them. He Loved them as they were. That's how fear of not being enough dissolves: when someone sees your worth even when you don't.

Why "Not Enough" Persists

The fear is sticky because it taps into a universal human wound. Even outside religion, we fear inadequacy. Capitalism exploits it by telling us we're not thin enough, rich enough, young enough, successful enough. Social media amplifies it by showing us everyone else's highlight reels. Religion just added eternal consequences to the mix.

And so the fear lingers, even long after people leave church pews. The inner critic, armed with decades of programming, keeps whispering, "Not enough."

Other Traditions on Enoughness

The Bhagavad Gita teaches that each person's dharma – their unique path – is sacred. You don't need to do someone else's work; your way is enough. Buddhism insists that enlightenment isn't about becoming something new but realizing what you already are. Sufi mystics sing of the beLoved already dwelling within, enough and whole. Across traditions, wisdom dismantles the myth of inadequacy.

Imagine if Jeshua had walked around saying, "You know, folks, you're all terrible. You'll never be enough. Good luck with eternal failure!" He wouldn't have gathered followers, he'd have started the first mass therapy clinic. Luckily, his actual message was the opposite: you are already beLoved.

Practices to Reclaim Enoughness

How do we step out of this trap in daily life?

1. **Declare Wholeness Daily.** Start the morning with: *"I am whole. I am Loved. I am enough."* Repeat until the old voice loses its grip.
2. **Celebrate Small Wins.** Don't wait for perfection. Celebrate progress. Each act of kindness, each moment of presence is enough.
3. **Redefine Success.** Instead of measuring worth by rules or achievements, measure by Love. Did you Love today? Then you're enough.
4. **Practice Self-Compassion.** When you fail, talk to yourself like you would a beLoved child. Gentle, forgiving, encouraging.
5. **Sit in Love.** Presence itself is proof of enoughness. When you sit quietly and feel the divine within, you realize you lack nothing.

A Personal Shift

I remember one particular morning where I sat with the phrase, *"The Kingdom of Heaven is within you."* I let it echo in silence. Slowly, the weight of "not enough" started melting. I realized the voice that told me I was inadequate was not God, it was programming. And programming can be rewritten. That moment didn't erase the fear forever, but it gave me a new anchor: Love as enoughness.

The Drumbeat Truth

Let's anchor this with repetition:

- You are not broken. You are whole.
- You are not unworthy. You are beLoved.
- You are not lacking. You are enough.
- Jeshua's Way is not about striving to be enough. It's about realizing you already are.

Stop listening to the voice of "not enough." Stop running on the treadmill of inadequacy. Start living from wholeness. Start trusting that the Kingdom is already within you. Jeshua's Way is not about becoming what you're not. It's about awakening to what you already are.

That's freedom from the fear of not being enough — and it's one of the most liberating steps on the path.

Living Beyond Fear

We've walked through fear's many disguises: fear of death, fear of judgment, fear of the unknown, fear of not being enough. Each one has been unmasked as an illusion, a tool of control, a shadow over the light of Love. Now comes the deeper question: what does it mean to live beyond fear altogether? Not just to manage fear, not just to wrestle it into submission, but to step into a life where fear no longer calls the shots.

What "Beyond Fear" Really Means

Living beyond fear doesn't mean you never feel fear again. Fear is part of being human. If a bear chases you in the woods, you should run — that's survival, not sin. The freedom we're talking about isn't the absence of fear, but the absence of fear's rule. Fear may knock on the door, but it doesn't get to move in and redecorate. Fear may whisper, but it doesn't get to steer the car. Living beyond fear means you stop being driven by fear and start being guided by Love.

Imagine your life as a car. Fear is allowed to ride in the backseat, buckled up. It's not allowed to drive, not allowed to touch the radio, and definitely not allowed to grab the wheel. That's what living beyond fear looks like: you acknowledge its presence but refuse its control.

Jeshua as the Model

Jeshua embodied this perfectly. He didn't deny fear. In Gethsemane, it's said he sweated drops of blood, begging for another way. But he didn't let fear stop him. He walked forward anyway, rooted in Love deeper than his dread. That's the key: living beyond fear doesn't mean pretending you're fearless. It means acting from Love even when fear screams in your ear.

Over and over, Jeshua told people, *"Do not be afraid."* Not as a command, but as an invitation. As if to say, "You don't have to live like this anymore. You don't have to be ruled by shadows. Step into the light with me."

My Own Experience

I'll be honest: fear still shows up for me. Fear of failure. Fear of ridicule. Fear of stepping fully into the work I feel called to. But the difference now is that fear doesn't run the show. I see it, I name it, I laugh at it when I can, and I choose Love anyway. The more I do this, the smaller fear gets. It's like a balloon losing air: still visible but shrinking fast.

How Fear Shrinks Life

When fear drives, life shrinks. You avoid risks. You suppress dreams. You stay silent when you should speak. You cling to security instead of stepping into growth. Fear convinces you that safety is more valuable than freedom. But safety built on fear isn't safety at all – it's a cage.

Living beyond fear means refusing the cage. It means opening the door, flying out, and realizing the world is bigger, scarier, and far more beautiful than you imagined.

The Practices of a Fear-Free Life

So how do we cultivate this in daily living?

1. **Presence Practice.** Fear always lives in the future or past. Anchor yourself in the now, where fear has no foothold.
2. **Reframe Risk.** Instead of asking, "What if I fail?" Declare, "I am flying!" Shift the narrative from loss to achievement.

3. **Courageous Action.** Take one small step each day that fear resists. Call the friend. Speak the truth. Launch the project. Each act shrinks fear's grip.
4. **Community of Love.** Surround yourself with people who encourage courage. Fear shrinks faster in groups of Love.
5. **Humor Therapy.** Laugh at fear. Mock it. Turn it into a cartoon villain, twirling its mustache, in your imagination. Laughter disarms what once terrified.
6. **Trust the Flow.** Deep down, living beyond fear means trusting Love's current. The river carries you, even when you can't see around the bend.

Other Traditions on Life Beyond Fear

Buddha taught that fear dissolves when you see reality clearly — impermanence embraced, attachment released. The Bhagavad Gita speaks of the yogi who is "*fearless, pure-hearted, and steady in meditation.*" Sufi mystics insist that Love burns away fear until only God remains. And modern voices echo the same: FDR's famous line, *"The only thing we have to fear is fear itself,"* could've been straight out of Jeshua's playbook.

Imagine if churches replaced their "fear God" sermons with "laugh at fear" classes. Parishioners would leave each Sunday chuckling, free, and far less manipulable. Attendance might actually go up.

What Life Beyond Fear Looks Like

Living beyond fear looks like:

- Speaking your truth even if your voice shakes.
- Creating without worrying about critics.
- Loving even when you risk rejection.
- Forgiving even when you fear being hurt again.
- Trusting even when outcomes are unclear.

It looks like living boldly, joyfully, playfully — because fear no longer sets the rules.

A World Beyond Fear

And here's the bigger vision: imagine whole communities living beyond fear. No more manipulated masses terrified of hell. No more politics driven by fear of "the other." No more economies fueled by fear of scarcity. A world beyond fear would be a world of creativity, generosity, and Love. That's not utopia. That's Jeshua's Kingdom – heaven on earth.

The Drumbeat Truth

Let's engrain this:

- Fear is not your master. Love is.
- Fear is not truth. Love is.
- Fear shrinks. Love expands.
- To live beyond fear is to live free.

So here's the invitation: recognize fear, yes. Respect it as a signal, yes. But don't let it rule you anymore. Step into a life where Love leads. Step into a life where you laugh at shadows. Step into a life where freedom is your birthright.

Living beyond fear isn't just a personal achievement. It's a collective revolution. When enough of us refuse fear, systems of control collapse. When enough of us live in Love, the world changes.

That's the promise of Jeshua's Way. That's the freedom you were born for.

That's what it means to live beyond fear.

Chapter 13: Living in Presence

The Power of Now

If fear is the shadow that has stalked humanity through religion, then presence is the light that dissolves it. Presence is where Jeshua pointed again and again: *Take no thought for tomorrow... the Kingdom of Heaven is within you... sufficient for the day is its own trouble."* Over and over, he was teaching one radical truth – that life, freedom, Love, and power exist only in the now.

Why Presence Is So Hard

We humans are professional time travelers. Our minds love to run backward into regret or forward into anxiety. We replay mistakes, re-litigate conversations, and marinate in "what if." Or we fast-forward into the future, spinning scenarios of catastrophe and disappointment. The present moment? That gets about five minutes of attention a day, usually while standing in line at the DMV.

Religion reinforced this distraction. Instead of teaching people to live here and now, it shoved their attention into the past (original sin, inherited guilt) or the future (final judgment, heaven, hell). Presence got buried under timelines of shame and terror.

Imagine if religion held annual "Now" conferences. Instead of debating doctrine, everyone just sat quietly, breathed deeply, and actually noticed they were alive. Attendance would plummet at first, because fear sells better than silence, but those who stayed would leave free.

Jeshua's Radical Simplicity

Jeshua was a master of presence. He never seemed rushed, even with crowds pressing in. He never seemed paralyzed by regret, even when rejected. He moved through life fully awake, fully aware, fully here. When asked tricky theological questions, he often sidestepped with stories about seeds, birds, and bread – everyday reminders of presence.

When he said, *"Do not worry about tomorrow,"* he wasn't advocating irresponsibility. He was revealing the futility of living outside the now. Tomorrow doesn't exist yet. Yesterday is gone.

The only space where Love, healing, and creation are possible is here, now.

My Own Journey into Presence

For years, my mind was everywhere but here. I worried constantly about salvation, about sins remembered and forgotten, about whether I was living up to God's expectations. The present moment felt like a waiting room for eternity.

It wasn't until I began practicing "sitting in Love" that presence cracked open for me. Sitting quietly, breathing, letting Love fill the space, suddenly the racing thoughts slowed. I wasn't waiting for God to show up someday. God was already *here*. I wasn't preparing for heaven later. Heaven was already within. That shift, from someday to now, changed everything.

Other Voices on Presence

The power of now is echoed across traditions. Buddha said, *Do not dwell in the past, do not dream of the future, concentrate the mind on the present moment."* The Bhagavad Gita insists that right action must be done without attachment to outcomes – which means in the present. The Tao Te Ching says, *If you are depressed you are living in the past, if you are anxious you are living in the future, if you are at peace you are living in the present."* Jeshua was not alone – all wisdom points here.

Imagine if smartphones came with a pop-up reminder: "Warning: prolonged use may cause loss of present moment." Jeshua's updated Sermon on the Mount might include, *Blessed are those who put down their phones, for they shall actually see the world around them."*

Why Presence Frees Us from Fear

Fear can't survive in presence. Think about it: fear always imagines a future – the worst-case scenario, the disaster waiting around the corner. But when you anchor in now, most of the time you realize, "I'm okay. Right now, I'm breathing. Right now, I'm safe. Right now, Love is possible."

Presence isn't about denying real problems. It's about meeting them from a place of calm awareness instead of frantic projection.

Jeshua could face storms, mobs, even death because he was anchored in presence. That's why fear had no hold on him.

Practices for Living the Power of Now

So how do we cultivate presence?

1. **Breath Awareness.** Start by noticing your breath. It's always here, always now. Each inhale and exhale is an anchor.
2. **Sensory Grounding.** Notice what you see, hear, feel, taste, and smell in this moment. It draws your mind out of imagination and into reality.
3. **Thought Watching.** Instead of fighting thoughts, watch them pass like clouds. Presence isn't about stopping thoughts – it's about not chasing them.
4. **Sitting in Love.** Sit quietly, Exhale. Feel the natural state of Love within. Presence deepens naturally when Love is the focus.
5. **Interrupt the Future Spiral.** When your mind starts racing into "what if," ask: "*What is true right now?*" Usually, the answer is peace.

A Shift in Daily Living

Once you taste presence, everything changes. Meals become sacred because you're *tasting* them. Conversations become deeper because you're *listening*. Walks become meditations because you're *seeing*. Life, which once felt like a blur, slows into clarity.

Presence doesn't eliminate problems, but it changes how you meet them. Instead of reacting with fear, you respond with awareness.

Instead of drowning in anxiety, you act from centeredness. That's power – not control over the future, but freedom in the now.

The Drumbeat Truth

Let's repeat until it sticks:

- The past is gone. The future is not here. The *now* is all that exists.
- Fear lives in imagination. Freedom lives in presence.
- Jeshua's Way is not about preparing for someday. It's about awakening to now.

Stop running to yesterday, stop racing into tomorrow, and come home to now. The Kingdom of Heaven isn't later. It isn't after death. It isn't after judgment. It's here, within you, waiting in presence.

That's the power of now — the doorway to freedom, Love, and life as Jeshua taught it.

Escaping the Trap of Past and Future

If presence is freedom, then the greatest prison is the trap of past and future. Religion has specialized in this trap for centuries. It shackles you to yesterday's sins and chains you to tomorrow's judgment, leaving the present moment neglected and wasted. Instead of living here and now, people live in two places that don't even exist.

The Trap of the Past

The past is where guilt lives. Every mistake, every failure, every "sin" gets stored there, ready to be replayed at a moment's notice. Religion loves this because it turns memory into a courtroom. Confession booths, penance, indulgences — all designed to keep you revisiting the past over and over.

In CCD, I was taught that sins stick to your soul like dirt. Confession was like taking a shower, but here's the kicker — the dirt came back instantly, sometimes even before you left the confessional. I'd walk out feeling clean, only to remember something I forgot to confess, and suddenly I was "dirty" again. The past was never finished. It always reached forward to haunt the present.

Imagine if showers worked like confession. You scrub yourself clean, walk out sparkling, and suddenly dirt falls from the sky and covers you again. You'd never leave the bathroom. That's how I felt as a kid — permanently stuck in the confessional bathroom of guilt.

The Trap of the Future

If the past is guilt, the future is fear. Religion filled it with terrifying images: judgment day, hellfire, eternal separation. It also dangled the carrot of heaven — but only if you behaved perfectly now. So you lived every moment scanning the horizon for punishment or reward, never at peace in the present.

This future obsession wasn't limited to the afterlife. It also invaded daily life. "What if I sin before I die? What if I don't do enough good deeds? What if God is angry with me right now?" Anxiety spiraled endlessly, fueled by doctrines that made certainty impossible.

Jeshua's Escape Plan

Jeshua's teaching was an escape plan from both traps. Over and over, he said, *"Do not worry about tomorrow."* Over and over, he told people, *"Your sins are forgiven."* In other words: stop clinging to yesterday, stop obsessing over tomorrow. God is here, now. Love is here, now. The Kingdom is here, now.

When he healed people, he didn't give them a list of rituals to erase past sins. He simply declared, *Your faith has made you whole."* When people panicked about the future, he pointed to birds and flowers: *Look how they live without anxiety. Do the same."* Jeshua's Way was presence — a radical break from the religious fixation on past and future.

My Own Struggle

Breaking free from this trap wasn't easy for me. I carried the weight of past mistakes like that backpack full of bricks. And I constantly scanned the horizon for future punishments. It wasn't until I began practicing presence — breathing, sitting in Love, repeating Jeshua's words — that I realized the backpack was imaginary and the future monster was a shadow puppet.

One practice that helped was writing down what I still carried guilt about. Then I read Jeshua's words: *"The Kingdom of Heaven is within you."* And I asked myself: "If that's true, why am I carrying this?" Then I burned the paper. It was a ritual of release, a declaration that the past had no power over me anymore.

Other Voices

Across traditions, this wisdom echoes. Buddha taught that clinging to the past and grasping for the future are the roots of suffering. The Bhagavad Gita insists that one should act in the present without attachment to outcomes. Again, the Tao Te Ching says, *If you are depressed you are living in the past, if you are anxious you are living in the future, if you are at peace you are living in the present."* Jeshua stood in that same stream: live here, not there.

Imagine if therapists billed by the "thought trip." "That'll be $200 for your journey into the past, and another $300 for your anxiety vacation into the future." We'd all go broke. Luckily, presence is free.

Why the Trap Persists

Why do we stay stuck? Because past and future feel safer than now. The past gives us identity: "I am my mistakes, my wounds, my history." The future gives us illusion: "Someday I'll be okay, someday I'll be Loved, someday I'll arrive." The now? The now demands we live. It demands we feel. It demands we awaken. That's scarier to the ego than hellfire.

Institutions know this. If you live in the now, you don't need them. If you realize Love is already here, their threats lose power. That's why religion keeps pulling you backward and forward like a soul tug-of-war — because the present is freedom.

Practices to Escape the Trap

So how do we live free?

1. **Release the Past Daily.** Each morning, consciously say: "*The past is gone. It does not define me.*"
2. **Forgive Yourself.** Write letters of forgiveness to your younger self. Replace guilt with compassion.
3. **Stop Forecasting Doom.** When your mind projects disaster, ask: "*Is this real now, or imaginary?*" Most of the time, it's fantasy.
4. **Anchor with Breath.** Each inhale is proof of life now. Each exhale releases past and future.
5. **Create Rituals of Presence.** Eat slowly, walk attentively, listen deeply. Each act pulls you back to now.

A Shift in Living

Once you escape the trap, life expands. The weight of past mistakes drops. The terror of future judgment fades. What's left is presence — clear, open, full of possibility. Relationships deepen because you're not dragging old baggage or projecting fears. Work becomes more meaningful because you're actually engaged. Joy blossoms because you finally let yourself be alive.

The Drumbeat Truth

Let's repeat until it sticks:

- The past is gone. It cannot be changed.
- The future is not here. It cannot be controlled.
- The now is real. It is where life, Love, and freedom exist.
- Escaping the trap of past and future is the heart of Jeshua's Way.

Drop the backpack of the past. Stop staring into the fog of the future. Step into the only space that's real: now. Jeshua isn't waiting in your memories or in some distant tomorrow. He's here, within, in presence.

That's how we escape the trap — by walking free into the present moment where Love lives.

Presence as Connection to God

If there's one thing religion has gotten spectacularly wrong, it's this: the idea that connecting to God requires intermediaries, rituals, or special circumstances. Priests, temples, liturgies, catechisms — all supposedly the gateways to the Divine. But Jeshua flipped the script. He said the Kingdom of Heaven is *within you.* He said the Father knows what you need before you ask. He said when you pray, go into your room, shut the door, and simply be. In other words: presence itself is connection to God.

Why Religion Distrusts Presence

Presence is dangerous to institutions because it makes them unnecessary. If you can sit quietly, breathe, and feel God within, what need do you have for elaborate systems? If you can taste Love in the stillness of your own heart, why buy indulgences? Presence democratizes spirituality. It says everyone has equal, immediate access to the Divine. That's liberating for people but terrifying for hierarchies.

So instead of teaching presence, religion distracted people with activity. Endless prayers, rituals, and rules. Confessions, penances, fasts, feasts. The busier you are, the less likely you are to notice the quiet whisper of God already here. Presence got buried under performance.

Imagine if churches actually encouraged presence. Sunday services would consist of sitting in silence for an hour. No sermons, no songs, no collection plates. Just presence. Attendance would probably plummet at first – no entertainment value – but those who stayed would be transformed.

Jeshua and Presence

Jeshua modeled presence constantly. He withdrew to quiet places to pray. He spent nights on mountaintops in silence. He sat with people one-on-one, fully attentive. He noticed small details – lilies in fields, sparrows falling, coins in widows' hands. His miracles flowed not from frantic effort, but from calm awareness. Presence was his source.

When Martha was bustling in the kitchen, anxious about serving, Jeshua gently told her, *You are worried about many things, but only one thing is needed."* Mary, who simply sat at his feet, had chosen it. That "one thing" wasn't ritual. It was presence.

My Own Experience

For years, I thought connection to God required effort. Prayers recited perfectly. Mass attended faithfully. Confessions made exhaustively.

And yet, after all the effort, I often felt emptier, not fuller. It wasn't until I started sitting in silence, breathing deeply, and simply resting in Love that I realized: this is it. Connection isn't earned. It's noticed.

When "sitting in Love" for ten, fifteen, thirty minutes where I stop performing and just *be*, inevitably something shifts. Fear softens. Guilt loosens. Joy arises. Not because I did the right ritual, but because I finally got out of my own way and let presence reveal God already here.

Other Voices on Presence and God

Mystics across traditions affirm this. Meister Eckhart said, *The eye with which I see God is the same eye with which God sees me."* The Bhagavad Gita insists God is nearer than breath, closer than hands and feet. Sufi poets sing of God as the BeLoved found in stillness.

Buddhist teachers speak of awakening as seeing reality as it is – which is another way of saying presence. Everywhere, mystics bypass institutions and point to direct experience.

Imagine if God had a voicemail system: "Press 1 for forgiveness, press 2 for blessings, press 3 for salvation. Due to high call volume, wait times are longer than usual." Presence bypasses the phone tree. It's direct connection – no Muzak required.

Why Presence Feels Difficult

If presence is so simple, why do we resist it? Because silence feels uncomfortable. Stillness makes us notice our fears, our doubts, our inner noise. And because we've been conditioned to think God is external, we don't trust the quiet voice within. Institutions thrive on this discomfort, offering rituals and distractions as substitutes. But the only real way forward is to sit through the discomfort until presence becomes familiar. "*Be still and know that I AM God.*"

Practices to Deepen Connection

So how do we cultivate presence as connection to God?

1. **Daily Silence.** Commit to a few minutes each day of quiet. Sit, breathe, be. Start small and grow.
2. **Nature Presence.** Step outside, notice creation, and let the beauty draw you into God's nearness.
3. **Attentive Listening.** When talking with someone, listen fully. Presence with others is presence with God.
4. **Breath Prayer.** With each inhale, imagine breathing in God's Love. With each exhale, release fear.
5. **Journal the Now.** Write daily: "*Right now, I notice...*" This trains awareness of God in the present.

A Shift in Daily Life

The more you practice presence, the more it bleeds into everything. Washing dishes becomes prayer. Driving becomes meditation.

Conversations become sacred encounters. You realize God isn't hidden in churches or rituals. God is hidden in plain sight – in every moment you're awake enough to notice.

Presence vs. Absence

Here's the paradox: God is never absent. Only our awareness is. Presence isn't about summoning God – it's about realizing God was never gone. It's like tuning a radio. The music was always playing; we just weren't on the right frequency. Presence tunes us back to Love's channel.

The Drumbeat Truth

Let's engrain this:

- Presence is not optional. It is the heart of connection.
- Presence doesn't require rituals. It requires awareness.
- God is not distant. God is here, now.
- The Kingdom isn't accessed by effort. It's awakened by presence.

So again, I invite you to stop chasing God through rituals and doctrines. Stop outsourcing connection to intermediaries. Sit. Breathe. Be. Discover that presence itself is connection. Jeshua's Way wasn't about climbing ladders to heaven. It was about realizing heaven is here, within, in presence.

That's the secret religion feared most. That's the freedom Jeshua offered. And that's the life waiting for you now.

The Obstacles to Presence

If presence is so natural, if it is the direct connection to God, the Kingdom within, the path Jeshua taught, then why is it so hard to live in it? Why do our minds slip back into guilt about yesterday and worry about tomorrow within seconds of trying to be still? Because there are obstacles. Real, sticky, stubborn obstacles. Jeshua knew them. The mystics knew them. And if we're honest, we know them too.

The Main Obstacles

Let's name them clearly:

1. **Distraction.** Our world is engineered to pull attention everywhere except here.

2. **Busyness.** We wear productivity like a badge, but it keeps us from being.
3. **Fear.** Presence threatens the ego, which thrives on fear about past and future.
4. **Guilt.** Old programming convinces us we're not worthy to sit with God directly.
5. **Expectation.** We think presence must feel like fireworks, when often it feels simple and quiet.

Each of these blocks the doorway to presence, but none of them are stronger than the truth: Love is here now.

Imagine trying to meditate in the middle of Times Square. Billboards flashing, horns honking, tourists taking selfies with Elmo. That's what our inner world looks like most days. And yet, even there, presence is possible. Jeshua found it in crowds. So can we.

Distraction: The Noise Machine

We live in the noisiest age in human history. Notifications, advertisements, endless entertainment. Our devices are designed to monetize distraction. The more attention we spend on screens, the less we notice the present moment.

Religion added its own noise: endless prayers, rituals, and obligations. Instead of sitting quietly and noticing God within, people were trained to keep busy with spiritual chores. Distraction wasn't accidental. It was engineered.

The cure? Silence. Even a few minutes of intentional quiet each day begins to weaken distraction's hold.

Busyness: The Idol of Productivity

Busyness is the socially acceptable drug. We brag about how busy we are, as if exhaustion proves our worth. But busyness is the enemy of presence. When every moment is packed, there's no space to notice Love here and now.

Religion reinforced this by equating holiness with activity: more prayers, more devotions, more volunteering, more rules. Jeshua pushed back. When Martha scurried around serving, anxious about being productive, Jeshua pointed to Mary sitting still and said, *"She has chosen the better part."* Presence outranks performance.

If Jeshua visited a modern corporate office, he'd probably say, "What good is answering 300 emails if you miss the one person who needed your presence today?" Then he'd probably take everyone outside for a walk and a picnic.

Fear: The Ego's Last Stand

The ego hates presence because it thrives on fear. Fear needs time to survive — fear of what happened, fear of what's coming. In the now, fear evaporates. That's why the moment you sit in presence, your mind screams, "This is boring! This is dangerous! You're wasting time!" It's ego panic.

Religion weaponized this by teaching that silence is suspicious. "Idle hands are the devil's workshop." Better to keep people fearful and busy than let them discover the freedom of presence. Jeshua countered: *Do not be afraid."*

Guilt: The Unworthiness Trap

Another obstacle is the belief that we're not worthy of presence. Raised in guilt-based systems, many people feel they must "clean themselves up" before approaching God. The mind whispers, "You're too sinful, too broken, too distracted." And so we avoid presence because it feels presumptuous.

But Jeshua constantly shattered this lie. He welcomed sinners, outcasts, and failures into presence. He never required perfection first. Presence heals guilt — not the other way around.

Expectation: The Subtle Block

Finally, expectation derails presence. People imagine mystical fireworks: visions, voices, raptures. When presence feels simple — just breathing, just being — they think they're failing. Religion reinforced this by glorifying ecstatic saints while dismissing ordinary presence. But Jeshua taught that the Kingdom is like a mustard seed, small, humble, unnoticed, but alive. Presence is often subtle. Quiet. Ordinary. That's its power.

My Own Experience with Obstacles

When I first tried to practice presence, I hit every obstacle. My phone buzzed. My mind raced. Guilt told me I wasn't holy enough. Fear told me I was wasting time. Expectation told me it should feel like floating in bliss. None of it matched reality.

But slowly, I realized the obstacles weren't failures — they were teachers. Every distraction became a chance to return. Every wave of guilt became a chance to declare Love. Every surge of fear became a chance to breathe. Over time, the obstacles lost their power. Presence grew.

Other Voices

Buddhists call them the "hindrances": desire, aversion, restlessness, sloth, doubt. The desert fathers spoke of "logismoi", distracting thoughts to be gently dismissed. Sufi poets wrote of veils covering the BeLoved, removed one by one. Jeshua named them as worries about tomorrow, anxiety about food and clothing, obsession with status. Everyone agrees: the obstacles are real, but presence is stronger.

Practices for Dismantling Obstacles

1. **Digital Sabbath.** Turn off devices for set times. Let silence return.
2. **Busyness Audit.** Ask: "*Is this activity necessary, or is it avoiding presence?*"
3. **Fear Naming.** When fear arises, say out loud, "*This is fear, not reality.*" Then return to breath.
4. **Guilt Reversal.** When guilt says, "You're not worthy of presence," reply, "*Presence is what heals me.*"
5. **Expectation Release.** Let presence be ordinary. Celebrate the quiet instead of chasing the spectacular.

The Freedom Beyond Obstacles

The more you practice, the less power these obstacles hold. Distraction loses its grip. Busyness loses its glamour. Fear loses its sting. Guilt loses its authority. Expectation loses its demands. What's left is the simple, spacious, healing reality of presence.

The Drumbeat Truth

Let's repeat it until it anchors deep:

- Distraction is noise. Presence is silence.
- Busyness is slavery. Presence is freedom.
- Fear is illusion. Presence is truth.
- Guilt is a lie. Presence is grace.
- Expectation is pressure. Presence is gift.

So don't be surprised by obstacles. Expect them. See them not as failures, but as doorways. Every time you notice distraction, busyness, fear, guilt, or expectation, you have a chance to return. Presence doesn't demand perfection. It invites persistence. That's how obstacles become teachers. That's how we move deeper into presence.

Practices of Presence

If presence is the key to freedom, the direct connection to God, and the antidote to fear, then we need more than inspiration – we need practice. Jeshua didn't just preach presence; he embodied it, lived it, modeled it. And every wisdom tradition agrees: presence isn't something you simply understand intellectually. It's something you practice until it becomes your way of being.

This section is about the "how." Because let's face it – *knowing* that presence matters and actually *living* in it are two very different things. The modern world does not make presence easy. Religion hasn't made it easy either. Both have conspired to keep us distracted, anxious, and anywhere but here. But the Way of Jeshua is simple, practical, and always accessible. You don't need a monastery, a seminary, or a Himalayan cave. You need willingness, a little humor, and a handful of practices you can actually use.

Jeshua's Practices of Presence

Let's start with Jeshua himself. What did he actually *do* that demonstrated presence?

- **Silence.** Jeshua often withdrew to solitary places to pray. Presence requires stepping away from noise.
- **Nature.** He pointed constantly to birds, lilies, seeds, weather. Presence notices creation.
- **Stories.** His parables drew people's attention to simple, everyday realities – bread, coins, wine. Presence sees the sacred in the ordinary.
- **Meals.** Jeshua ate slowly, intentionally, and with others. Meals became moments of presence.
- **Touch.** He touched lepers, children, the sick – fully present with each one.

Notice how grounded all of this is. Jeshua's practices weren't mystical techniques. They were simple, embodied ways of showing up to life fully.

My Own Journey with Practice

When I first started trying to live in presence, I assumed it required complicated meditation methods or special conditions. But the more I experimented, the more I realized presence is accessible anywhere. Sometimes the simplest practice — a deep breath, a quiet moment, a genuine laugh — carried me further into presence than any elaborate ritual.

"Sitting in Love" is nothing fancy. Just sitting quietly, breathing deeply, and letting myself rest in Love's awareness. At first, my mind raced like a caffeinated squirrel. But over time, the racing slowed. Stillness deepened. And I realized: this is it. This is the Kingdom within.

Practical Practices for Daily Life

Here are some practices anyone can adopt, right now, to cultivate presence:

1. **Breath Awareness.** Set aside five minutes to simply notice your breathing. Don't change it, just notice. Each inhale: here. Each exhale: now. Fear and distraction dissolve when you return to breath.
2. **Sensory Grounding.** Pick one daily activity — brushing teeth, washing dishes, drinking coffee — and do it with full awareness. Notice textures, tastes, sounds. The ordinary becomes sacred when seen through presence.
3. **Gratitude Pause.** A few times a day, stop and name three things you're grateful for right now. Gratitude is a magnet for presence.
4. **Love Lens.** When you encounter another person, silently say, "*The Kingdom of Heaven is within you.*" This simple recognition pulls you into presence with them.
5. **Digital Sabbath.** Set times each day with no screens. Silence the noise. Presence thrives in quiet.
6. **Humor Breaks.** Laughter is one of the fastest routes to presence. Intentionally watch something funny, share a joke, or laugh at yourself daily.

7. **Evening Reflection.** Before bed, review the day. Where was I present? Where was I distracted? Celebrate the wins, forgive the misses, and commit to tomorrow.

The Simplicity of Presence

Imagine Jeshua leading a modern mindfulness workshop. Instead of incense and chanting, he takes everyone outside, points to a sparrow, and says, "See? It's not freaking out about the stock market. Learn from that." Half the participants would roll their eyes; the other half would have an awakening. That's how simple presence can be.

Why Practice Matters

Presence isn't automatic. The ego loves to pull us into past and future. Fear loves to hijack attention. Without practice, presence remains an occasional glimpse. With practice, it becomes a way of life.

Think of it like physical fitness. If you exercise once a year, you won't get strong. But consistent, simple practices change your body over time. Presence is spiritual fitness. Every breath, every pause, every moment of awareness builds strength.

Other Traditions on Practice

The Buddhists developed mindfulness meditation. The Hindus developed yoga. The Sufis developed chanting and dance. The desert fathers developed contemplative prayer. Different forms, same purpose: training the mind and heart to stay present. Jeshua's simple practices fit right into this stream – silence, awareness, Love.

Common Struggles

People often say, "I tried presence, but my mind wandered." Of course it did. That's what minds do. The point isn't to stop wandering. The point is to notice and return. Each return is the practice.

Another struggle: "I don't feel God in presence." That's okay. Presence isn't about chasing feelings. It's about showing up. Sometimes presence feels blissful. Sometimes it feels boring. Both are fine. God is here regardless.

Imagine if gym memberships worked like spirituality. People sign up, go once, get sore, then quit and say, "Exercise doesn't work for me." That's how most people approach presence. The truth is that you need repetition. That's how growth happens.

My Favorite Daily Routine

Here's a practice flow I often recommend:

- **Morning:** Begin with a restorative exhale and declare, *"The Kingdom of Heaven is within me."*
- **Midday:** Take a five-minute gratitude pause. Notice three blessings right now.
- **Evening:** Sit in Love quietly for ten minutes, breathing and resting in Love.
- **Before Bed:** Reflect on presence moments. Forgive distractions. Rest in gratitude.

That's less than 30 minutes total, but it transforms the entire day.

The Fruit of Practice

Over time, practices of presence bear fruit:

- Anxiety softens.
- Joy increases.
- Relationships deepen.
- Creativity expands.
- Fear dissolves.
- God becomes near, not distant.

The more you practice, the more you realize presence isn't something you do occasionally. It becomes your natural state.

The Drumbeat Truth

Let's repeat it until it anchors deep:

- Presence requires practice.
- Practice doesn't need to be complicated.
- Small, daily acts accumulate into transformation.
- Presence practice connects you directly to God, no intermediaries required.

So don't just admire presence. Practice it. Don't just talk about it. Train in it. Jeshua's Way wasn't a theory. It was a practice of Love, silence, awareness, and connection. And the more you practice, the more you realize the Kingdom is not coming someday – it's here, now, waiting to be lived.

That's the practices of presence — the simple, daily ways we train ourselves into the freedom Jeshua promised.

The Fruit of Presence

Practices are the soil and water, but presence itself is the seed of transformation. And just like seeds, presence bears fruit. You don't sit in Love, breathe into the now, or return from distraction just to feel calm for a few minutes — though that's a fine start. You do it because presence produces something in you and around you that ripples outward. Jeshua knew this. The mystics knew this. And anyone who has tasted true presence has glimpsed it: presence transforms everything it touches.

The Fruit in the Individual

The first fruit of presence is personal. Something shifts inside you. Anxiety softens. Guilt loosens. Fear loses its grip. Joy sneaks in where worry used to dominate. It doesn't happen overnight. At first, you might just notice a little more calm in your day, a little more patience with people, a little more clarity in decisions. But over time, these little shifts accumulate into a new way of being.

Presence gives you back yourself. Without it, you're lost in memories and projections, always missing the only time you're actually alive: *now*. With it, you return to the truth: you are alive, you are whole, you are here. That recognition changes everything.

Imagine your mind as a puppy that keeps running into the past or future. Presence is the gentle leash that says, "Nope, right here." Over time, the puppy learns to heel. Still excitable, but a lot less likely to drag you into traffic.

The Fruit in Relationships

Presence doesn't just change you. It changes how you relate to others. When you're actually present with someone, they feel it. They feel seen, heard, valued. Presence is one of the rarest gifts in today's distracted world.

Think about conversations. Most of the time, people aren't listening, they're rehearsing their response, checking their phone, or drifting into their own thoughts. But when someone listens with full presence, it's healing. It communicates: *You matter. You are worthy of my attention. You are Loved.*

Jeshua embodied this fruit constantly. People flocked to him not just because he healed or preached, but because he *saw* them. The woman at the well. Zacchaeus up in the tree. Children brought to him. Lepers cast out of society. Each one felt the fruit of his presence — unconditional regard.

The Fruit in Communities

When enough individuals practice presence, communities change. Gossip fades because people actually listen. Fear-based divisions shrink because people engage openly. Compassion increases because people notice suffering in real time instead of numbing out.

The early Christian communities were marked by this fruit. Outsiders marveled, *"See how they Love one another."* That wasn't the result of fear-driven rule-following. It was the fruit of people living in presence: sharing meals, caring for the sick, honoring each person.

Imagine a modern HOA meeting conducted in presence. Instead of yelling about lawn heights and barking dogs, neighbors breathe, listen, and seek solutions. Miracles would happen. Even the guy with the neon pink house would get understanding.

The Fruit in Society

Presence scales. When individuals and communities embody it, entire societies shift. Fear-based politics lose power. Consumerism loses its stranglehold. Systems rooted in greed and manipulation crumble.

Why? Because presence cuts through illusion. People who live in the now are harder to control. They don't buy lies about the past or fearmongering about the future. They live awake.

Think of leaders like Gandhi or Martin Luther King Jr. Their activism was rooted in presence — the refusal to be driven by fear, the choice to stand calmly in Love even in the face of violence. That's fruit.

Presence transformed not just their inner lives, but history itself.

The Fruit of Creativity

Another fruit of presence is creativity. When your mind isn't trapped in regret or anxiety, space opens for imagination. Artists, writers, inventors, and problem-solvers all testify: their best work comes when they're fully present, "in the flow." Jeshua's parables were creative brilliance, born not of academic study, but of presence to the world around him.

Presence makes life itself a canvas. Meals become art. Conversations become music. Work becomes play. That's fruit.

The Fruit of Spiritual Freedom

At the deepest level, the fruit of presence is freedom. Freedom from fear, freedom from guilt, freedom from manipulation. When you realize the Kingdom is here now, no one can scare you into obedience with threats of tomorrow. When you feel Love in this breath, no one can convince you you're unworthy. Presence liberates you from the chains of control and returns you to your divine inheritance: wholeness.

My Own Experience of the Fruit

I've seen this fruit in my own life. The more I sit in presence, the less I react with anger, the more I respond with humor. The less I obsess over outcomes, the more creative ideas flow. The less I live in regret or worry, the more I savor simple joys – a meal, a laugh, a walk. And in relationships, presence has changed everything. People tell me "I feel calmer around you," or "I feel seen." That's not me being special. That's presence bearing fruit.

Practices to Cultivate Fruit

The fruit isn't something you manufacture. It grows naturally when you practice presence. But you can nurture the growth:

1. **Notice Small Shifts.** Pay attention to moments of peace, patience, or joy. Celebrate them as fruit.
2. **Practice Gratitude.** Thank God for each fruit, however small. Gratitude multiplies growth.
3. **Share Presence.** Offer it to others by listening, noticing, and loving. Fruit grows best when shared.
4. **Trust the Process.** Trees don't bear fruit overnight. Neither do we. Patience is part of the practice.

Other Voices

Paul, in one of his good moments, described the "fruit of the Spirit" as Love, joy, peace, patience, kindness, goodness, faithfulness, gentleness, and self-control. Sounds a lot like the fruit of presence. Buddhist teachers describe equanimity, compassion, and joy as natural outcomes of mindfulness. Sufi mystics sing of Love, beauty, and generosity flowing from union with the BeLoved. Across traditions, presence leads to fruit.

The Drumbeat Truth

Let's engrain this:

- Presence changes you. That's fruit.
- Presence changes relationships. That's fruit.
- Presence changes communities. That's fruit.
- Presence changes the world. That's fruit.

Don't just practice presence for peace of mind. Practice it for the fruit it bears — in you, in your relationships, in your community, in the world. Jeshua's Way wasn't about private bliss. It was about living so present in Love that fruit overflowed everywhere you went.

That's the fruit of presence — the evidence that the Kingdom really is here, now, within.

Living Fully in the Present

We've explored the power of now, the traps of past and future, presence as connection to God, the obstacles that get in the way, the practices that help, and the fruit that presence produces. Now comes the heart of the matter: what does it actually look like to live fully in the present? Not just dabbling in presence during meditation, not just tasting it on a retreat, but making it the fabric of daily life. Jeshua didn't teach presence as a hobby. He lived it as a Way.

The Present as Home

The first truth about living fully in the present is this: the now is home. It's where you belong. When you leave it — when you wander into regret or anxiety — you become homeless, disconnected, adrift.

Living fully in the present is coming home again and again, realizing you never truly left.

Imagine your mind as a kid who keeps running out of the house barefoot. The present moment is the parent on the porch saying, "Come on back inside, dinner's ready." You might wander a hundred times a day, but each return is coming home.

Jeshua as the Example

Jeshua lived fully in the present. He didn't carry grudges about the past. He didn't panic about the future. He responded to each moment with Love. Hungry crowd? He fed them. Blind beggar? He healed him. Woman caught in adultery? He forgave her. Storm at sea? He calmed it. Jeshua wasn't rehearsing the past or predicting the future. He was alive, awake, here.

When he said, *"I am the way, the truth, and the life,"* it wasn't an invitation to memorize doctrines. It was an invitation to embody presence. He was showing us what it looks like to be fully here, fully alive, fully connected.

My Own Struggle

I'll be honest: living fully in the present has been the hardest and most rewarding discipline of my life. The old programming loves to pull me into fear about tomorrow or shame about yesterday. But the more I return to presence, the more I realize how much life I used to miss. Entire conversations, meals, and moments went by without me actually being there.

Now, when I practice presence, even the simplest things glow – sunlight on a wall, laughter with a friend, the taste of morning coffee. Life itself becomes sacramental.

The Qualities of a Present Life

So what does living fully in the present look like in practice?

- **Awareness.** You notice your surroundings, your breath, your feelings. You're awake to life unfolding.
- **Acceptance.** You stop fighting what is. Presence doesn't mean passivity, but it begins with accepting reality as it is.
- **Responsiveness.** You act from awareness instead of reaction. Love guides, not fear.

- **Simplicity.** The clutter of unnecessary worries falls away. What matters is clear.
- **Joy.** Presence makes ordinary life extraordinary. Gratitude blooms naturally.

Everyday Examples

Living fully in the present means:

- When you eat, you taste.
- When you listen, you truly hear.
- When you walk, you notice.
- When you work, you engage.
- When you rest, you rest.

It doesn't mean every moment feels blissful. It means every moment is lived.

Imagine a world where everyone was present. No one texting while driving. No one scrolling at dinner. No one zoning out during conversations. The divorce rate would drop, car accidents would plummet, and therapists would be out of work. That's how radical presence could be.

Obstacles Revisited

Living fully in the present doesn't mean obstacles vanish. Distraction still knocks, busyness still tempts, fear still whispers, guilt still nags. But instead of ruling you, they become reminders. Each time you notice them, you return. The present moment is endlessly patient. It always takes you back.

Practices for Daily Presence

Here are ways to anchor presence into every day:

1. **Morning Grounding.** Before touching your phone, take three breaths and notice where you are.
2. **Sacred Pauses.** Set reminders throughout the day to stop, breathe, and notice.
3. **Presence Meals.** Eat one meal a day without distractions, savoring each bite.
4. **Deep Listening.** Give at least one person your full attention daily. No multitasking.
5. **Evening Reflection.** Before bed, recall moments of presence. Thank God for them.

The Transformation of Presence

Over time, these simple practices shift everything. Stress decreases. Compassion increases. Creativity blossoms. Relationships heal. Fear dissolves. Guilt fades. The fruit of presence ripens more each day.

Living fully in the present doesn't mean life gets easier. Challenges remain. Pain still comes. But you face them differently. Instead of drowning in fear, you breathe into now. Instead of being consumed by regret, you act in Love. That shift changes everything.

Other Voices

Reminder: Buddhism calls this *mindfulness.* Hinduism calls it *yoga* — union with the divine in the present. Sufi mystics call it *remembrance.* Jeshua called it the *Kingdom within.* Different words, same reality: life is *now.* God is *now.* Love is *now.*

My Own Joy

For me, living fully in the present has brought a kind of joy I never knew in religion. It's not about earning approval. It's not about fearing punishment. It's about being alive in Love. And once you taste that, you never want to go back.

The Drumbeat Truth

Let's engrain it:

- The present is home. The past is gone. The future is illusion.
- Jeshua lived fully here, showing us the Way.
- Presence turns ordinary life into sacred life.
- Living fully in the present is the deepest freedom of all.

Stop dabbling in presence. Live it. Make it the heartbeat of your day. Jeshua didn't die to create a religion about the past or fear about the future. He lived to show us the Kingdom now.

To live fully in the present is to live the Way. And that's the doorway to everything this book is pointing toward: Love, freedom, and wholeness here and now.

Chapter 14: The Illusion of Separation

The Great Lie of Distance

If there is one lie that has caused more fear, guilt, and disempowerment than any other, it's this: that God is far away. That you are here, small and sinful, while God is somewhere else, distant and perfect. That gap, that supposed separation, is the stage on which religion built its entire empire. Without it, the whole system collapses. Because if God is already here, within you, then what use are intermediaries? What use are rituals to "bridge the gap"? What use is fear?

How the Lie Took Hold

In Jeshua's time, the Temple in Jerusalem was the epicenter of this illusion. God was thought to dwell in the Holy of Holies – a chamber so sacred only the high priest could enter, and only once a year.

Ordinary people were kept at a distance. Layers of curtains, walls, and rules reinforced the idea: God is separate, and you need a mediator to reach Him.

The early Church inherited this mindset and expanded it. Priests became gatekeepers. Sacraments became toll booths. Heaven became a gated community. The whole structure depended on convincing people that God was out there, and you needed the institution's help to get to Him.

Imagine if grocery stores worked this way. Instead of picking your own fruit, you'd have to pay someone to enter the "holy produce section" once a week and hand you an apple. That's what religion did with God – turned free access into controlled scarcity.

Jeshua's Message of Nearness

Here's the radical truth Jeshua taught: there is no distance. *The Kingdom of Heaven is within you."* Not far away. Not someday. *Within.*

When he forgave sins directly without Temple rituals, he was saying, "*The separation is an illusion.*" When he healed people on the margins, outside the official structures, he was saying, "*God is here too.*" When he tore down the hierarchies between priest and people, Jew and Gentile, clean and unclean, he was saying,

"*Nothing separates you from God but your own belief in separation.*"

And at the crucifixion, the Temple curtain — that symbol of separation — was torn in two. Presence was no longer hidden. It never was.

My Own Story of Distance

I grew up believing in a distant God. Heaven was far away. Hell was always threatening. God was up there somewhere with a cosmic clipboard. I was down here, guilty and inadequate. The gap felt unbridgeable. Every Mass, every confession, every prayer felt like trying to send smoke signals across the canyon, hoping God noticed.

And yet, in moments of stillness, in laughter, in Love, I felt something different. I felt nearness. I felt presence. I felt the Kingdom within.

Those glimpses terrified religion but freed me. Because if God was already here, what was all the fear for?

Why Separation Persists

The illusion of distance persists because it's profitable. Institutions thrive when people feel cut off. If you think you're separated from God, you'll pay for access. You'll obey for approval. You'll stay small and dependent.

It also persists because it feels safe to the ego. If God is far away, you can keep God theoretical. If God is within, you have to face the uncomfortable truth: you are divine. That's terrifying and liberating all at once.

Other Voices

The Bhagavad Gita says, *I am the Self, O Gudakesha, seated in the hearts of all creatures.*" The Tao Te Ching says, *You are not separate from the Way.*" Sufi poets sing, *I searched for God and found only myself. I searched for myself and found only God.*" Everywhere mystics whisper the same truth: separation is illusion.

Imagine if fish attended weekly services where priests told them, "Water is far away, and only we can give you access." That's religion in a nutshell. The truth is, you're already swimming in God.

Practices to Dissolve Separation

So how do we break this illusion in daily life?

1. **Declare Nearness.** Start the day declaring: *"The Kingdom is within me."* Say it until it feels real.
2. **Practice Presence.** Notice the breath, the heartbeat, the silence – God in each moment.
3. **Sacred Mirror.** Look in the mirror and say, "I see God in you." Scary at first, but transformative.
4. **See God in Others.** Whisper silently to each person you encounter: "*The Kingdom is within you. Namaste.*"
5. **Release Gatekeepers.** When old programming says you need intermediaries, remind yourself: nothing separates you from Love.

My Turning Point

One night, while drifting off to sleep, I felt the phrase rise up: *"There is no gap."* Not between me and God. Not between me and Love. Not between me and life. The distance was only in my mind. In that moment, I realized: I had never been outside God. I couldn't be. No one can. That realization shattered decades of fear in an instant.

The Drumbeat Truth

Let's engrain it:

- Separation is illusion.
- The Kingdom is within you.
- God is not distant. God is here.
- Nothing stands between you and Love.

Release the lie of distance. Stop paying tolls to gatekeepers. Stop imagining God as far away. Come home to the truth Jeshua taught and lived: the Kingdom is within you, here, now.

That's the great lie of distance – and the freedom of realizing it was never real.

The Role of Religion in Creating Separation

If the illusion of distance is the great lie, then religion has been its loudest storyteller. It didn't just casually suggest that God might be far away — it built entire empires on the idea. Separation became the cornerstone, and from it rose doctrines, rituals, hierarchies, and fear- based systems that convinced people they were cut off from the Divine and needed someone else to bridge the gap.

How the Separation Story Works

Here's the simple formula:

1. Convince people God is far away.
2. Convince them they are too sinful, broken, or unworthy to approach God directly.
3. Convince them the institution alone has the key to reconnect them.
4. Charge tolls — obedience, rituals, money, loyalty — for that access.

It's diabolically brilliant. If people believed they were already united with God, religion would lose its leverage. If they realized the Kingdom was within, the gatekeepers would be out of a job. So religion doubled down on the illusion: "You are separated. We are the bridge. Trust us."

Imagine a phone company that told you, "You actually can't talk directly to your friends. All calls must be routed through our operators — for a small monthly fee, of course." That's what religion did with God: turned free connection into a monopolized service.

Historical Roots of Separation

The Jewish Temple system already had this structure. God's presence was housed in the Holy of Holies, and only the high priest could enter once a year. Everyone else relied on intermediaries. Sacrifices, offerings, and rituals were the price of admission.

Christianity inherited this model and expanded it. Priests became the new mediators, sacraments became the new toll booths, and heaven and hell became the ultimate carrot and stick. By the Middle Ages, the Church was selling indulgences — literal payments for forgiveness. If God was already near, indulgences would've been laughable. But if God was distant, they became big business.

Jeshua's Disruption

Jeshua's entire ministry was a disruption of this system. He forgave sins without sacrifices. He healed people outside the

Temple. He declared the Kingdom was within. And when he died, it's said, the Temple curtain – the very symbol of separation – was torn in two. His message was unmistakable: the distance was never real.

That's why he was so dangerous to religious authorities. If people believed they could access God directly, the entire system of control and profit would collapse. Jeshua wasn't killed for telling people to be nice. He was killed for dismantling the illusion of separation.

My Own Experience with Religious Separation

Growing up Catholic, I felt this illusion constantly. God was "up there," distant, holy, terrifying. I was "down here," guilty, sinful, unworthy. The priest stood in the middle, the only one allowed to consecrate the Eucharist, the only one authorized to forgive sins. Even prayer felt like sending letters to a celestial P.O. box, hoping they'd get through.

I remember going to confession as a kid, listing every little sin – "I stole a cookie, I lied about homework" – and walking away still wondering if God heard me. The priest told me I was absolved, but I didn't feel close to God. I felt dependent on the system. That's the fruit of separation: dependency, not freedom.

Why Religion Clings to Separation

Institutions cling to separation for two main reasons:

1. **Power.** If people think they need you to reach God, you control them. You can dictate behavior, extract obedience, and silence dissent.
2. **Profit.** Separation is lucrative. Payments for indulgences, donations for Masses, offerings for rituals – all flow from the belief that access to God must be purchased.

It's not just ancient history. Modern churches still preach separation. "Without our pastor's covering, you're vulnerable." "Without tithing, you can't receive God's blessing." "Without our theology, you're outside the true faith." It's the same script with new branding.

Other Traditions' Warnings

This isn't unique to Christianity. Every religious hierarchy has exploited separation. Hindu priests once monopolized Vedic rituals. Buddhist monasteries charged for access to teachings. Sufi poets were often persecuted because they taught direct connection.

Wherever institutional religion rises, mystics appear to challenge it, reminding people: God is already here. You are not cut off.

Imagine if oxygen was treated this way. "Sorry, you can't breathe directly. You'll need to rent approved air from the official distributors." People would riot. And yet we've tolerated the same scam with spirituality.

The Psychological Effect

The illusion of separation doesn't just control behavior. It warps identity. People raised in separation-based religion internalize the message: I am not enough. I am distant. I am unworthy. That belief shapes relationships, careers, mental health. It's not just theology – it's trauma.

Presence heals this by returning us to the truth: we were never separate. The Kingdom was always within.

Practices to Heal Separation Wounds

1. **Direct Divine Conversation.** Talk to God as if already present. No intermediaries. Just you and Love.
2. **Inner Listening.** Sit in silence and trust the whispers of your own heart as sacred.
3. **Sacred Reading.** Read Jeshua's words about nearness aloud: *"The Kingdom of Heaven is within you."* Repeat until it sinks in.
4. **Reclaim Rituals.** If old practices still speak to you, do them as expressions of Love, not as tolls to bridge distance.
5. **Community of Equals.** Gather with people who affirm direct access. Practice presence together without hierarchy.

My Turning Point

For me, the breakthrough came when I realized the voice of separation was not God. It was programming. God's actual voice – the one I heard in stillness – always said, "*You are mine. You are enough. You are here.*" That voice didn't demand payment or rituals. It offered presence. Once I trusted that, the illusion of separation began to crumble.

The Drumbeat Truth

Let's repeat until it burns through the old programming:

- Separation is the great lie.
- Religion built systems on that lie.
- Jeshua exposed it by teaching God is within.
- You were never cut off. You are already home.

The illusion isn't real. So don't buy into it. Stop outsourcing your connection. Stop believing the story that you are far from God. Religion may have built its empire on separation, but Jeshua built his Way on union. The curtain is torn. The distance was never real.

That's the role of religion in creating separation — and the truth that dismantles it.

Experiencing Oneness

We've exposed the great lie of separation and traced how religion institutionalized it. But naming the illusion isn't enough. To be free, you have to *experience* the truth that dissolves it. And that truth is *oneness* — with God, with yourself, with others, and with creation. This isn't an abstract philosophy. It's a living reality you can taste in the present moment. Jeshua taught it, mystics across traditions echoed it, and it's available to each of us now.

What Oneness Means

Oneness doesn't mean uniformity. It doesn't erase individuality. It means that beneath the surface differences — body, personality, culture — there's a shared essence. You are not cut off from God but rooted in God. You are not cut off from others but connected through Love. You are not cut off from creation but part of its living web.

The illusion says: "You are separate, small, alone." Oneness says: "*You are whole, connected, infinite in Love.*" That shift changes everything.

Imagine drops of water arguing about who's more important, forgetting they're all part of the same ocean. That's humanity in a nutshell.

Oneness is remembering that we're the ocean, not just the drops.

Jeshua and Oneness

Jeshua constantly pointed to oneness. *I and the Father are one." "May they all be one, as we are one." The Kingdom of Heaven is within you."* These weren't metaphors. They were descriptions of reality.

When he broke bread and shared wine, it was more than ritual. It was the symbol of shared essence: "*We are one body.*" When he touched lepers and outcasts, he was collapsing the illusion of separation.

When he forgave sins directly, he was bypassing structures that divided people from God.

His whole life was a demonstration: God and humanity are not two. Love bridges every false divide.

My Own Taste of Oneness

There is a moment when sitting in Love where you feel the boundary between yourself and the world dissolve. For a few seconds, there is no "me" here and "God" there. There was only awareness, Love, presence. It wasn't dramatic. No angels, no visions. Just a quiet, overwhelming sense that you are not separate. You are part of something infinite.

That moment changed me. It wasn't theology. It was experience. And once you taste it, the illusion of separation can't hold you the same way again.

Why Oneness Feels Scary

Here's the irony: oneness sounds beautiful, but it can feel terrifying at first. Why? Because the ego thrives on separateness. It says, "I am me. You are you. God is far away. I must protect myself." Oneness threatens the ego's boundaries. If you're one with God, you can't cling to being small. If you're one with others, you can't cling to superiority. If you're one with creation, you can't exploit it. Oneness demands humility – and freedom.

Religion exploited this fear by insisting on separation. It's easier to control separate sheep than awakened beings who realize they're one with the shepherd.

Oneness in Other Traditions

The Bhagavad Gita teaches that the same divine Self dwells in all beings. Buddhism insists that the illusion of separateness is the root of suffering. The Tao Te Ching describes the Tao as the source of all, in which everything returns to unity. Sufi mystics sing of dissolving into the BeLoved. Across traditions, the mystics cry the same truth: you are not separate.

Imagine if the universe held a family reunion and everyone showed up — stars, trees, animals, humans. And God stands up and says, "Surprise! You're all related." That's oneness.

How to Experience Oneness

You don't have to wait for mystical visions. Oneness can be tasted in simple practices:

1. **Sit in Silence.** In stillness, notice the boundary between "you" and "God" softening. Feel Love holding everything.
2. **Eye Contact.** Look deeply into another person's eyes without distraction. Notice the shared humanity. The Kingdom in them is the same as in you.
3. **Nature Walks.** Walk slowly in nature. Realize the air in your lungs was breathed by trees. You are literally one with creation.
4. **Service.** Acts of Love dissolve separation. When you serve another, you serve yourself.
5. **Gratitude.** Thank everything — food, sunlight, friends. Gratitude awakens awareness of interconnectedness.

The Fruit of Oneness

Experiencing oneness changes how you live. Fear decreases because you realize nothing can separate you from God. Compassion increases because you see yourself in others. Joy increases because you feel connected to life itself. Oneness is the soil where Love naturally grows.

Jeshua knew this. That's why he said the greatest commandments are Love of God and Love of neighbor — because in truth, they're the same Love.

My Own Growth in Oneness

The more I practice presence, the more I notice moments of oneness daily. A laugh shared with a stranger. The hush of wind through trees. The peace of silence in meditation. Each one is a reminder: the separation I was taught was never real.

And every time I taste that oneness, fear shrinks. Guilt loosens. Love expands. That's how the illusion dies – not by argument, but by experience.

The Drumbeat Truth

Let's anchor it:

- Oneness is reality. Separation is illusion.
- Jeshua lived and taught union, not distance.
- Experiencing oneness dissolves fear and expands Love.
- The Kingdom within is the taste of oneness now.

I invite you to not settle for doctrines about separation. Taste the truth for yourself. Sit in silence. Look into eyes. Walk in creation.

Experience the oneness Jeshua described and lived. Once you do, the illusion of separation begins to crumble, and Love begins to reign.

That's oneness – the lived antidote to the great lie.

Psychological Impact of Separation

If the illusion of separation were just a theological quirk, it wouldn't matter much. People could shrug it off as one more weird religious idea, like whether angels dance on pinheads or whether Adam had a belly button. But the illusion of separation is not a harmless abstraction. It burrows deep into the psyche. It shapes how people see themselves, others, and the world. It wires fear and unworthiness into the nervous system. It haunts dreams, relationships, and choices. And for many, it leaves wounds that last a lifetime.

Separation as Identity

The first and deepest psychological effect of separation is identity distortion. When you're told from childhood that God is far away and you are sinful, you internalize it. You learn to see yourself not as beLoved but as broken. Not as whole but as lacking. Not as home but as exiled.

That distorted identity becomes the lens through which you see everything. You approach life not as a co-creator, but as a beggar. Not as someone empowered, but as someone deficient. And when that identity sinks in, it's hard to shake — even long after leaving the religion that planted it.

Imagine a kid told every day, "You're the worst student in class," even if he's brilliant. Eventually, he'll believe it and underperform just to fit the story. That's what separation does: it hands you a failing grade before you've even taken the test.

Separation and Anxiety

Separation fuels anxiety. If God is distant, then life feels uncertain. You're always worried: Am I good enough? Am I saved? Am I forgiven? Am I in or out? Anxiety festers because there's no stable ground. Every mistake feels catastrophic. Every doubt feels damning.

I remember as a kid lying in bed, terrified I'd missed a sin in confession. What if I died in my sleep? Would I wake up in hell? That's not spirituality. That's trauma. Separation wired anxiety into me before I even understood the word.

Separation and Guilt

Separation also amplifies guilt. If God is far away, every misstep feels like proof of distance. You think: "I sinned again, so God must be angry. I failed again, so God must be further." Guilt becomes a treadmill you can never get off. Confess, sin, confess, sin. Always chasing approval that never arrives.

The tragedy is that guilt can be useful in small doses; it points out when we've hurt someone. But separation-based guilt is toxic. It says, "You're not guilty because you hurt someone. You're guilty because you exist." That's not correction; that's condemnation of being.

Separation and Shame

Even deeper than guilt is shame. Guilt says, "I *did* wrong." Shame says, "I *am* wrong." Separation-based religion marinates people in shame. You're told you're inherently sinful, inherently broken, inherently unworthy. Shame eats away at self-esteem, mental health, and relationships.

I've seen countless people carry this shame into adulthood. Even after leaving church, they still feel unworthy of Love, success, or joy. That's the long shadow of separation — it lingers even when the theology is gone.

Separation and Relationships

The illusion of separation doesn't just damage your relationship with God. It spills into relationships with others. If you see yourself as broken and unworthy, you project that onto others. You become judgmental, competitive, fearful of intimacy. Or you become codependent, desperate for someone else to validate your worth.

Communities shaped by separation often become toxic. Fear-based rules breed gossip, exclusion, and control. Instead of Love and trust, people police each other's behavior, terrified of guilt by association. Separation poisons community.

Imagine if family dinners worked this way. "Sorry, Aunt Linda, you can't sit with us tonight. You missed church last week, so you're out." That's how separation logic works — absurd, but deadly serious in religious systems.

Separation and Mental Health

Modern psychology recognizes what religion long ignored: messages of unworthiness and fear damage mental health. Anxiety disorders, depression, scrupulosity (religious OCD), trauma responses — all can be fueled by separation theology. People live in constant fight-or-flight, bodies flooded with stress hormones, minds trapped in fear loops.

The saddest part is that many people seek help from the very systems that harmed them. They confess more, pray harder, volunteer more, hoping to quiet the anxiety. But the system can't heal what it created.

The wound of separation needs a different medicine: presence and Love.

Jeshua's Healing of the Psyche

Jeshua's Way was psychologically healing precisely because it dismantled separation. When he said, *"Your sins are forgiven,"* he wasn't just making a theological point. He was lifting shame. When he ate with outcasts, he was restoring worth. When he told people, *"Do not be afraid,"* he was calming anxiety. His entire ministry was one giant therapeutic intervention against separation trauma.

My Own Healing

For me, healing from separation meant relearning identity. I had to unlearn decades of programming and rewire my psyche around Jeshua's message: *"The Kingdom of Heaven is within you."* At first, I repeated it like a mantra. Then I began to feel it in moments of silence. Then it became a truth I could trust.

The shift was profound. Anxiety eased. Guilt loosened. Shame began to lift. Relationships deepened. I realized the biggest barrier wasn't God's distance – it was my belief in distance. Once that belief cracked, healing began.

Practices for Healing the Psychological Impact

1. **Identity Declarations.** Declare Daily: "*I am beLoved. I am whole. I am not separate.*"
2. **Release the Past.** Reassure the child in you who was taught separation. Speak words of Love.
3. **Body Awareness.** Notice where anxiety or guilt lives in your body. Breathe presence into those places.
4. **Rewrite the Story.** Journal about separation messages you absorbed. Then write Jeshua's truth beside them.
5. **Seek Support.** Therapy, community, and mentors can help unravel separation's psychological grip.

Other Voices

Modern psychology echoes what mystics have always known. Carl Jung said the deepest wound is the loss of connection to the Self – which sounds a lot like the illusion of separation. Contemporary trauma studies emphasize safety, connection, and presence as keys to healing. Buddhist psychology teaches that suffering arises from the illusion of separateness. All point to the same solution: return to union, return to presence.

The Drumbeat Truth

Let's anchor it:

- Separation distorts identity.
- Separation fuels anxiety, guilt, and shame.
- Separation poisons relationships and communities.
- Separation wounds mental health.
- Jeshua's Way heals by restoring oneness.

Recognize the psychological impact of separation in your own life. Name the anxiety, the guilt, the shame. Don't let religion's lie define you any longer. Begin to live into Jeshua's truth: you are not separate, never were, never will be. Presence heals. Love restores.

That's how we undo the psychological impact of separation – by replacing illusion with lived truth.

Unity in Diversity

When people first hear the word *oneness*, they sometimes get nervous. They imagine a gray, uniform world where everyone talks the same, dresses the same, prays the same, eats the same bland casserole at every meal. But oneness is not sameness. Jeshua didn't come to create clones. He came to awaken people to Love so deep that diversity no longer divides. Unity in diversity is the real fruit of dissolving separation: the realization that difference does not mean distance.

The Fear of Difference

Human beings have always been suspicious of difference. Skin color, language, customs, gender, beliefs – we fixate on them. Religion amplified this by declaring insiders and outsiders, saved and damned, pure and impure. Separation became not just about God but about each other.

The psychological wiring runs deep: the ego likes to divide the world into "us" and "them." It feels safer when people look and act the same. But that safety is counterfeit. It shrinks life, it breeds fear, and it justifies cruelty. History's ugliest chapters – slavery, wars, inquisitions, genocides – all grew from separation amplified by fear of difference.

Imagine if the animal kingdom worked this way. "Sorry, giraffes, you can't graze here. This is a lion-only zone." Nature would collapse in weeks. Diversity is how ecosystems thrive. But humans? We've tried to make monocultures of the soul.

Jeshua and Diversity

Jeshua consistently dismantled divisions. He spoke to Samaritans – people his culture despised. He praised the faith of a Roman centurion – a foreign oppressor. He healed women and men alike, rich and poor, Jew and Gentile. His table fellowship scandalized the religious elite because he ate with tax collectors, prostitutes, zealots, and Pharisees.

He wasn't saying differences don't exist. He was saying differences don't define worth. Love transcends them. Unity isn't about erasing identity. It's about affirming identity within the larger reality of oneness.

My Own Awakening to Unity

Growing up, my world was small. Catholic meant "good," everyone else was suspect. But as I stepped outside those boundaries, I met people whose Love, wisdom, and presence rivaled any priest I'd known.

Buddhists, atheists, Muslims, Hindus – each carried light. At first, it shook me. If they were supposed to be "outside" God's grace, how could they radiate so much of it? Then I realized: the illusion of separation was crumbling. God was in them too.

Now, I see diversity as sacred. The Kingdom doesn't look like a monoculture. It looks like a banquet table where every dish from every culture is offered.

Unity Without Uniformity

Unity in diversity doesn't demand everyone agrees on everything. It doesn't mean watering down differences into mush. It means honoring difference without letting it divide.

Think of music. A symphony isn't beautiful because every instrument plays the same note. It's beautiful because each plays its part in harmony. Unity doesn't erase diversity; it orchestrates it. Jeshua's vision was a symphony of Love, not a solo of conformity.

Other Voices

The Bhagavad Gita teaches that the One takes on countless forms, yet all are expressions of the same Self. Buddhism emphasizes interdependence – no being exists in isolation. The Quran says, *"We made you into nations and tribes so that you may know one another."* The Tao Te Ching celebrates the ten thousand things as expressions of the Tao. Everywhere, wisdom traditions affirm that diversity is not a threat to unity but an expression of it.

Imagine heaven as a potluck. If everyone brought the same casserole, it'd be boring. Diversity makes the feast. God's table isn't picky — it welcomes all flavors.

Why Religion Fears Diversity

Institutions often fear diversity because it threatens control. If people realize God speaks in many voices, no single group can claim monopoly. Religions exaggerate difference: "We alone have the truth. They are wrong, dangerous, damned." Unity in diversity dismantles this exclusivity. It frees people to honor wisdom wherever it appears.

The Fruit of Unity

When people embrace unity in diversity, fear decreases. Compassion increases. Curiosity blooms. Instead of judging others for differences, you learn from them. Instead of clinging to tribal identity, you expand into global humanity. Instead of defending rigid boundaries, you celebrate shared essence.

Communities that live this way shine. Outsiders feel welcome. Conversations deepen. Conflict diminishes. Creativity flourishes. It's not utopia — disagreements still happen — but they happen in Love, not fear.

My Own Growth

I've found that the more I live in presence, the more I experience unity in diversity naturally. Sitting in Love, I feel connected not just to "my people" but to everyone. The boundaries religion drew — Catholic vs. Protestant, believer vs. unbeliever — start to look absurd. Presence makes me see: the same divine spark animates all.

And in daily life, this shifts relationships. I listen more. I judge less. I find joy in differences rather than threats. That's the fruit Jeshua promised when he prayed, *"That they may all be one."*

Practices for Unity in Diversity

1. **See God Everywhere.** Consciously affirm the divine spark in each person you meet.
2. **Cross Boundaries.** Intentionally spend time with people outside your tradition, culture, or comfort zone.
3. **Listen Deeply.** Instead of debating, listen to understand. Presence dissolves defensiveness.
4. **Celebrate Difference.** Instead of minimizing diversity, honor it as part of God's creativity.
5. **Shared Service.** Work alongside people of different backgrounds. Unity grows through action.

The Drumbeat Truth

Let's engrain it:

- Oneness does not erase difference.
- Unity flourishes in diversity.
- Fear divides. Love unites.
- The Kingdom is a banquet, not a monoculture.

Differences are nothing to fear. Stop letting religion's boundaries dictate who's in and who's out. Embrace unity in diversity. See God in every face, hear God in every voice, taste God in every culture.

Jeshua's Way was never about building walls. It was about setting tables.

That's unity in diversity – the antidote to separation among people.

Practices to Dissolve Separation

We've unmasked the illusion of separation, explored its psychological impact, and celebrated unity in diversity. But knowing the truth and living the truth are two different things. Separation isn't just a doctrine in a dusty theology book – it's a habit of mind and heart. It creeps into thoughts like, "I'm unworthy;" into relationships like, "They're not like me;" into spirituality like, "God is far away." To dissolve separation, we need practice. Real, daily, embodied practices that retrain the mind, rewire the heart, and return us to oneness.

Why Practice Matters

Separation is sticky. Even after leaving a fear-based religion, people often carry the old programming. They may reject doctrines intellectually but still feel distant from God emotionally. They may say, "I believe all people are one," but still live in judgment. Practice is what bridges that gap. It moves truth from the head into the body, the heart, and daily life.

Imagine trying to learn guitar by reading books about music but never touching the strings. That's how many people approach spirituality – lots of theory, no practice. Oneness isn't something you just "get." It's something you live into.

Jeshua's Practical Way

Jeshua was endlessly practical. He didn't give his disciples abstract theology lectures. He gave them things to do: forgive, serve, share meals, pray simply, Love enemies, be present. Every teaching was embodied practice designed to dissolve separation – between people, between classes, between God and humanity.

When he washed his disciples' feet, it wasn't symbolic pageantry. It was practice. It shattered hierarchies, dissolved the illusion of superiority, and embodied oneness.

My Own Journey

When I first realized separation was an illusion, I thought insight alone would free me. But the old voices lingered: "God is far." "You're not enough." "They're not like you." It wasn't until I started daily practices that things shifted. Sitting in Love, declaring my truth, looking people in the eye with presence – these habits rewired me. Slowly, the illusion lost its grip.

Practices for Daily Life

Here are practices I recommend for dissolving separation, drawn from Jeshua's Way, other traditions, and my own path:

1. **Presence Sitting.** Set aside 10–20 minutes daily to sit quietly, breathe, and rest in Love. Each time your mind drifts into fear or distance, gently return. This is the cornerstone. Presence itself dissolves separation.
2. **The Mirror Exercise.** Look into your own eyes in a mirror. Say out loud: *"The Kingdom of Heaven is within you. You*

are not separate. You are beLoved." At first it feels awkward. Over time, it sinks deep.

3. **Eye Contact Practice.** When speaking with someone, give them your full attention. Silently affirm: *"The Kingdom is within you too."* This turns ordinary conversations into experiences of union.
4. **Gratitude Walks.** Walk outside and consciously thank creation — trees, sky, birds, air. Notice you are not separate but part of this web.
5. **Forgiveness Ritual.** Write down resentments or judgments you hold. Then burn or bury the paper, saying: *"I release separation. I choose oneness."*
6. **Simple Service.** Do acts of kindness daily — not for reward, not for ego, but to dissolve the illusion of separateness. Serving another is serving yourself.
7. **Affirmations of Union.** Repeat throughout the day: *God and I are one. I and others are one in Love. Separation is illusion."*
8. **Community of Equals.** Gather with people not to debate doctrine but to practice presence, Love, and service together. True community dissolves separation.

Imagine if religious services were restructured around these practices. Instead of sermons about sin, everyone would do mirror affirmations: "*You are beLoved*!" Instead of confessions of guilt, people would confess the ways they forgot their oneness and commit to remembering. Attendance might shrink at first, but those who came would actually heal.

Other Voices on Practice

Mystics across traditions prescribe similar practices. Buddhists use mindfulness meditation to dissolve the illusion of a separate self. Sufis use chanting and whirling to experience union with the BeLoved. Hindus use yoga to unite body, mind, and spirit. Christian mystics use contemplative prayer. Different forms, same goal: dissolving separation through practice.

The Challenge of Consistency

The hardest part isn't starting. It's continuing. Old habits of separation creep back. The ego resists. Life gets busy. That's why practice must be simple and daily. Even five minutes of presence a day is better than none. Like exercise, consistency matters more than intensity.

Think of presence like dental hygiene. If you brush once a year, you'll have cavities. If you brush daily, your teeth stay healthy. Separation is like plaque – it builds up fast. Practices are spiritual toothbrushes.

The Fruit of Practice

Over time, these practices bear fruit. Anxiety lessens because you feel God's nearness. Compassion deepens because you see yourself in others. Joy increases because you feel connected to creation. Guilt fades because you know you're already beLoved. Fear shrinks because nothing can separate you from Love.

I've seen it in my own life and in others': people who practice dissolving separation become calmer, kinder, freer. They radiate presence. They embody Jeshua's Way more than any sermon ever could.

My Turning Point

One day, during a mirror exercise, I looked into my own eyes and actually believed it: *"The Kingdom of Heaven is within me."* For the first time, it wasn't just words. It was real. Tears came. Decades of programming cracked. That moment didn't fix everything overnight, but it shifted the foundation. The illusion had been pierced.

The Drumbeat Truth

Let's engrain it:

- Separation is illusion, reinforced by habit.
- Practices dissolve the habit and reveal truth.
- Presence is the foundation of every practice.
- Consistency matters more than perfection.
- You are already one – practice simply uncovers it.

Don't just agree with the idea of oneness. Live it. Practice it. Make it daily. Jeshua didn't teach separation as theory; he embodied union as practice. You can too. Sit in Love. See God in yourself. See God in others. Walk in gratitude. Serve in simplicity.

Each practice is a small act of rebellion against separation and a step into freedom. And the more you practice, the more you realize: the gap was never real. Love was always here.

That's how we dissolve separation – not just in theory, but in lived reality.

Living in Wholeness

We've unmasked the lie of separation, explored how religion reinforced it, tasted oneness, examined the psychological damage, celebrated unity in diversity, and practiced dissolving the illusion. But all of that points to something bigger: living in wholeness. Not just moments of union, not just glimpses of presence, but a way of life grounded in the truth that you are never separate, never broken, never cut off. Wholeness is the natural state beneath the illusion.

Living in it is the fruit of the Way.

What Wholeness Means

Wholeness doesn't mean perfection. It doesn't mean you never feel fear, never get distracted, never make mistakes. Wholeness means you no longer see yourself as divided, lacking, or defective. It means you accept yourself as an integrated being – body, mind, spirit, all connected to God and part of the great flow of life.

The illusion of separation fractures identity. It says: You're split from God. You're at war with yourself. You're cut off from others.

Wholeness heals that fracture. It says: *You and God are one. You and yourself are reconciled. You and others are connected.*

Imagine a mirror shattered into a hundred pieces, and religion comes along saying, "Look, you're broken! Only we can glue you back together – for a small fee." Wholeness says, "You were never broken glass in the first place. You're a diamond – you just forgot to shine."

Jeshua and Wholeness

Jeshua constantly invited people into wholeness. His healings weren't just physical. They were symbolic acts of restoring wholeness. The leper cast out of community? Jeshua touched him, saying, "*You're not separate.*" The woman caught in adultery, shamed and condemned? Jeshua lifted her up, saying, "*You are whole.*" The paralytic lowered through the roof? Jeshua forgave his sins, dissolving shame, and said, "*Stand up.*"

He never reinforced the illusion of separation. He always revealed wholeness. That's why people flocked to him. They didn't just hear about God's Love. They *felt* whole in his presence.

My Own Path Toward Wholeness

For years, I lived fractured. On the outside, I tried to look "together." On the inside, I felt divided – guilty before God, inadequate before others, and at war with myself. The illusion of separation made me feel like a puzzle with missing pieces.

But as I practiced presence, sat in Love, and declared oneness, I began to feel different. I realized I didn't need fixing. I needed *remembering*. Slowly, wholeness stopped being an idea and started being a lived reality.

I still stumble. Old programming still whispers, "You're not enough." But now I know it's an echo, not the truth. The truth is wholeness – here, now, within.

The Psychology of Wholeness

Modern psychology confirms what mystics knew: integration is health. Trauma fragments us. Fear splits us. Shame hides parts of us.

Healing comes when we reintegrate – when we accept every part of ourselves with compassion. Jeshua's Way of presence and Love is profoundly therapeutic. It doesn't demand we erase our wounds. It invites us to bring them into Love, where they are embraced, not condemned.

Wholeness and Relationships

Living in wholeness changes how you relate. If you see yourself as divided, you project division outward. But when you embrace your own wholeness, you see others differently. You no longer need to judge, control, or compare. You meet people as fellow whole beings. Conflicts still arise, but they're navigated from Love, not insecurity.

Imagine if couples fought from wholeness. "Honey, I'm feeling whole right now, but I disagree with your choice of curtains." Arguments would turn into design discussions instead of wars.

Wholeness doesn't eliminate difference — it eliminates the illusion that difference threatens Love.

Wholeness in Community

Communities shaped by separation police each other's behavior, terrified of impurity. Communities shaped by wholeness celebrate each person's uniqueness while affirming shared oneness. That's what the early followers of Jeshua tasted — a radical community where insiders and outsiders ate together, shared possessions, and cared for the vulnerable. Wholeness scales from self to community.

Practices for Living Wholeness

How do we make wholeness more than an idea?

1. **Daily Presence.** Anchor in the now, where wholeness is always accessible.
2. **Self-Compassion.** Speak to yourself with kindness. When flaws appear, affirm: "*I am still whole.*"
3. **Body Awareness.** Treat the body as sacred, not separate from spirit. Movement, rest, and care are acts of wholeness.
4. **Inclusive Love.** Extend compassion to people outside your comfort zone. Their wholeness reflects yours.
5. **Integrative Journaling.** Write to reconcile parts of yourself — fears, doubts, hopes — into a unified whole.
6. **Celebrate Diversity.** Honor difference in others as part of the larger whole.
7. **Gratitude for Now.** Daily thankfulness for breath, life, and Love affirms present wholeness.

The Fruit of Wholeness

Living in wholeness produces peace. Not the fragile peace of avoiding conflict, but the deep peace of knowing nothing can separate you from Love. It produces joy, not as fleeting pleasure but as the steady gladness of belonging. It produces courage, because fear shrinks when you know you are whole.

It also produces creativity, generosity, and resilience. People rooted in wholeness are harder to manipulate, harder to divide, harder to control. That's why Jeshua's Way was such a threat — whole people don't bow to fear.

My Turning Point in Wholeness

One day, during meditation, I repeated the affirmation: *"The Kingdom of Heaven is within me."* Suddenly it clicked. Not partially. Not someday. Now. In me. The war ended, if only for a moment. That glimpse of wholeness was enough. It showed me what's always true, even when I forget.

Other Voices

Mystics echo the same. Meister Eckhart: *The eye with which I see God is the eye with which God sees me."* Rumi: *You are not a drop in the ocean. You are the entire ocean in a drop."* The Upanishads: *That Thou Art."* All voices point to the same reality: wholeness is our essence.

The Drumbeat Truth

Let's engrain it:

- Separation fractures. Wholeness heals.
- You are not broken. You are whole.
- Jeshua's Way restores wholeness.
- Living in wholeness is freedom.

Stop chasing wholeness as if it's missing. Live it. Right now. See yourself as whole, not fractured. See others as whole, not enemies. See God not as distant but as your wholeness itself.

Living in wholeness is the fruit of dissolving separation. It's the life Jeshua embodied and invited us into. And it's the life available now, in every breath, in every moment, in every act of Love.

That's living in wholeness – the end of the illusion, the beginning of freedom.

Chapter 15: The Power of Love

Love as the Core Teaching

If separation is the great lie, then Love is the great truth. Love is the thread running through Jeshua's life, words, and actions. Strip away the doctrines, the rituals, the centuries of theological dust, and what remains is this: *Love God, Love yourself, Love others.* That's it. Not complicated. Not hidden. Just Love.

Jeshua's Radical Simplicity

When asked the greatest commandment, Jeshua didn't quote obscure laws or invent new rules. He said, *Love the Lord your God with all your heart, soul, mind, and strength. And Love your neighbor as yourself. All the law and prophets hang on this."* In other words: every ritual, every command, every story boils down to Love.

This was radical. Religion thrived on rules, rituals, and hierarchies. Jeshua cut through it all with one word: Love. No wonder authorities hated him. Love collapses control. Love empowers people. Love renders gatekeepers irrelevant.

Imagine if you went to the DMV and instead of fifty forms, the clerk smiled and said, "Just Love each other, and you're good to go." Bureaucracies would collapse overnight. That's how disruptive Jeshua's message was to religious bureaucracy.

Love in Action

Jeshua didn't just talk about Love. He embodied it. He touched lepers no one else would touch. He ate with outcasts no one else would eat with. He forgave enemies no one else would forgive. He treated women, children, and foreigners with dignity in a culture that marginalized them. Love wasn't theory. It was practice.

Every healing was an act of Love. Every parable was an invitation to Love. Even his confrontations with authorities were rooted in Love for the people being oppressed. Jeshua's whole life was Love made flesh.

My Own Awakening to Love

For years, I thought spirituality was about avoiding sin, pleasing God, and following rules. Love was mentioned, but it was buried under guilt and fear. It wasn't until I began sitting in Love – literally practicing presence and resting in Love – that I realized: this is the point. Not fear, not separation, not guilt. Love.

The first time I felt Love fill the silence of meditation, I cried. Not because it was sentimental, but because it was freeing. Love didn't demand performance. Love didn't demand perfection. Love simply said, "*You are mine. You are enough.*" That was the core Jeshua had been pointing to all along.

Other Voices

Mystics across traditions echo the same. The Upanishads speak of the Self as pure Love. The Buddha emphasized compassion as the highest path. Rumi wrote, *Love is the bridge between you and everything."* Paul wrote, *If I have not Love, I am nothing."* Strip away cultural differences, and the message aligns: Love is the core.

Imagine if all the world's religious leaders met in a stadium and the only agenda item was, "Be nice." The meeting would end in five minutes. But then no one could write ten-volume commentaries or argue for centuries. Simplicity doesn't sell books – but it does set people free.

Why Love Gets Complicated

If Love is so simple, why does religion complicate it? Because Love can't be controlled. You can't sell indulgences with Love. You can't scare people into obedience with Love. You can't build empires on Love, so institutions buried Love under fear, guilt, and ritual.

Love also scares the ego. If you really Love yourself, you stop chasing approval. If you really Love others, you stop competing. If you really Love God, you stop fearing. Love dismantles the ego's entire operating system. No wonder we resist it.

Practices for Living Love

1. **Daily Declaration.** Begin each day: *"I choose Love."* Simple, but powerful.

2. **Small Acts.** Hold a door. Offer a smile. Call a friend. Love lives in the small.
3. **Forgive.** Release resentments. Each act of forgiveness dissolves separation.
4. **Listen.** Presence is Love. Listening deeply affirms worth.
5. **Sit in Love.** Spend time daily resting in Love's presence. Let it wash over you.

The Fruit of Love

Love transforms everything. Fear shrinks. Guilt fades. Joy rises. Relationships heal. Communities thrive. Societies shift. Love doesn't just improve life – it recreates it. That's why Jeshua said Love fulfills the law. You don't need a thousand rules when you Love.

My Turning Point

One day I asked: "What is the path forward?" The answer came, not as words, but as a wave: Love. Everything else – presence, healing, wholeness – flows from Love. That moment reframed my entire journey. Love wasn't one piece of the puzzle. It was the whole picture.

The Drumbeat Truth

Let's engrain it:

- Love is the core. Everything else hangs on it.
- Jeshua embodied Love, not rules.
- Love is simple, but revolutionary.
- Fear controls. Love frees.

Let go of complicated doctrines. Stop fearing distant judgment. Stop carrying guilt. Come home to Love, the core teaching Jeshua lived and died for. Love God. Love yourself. Love others. Everything else is commentary.

That's the power of Love: the beginning, the middle, and the end of the Way.

Love Versus Fear

If Love is the core teaching, then fear is the counterfeit. They are the two great forces shaping human life: Love expands, fear contracts; Love frees, fear enslaves. Jeshua's entire ministry can be seen as a battle between these two forces – not cosmic armies in the sky, but the daily choices of the human heart. Religion, tragically, often sided with fear. Jeshua always pointed to Love.

The Nature of Fear

Fear isn't always bad. At its simplest, fear is a survival instinct. A snake on the path triggers fear, and you jump back. Useful. But when fear becomes the operating system of the soul, it distorts everything. Fear sees scarcity, danger, separation everywhere. Fear convinces you you're not safe, not worthy, not Loved.

Religion realized long ago that fear is a powerful motivator. Fear of punishment. Fear of rejection. Fear of death. Fear of hell. Keep people afraid, and you can keep them compliant. Fear-based religion thrives because terrified people will cling to authority.

Imagine a gym that motivates with fear: "Work out or you'll burn in eternal flabbiness." Membership would skyrocket. That's how fear works – it sells.

The Nature of Love

Love, on the other hand, isn't about survival. It's about thriving. Love expands awareness. Love trusts abundance. Love connects. Love heals. Jeshua's teaching wasn't "be afraid so you'll behave." It was "*be Loved so you'll live.*"

"Perfect Love casts out fear," wrote John. Jeshua embodied that truth. In his presence, people felt safe. Fear dissolved. The woman caught in adultery, who expected stones, found forgiveness. The disciples in a storm, expecting drowning, found calm. Love undid fear again and again.

Jeshua's Encounters with Fear

The Gospels are full of fear-Love showdowns:

- **The storm at sea.** The disciples panicked. Jeshua calmed the storm – and their fear.
- **The synagogue healings.** People feared breaking Sabbath law. Jeshua healed anyway, showing Love is greater than fear of rules.

- **The crucifixion.** Authorities used death – the ultimate fear – to silence him. Jeshua met it with forgiveness, showing Love stronger than fear itself.

His constant refrain: *Do not be afraid."* Not because life is easy, but because Love is present.

My Own Fear-Love Battle

Fear was baked into my upbringing. Fear of sin, fear of hell, fear of my father, fear of displeasing God. I was told fear was holy, that it kept me safe. But it didn't keep me safe. It kept me small. It kept me anxious.

When I began practicing presence, sitting in Love, I felt the difference. Fear constricted my chest. Love expanded it. Fear whispered, "You're not enough." Love said, "*You are already mine.*" Fear drove me to strive endlessly. Love invited me to rest. Slowly, I began choosing Love over fear. Not always perfectly. But enough to taste freedom.

Other Voices

Across traditions, teachers draw the same contrast. The Bhagavad Gita teaches that fear arises from attachment and ignorance, while Love (bhakti) is union with the divine. The Buddha taught compassion dissolves fear. Rumi wrote, *Move outside the tangle of fear-thinking. Live in silence. Flow down and down in always widening rings of being."* Everywhere, the mystics align: fear shrinks, Love expands.

Imagine if customer service reps answered the phone with, "What would Love do?" instead of scripts designed to upsell through fear. Complaints would turn into therapy sessions. Love is disarming.

Why We Choose Fear

If Love is so freeing, why do we cling to fear? Because fear feels familiar. Fear pretends to protect us. Fear offers certainty: follow the rules and maybe you'll be safe. Love is riskier. Love requires trust.

Love means letting go of control. That terrifies the ego.

Institutions exploited this. Fear-based sermons keep pews full. Fear- based politics win elections. Fear-based advertising sells products.

Fear works. But Love transforms.

Practices to Choose Love Over Fear

1. **Breath Reset.** When fear rises, pause. Breathe deeply. On the inhale, say "*Love in.*" On the exhale, say "*Fear out.*"
2. **Fear Naming.** Write down specific fears. Then write: "*This is not ultimate truth. Love is stronger.*"
3. **Love Questions.** When making decisions, ask: "*Am I choosing from fear or from Love?*"
4. **Declare Love Daily.** Start mornings with: "*Perfect Love casts out fear. Today I choose Love.*"
5. **Act from Love.** Do one thing daily that scares you but is rooted in Love – forgiving, reaching out, speaking truth.

The Fruit of Choosing Love

When you start living from Love instead of fear:

- Anxiety loosens its grip.
- Relationships deepen.
- Creativity blossoms.
- Compassion grows.
- Joy increases.

It doesn't mean fear vanishes. But Love stops letting fear drive the bus. Fear can sit in the back seat, but Love holds the wheel.

My Turning Point

One night, I came to a profound realization: *"Everything you fear is a shadow. Only Love is real."* In that moment, I saw how much energy I'd wasted living in fear. Not that fear disappeared forever, but I had a new compass. Since then, every time fear rises, I return to Love. Again and again.

The Drumbeat Truth

Let's anchor it:

- Fear contracts. Love expands.

- Fear enslaves. Love frees.
- Religion often chose fear. Jeshua always chose Love.
- Perfect Love casts out fear.

Fear no longer runs your life. Stop obeying fear disguised as holiness. Start choosing Love – in thought, in action, in relationships. Jeshua didn't come to terrify people into obedience. He came to liberate people into Love.

That's the battle of Love versus fear – and Love always wins when you choose it.

Love as Action, Not Just Emotion

When most people hear the word *Love*, they think of a feeling. Butterflies in the stomach. Warm fuzzies. Romantic songs on the radio. That's fine – feelings of affection and connection are real. But when Jeshua talked about Love, he wasn't talking about a passing mood. He was talking about a way of living. Love wasn't just an inner emotion; it was an outer action.

Why Emotion Isn't Enough

Emotions are fleeting. They come and go like weather. One moment you feel affectionate toward someone, the next you're annoyed. If Love were only emotion, it would collapse at the first conflict. Jeshua knew that. That's why he commanded *"Love your neighbor as yourself,"* not as a suggestion for when you're in the mood, but as a practice regardless of mood.

Imagine if marriages ran only on emotion. "Sorry honey, I don't feel in Love today, so you're on your own." That wouldn't last a week. Love as emotion is fragile. Love as action endures.

Jeshua's Love in Action

Jeshua's life was filled with action-Love:

- He fed hungry crowds instead of sending them away.
- He healed the sick instead of ignoring them.
- He touched lepers instead of avoiding them.
- He forgave enemies instead of retaliating.
- He served his disciples by washing their feet.

Each act was Love embodied. Not just a feeling in his heart, but a choice in his hands.

The Challenge of Loving Enemies

Nowhere is Love-as-action clearer than in Jeshua's command: *"Love your enemies."* You can't wait to *feel* like loving enemies; you'll be waiting forever. Loving enemies means choosing to act with compassion even when your emotions resist. Forgiveness is an action. Prayer for persecutors is an action. Nonviolence is an action.

This is why Jeshua's Love was revolutionary. Anyone can Love friends when emotions are warm. The Way is proven when you Love those who don't deserve it – because that's when Love is most needed.

My Own Struggles with Action-Love

I'll admit I used to think Love meant feeling kindly toward people. But when someone cut me off in traffic or insulted me, those feelings evaporated. It was only when I realized Love is action that things shifted. I don't have to *feel* warm toward the driver who swerves in front of me. I can still choose patience. I don't have to *feel* affection for someone who gossips about me. I can still choose forgiveness. Action is within my control.

That realization liberated me. Feelings come and go. But action-Love anchors me in the Way regardless of mood.

Love in Relationships

In daily life, Love-as-action shows up in simple ways: listening fully to a friend, even when tired; helping a neighbor, even when busy; speaking kindly, even when frustrated. These choices create trust and healing. Relationships thrive not because emotions never fluctuate, but because actions of Love build consistency.

Imagine if your dog Loved you only when in the mood. One day he greets you wagging, the next he glares and says, "Not feeling it today." Thankfully, dogs embody action-Love – consistent affection regardless of mood. Jeshua was more like a golden retriever than a moody cat.

Other Traditions on Love-as-Action

The Bhagavad Gita calls this *karma yoga* – Love expressed through selfless action. Buddhism emphasizes *metta* – loving-kindness practice that involves intentional actions of compassion.

Sufi mystics describe service as the highest form of Love. Even modern psychology agrees: Love isn't just a feeling, it's a behavior pattern that sustains relationships.

Why Action Matters More Than Words

Words about Love are cheap. Actions prove them. Jeshua critiqued religious leaders for saying the right things but failing to Love in practice. He told a parable of two sons – one who said he'd obey but didn't, and one who initially refused but acted anyway. The point?

Action matters more than lip service.

Churches today often preach Love but act in fear or exclusion. Jeshua flipped it: he embodied Love even when words failed.

Practices for Living Love-as-Action

1. **Daily Love Intention.** Each morning, ask: "*What action of Love can I take today?*"
2. **Small Gestures.** Hold doors, smile, send kind notes. Small actions ripple widely.
3. **Forgiveness Practice.** Choose one person weekly to forgive, even if just in your heart.
4. **Active Listening.** In conversations, give full attention. Listening is a powerful act of Love.
5. **Service Habit.** Commit to regular acts of service – volunteering, helping neighbors, mentoring.
6. **Love Check.** At day's end, review: *"Where did I act from Love today? Where did I miss?"* Celebrate progress, not perfection.

My Turning Point

One turning point for me was realizing that sitting in Love wasn't enough if it didn't translate outward. It filled me with peace, but the real test was how I treated people afterward. The shift came when I started asking: *"How can I embody Love right now?"* That question changed my daily life – in traffic, in conversations, in conflicts. Love became less about inner warmth and more about outer choice. I began ACTING in Love.

The Fruit of Action-Love

When Love becomes action, everything shifts:

- **Relationships strengthen.** Trust grows through consistent action.
- **Communities thrive.** Service creates bonds beyond words.
- **Enemies disarm.** Forgiveness breaks cycles of retaliation.
- **Society changes.** Nonviolent movements prove Love in action transforms history.

Think of Gandhi, Martin Luther King Jr., or Mother Teresa. Their Love wasn't sentimental. It was action. And it reshaped the world.

Jeshua's Final Act of Love

The cross itself was Love-as-action. Jeshua didn't die to satisfy theological equations. He died embodying forgiveness and refusing violence, even under torture. His final words: "*Father, forgive them*" weren't feelings. They were action. That's the power of Love made flesh.

The Drumbeat Truth

Let's engrain it:

- Love is not just emotion. It is action.
- Jeshua embodied Love in what he did, not just what he said.
- Feelings fluctuate. Actions can remain steady.
- The Way is proven when Love becomes practice.

To live loving is a choice. Don't just talk Love – act it. Jeshua's Way isn't about warm fuzzies. It's about choosing forgiveness, service, compassion, and presence in every moment.

That's Love as action, not just emotion – the heartbeat of transformation.

Love as Forgiveness

If Love is the core of Jeshua's teaching, forgiveness is Love's sharpest edge and deepest proof. It's easy to talk about Love in the abstract, easy to Love people who already like us, easy to Love when nothing's at stake. But forgiveness? That's Love put to the test. Forgiveness is where Love stops being a slogan and becomes a revolution.

The Scandal of Forgiveness

Forgiveness sounds nice on paper, but it's scandalous in practice. Think about it: the very people who hurt you, betrayed you, humiliated you — Jeshua says Love them by forgiving them. Not just once, but *"seventy times seven."* That's not math, that's infinity. Forgiveness is radical because it refuses to let resentment or revenge define the story.

Religions often complicate forgiveness by turning it into a transaction: confess here, perform this ritual, pay this penance. Jeshua shattered that model. He forgave freely, directly, abundantly. He told parables of kings canceling debts and fathers running to embrace prodigal sons. Forgiveness, to him, wasn't earned. It was given.

Imagine if banks operated like Jeshua. "Oh, you defaulted on your loan? No problem. We'll throw you a party." Wall Street would collapse in a week — but the Kingdom would thrive.

Jeshua's Forgiveness in Action

The Gospels overflow with forgiveness stories:

- The paralyzed man: Jeshua forgave his sins before healing his body, showing that inner freedom matters as much as outer.
- The woman caught in adultery: Jeshua refused to condemn her, exposing the hypocrisy of her accusers.
- Peter: After denying him three times, Peter was restored with Love and given responsibility, not shame.
- The cross: Jeshua's ultimate act — "*Father, forgive them, they know not what they do.*"

Each story dismantles fear and shame, replacing them with Love and dignity. Forgiveness wasn't an idea to Jeshua. It was his way of life.

My Own Wrestling with Forgiveness

Forgiveness has been one of the hardest practices for me. Growing up Catholic, forgiveness felt like a transaction — confess your sins, say your Hail Marys, pay your penance, and maybe God forgives you. But I rarely felt free. It felt like probation, not forgiveness.

When I began to explore forgiveness as Love, I realized how much resentment I carried – toward institutions that burdened me, toward people who hurt me, even toward myself. Letting go wasn't easy. But every time I chose forgiveness, something lifted. The weight of separation lightened.

One of the most powerful shifts came when I forgave myself. That was harder than forgiving anyone else. But when I did, I tasted freedom I'd never known. Forgiveness isn't just something you extend outward.

It's something you give inward too.

Why Forgiveness Feels Impossible

Forgiveness feels impossible because our culture equates it with condoning or excusing harm. But forgiveness doesn't mean pretending nothing happened. It doesn't mean trusting abusers or tolerating injustice. It means refusing to let resentment poison your soul. It means breaking the chain of hatred. It means choosing Love over fear, again and again.

Religion often weaponized forgiveness, pressuring victims to forgive prematurely or without justice. That's not Love – that's control. True forgiveness arises from freedom, not coercion.

Imagine if forgiveness were a product sold on late-night TV: "For only three payments of $29.99, you too can release resentment!" The irony is that forgiveness really is free – it just costs the ego its favorite grudge.

Other Voices on Forgiveness

The Buddha said, *Holding onto anger is like drinking poison and expecting the other person to die."* Gandhi said, *The weak can never forgive. Forgiveness is the attribute of the strong."* Rumi wrote, *Raise your words, not your voice. It is rain that grows flowers, not thunder."* Across traditions, forgiveness is seen as the highest act of Love and the surest path to freedom.

Practices for Forgiveness

Here are practices that help move forgiveness from theory to reality:

1. **The Letter You Don't Send.** Write a letter to the person who hurt you, expressing everything. Then burn it, releasing resentment.
2. **The Mirror Exercise.** Forgive yourself by looking in the mirror and saying: *"I release you. You are forgiven. You are whole."*
3. **The Breath Release.** On each exhale, imagine resentment leaving your body. On each inhale, imagine Love filling you.
4. **Prayer for the Enemy.** Each day for a week, pray for someone you resent. Not a prayer that they change, but that they be blessed.
5. **Forgiveness Journal.** Write a list of old grudges. Each week, choose one to release. Even if imperfect, the intention matters.

The Fruit of Forgiveness

Forgiveness dissolves fear and guilt. It restores relationships when possible, and inner peace when not. It frees energy trapped in resentment. It heals the psyche and even the body – studies show forgiveness lowers blood pressure and stress. Most importantly, forgiveness aligns you with Love.

I've seen hardened hearts soften through forgiveness. I've seen estranged families reunited. I've seen people who carried shame for decades finally breathe free. Forgiveness is Love in its most transformative form.

My Turning Point

One of my turning points came when I forgave the Church. For years, I carried bitterness toward the institution that burdened me with fear. But holding that resentment only kept me tied to it. Forgiving didn't mean excusing abuse. It meant freeing myself. When I let go, I felt light. I could carry the wisdom of my journey without carrying the chains of anger.

The Drumbeat Truth

Let's engrain it:

- Forgiveness is Love in action.
- Forgiveness is not condoning – it is freeing.

- Forgiveness heals the forgiver as much as the forgiven.
- Jeshua embodied forgiveness to the end.

So don't just talk about Love. Live it through forgiveness. Release resentments, forgive yourself, forgive others. Let forgiveness dismantle the illusion of separation. Jeshua's Way wasn't about keeping score. It was about canceling debts.

That's Love as forgiveness – the deepest proof that Love is stronger than fear, stronger than shame, stronger than hate.

Love as Service

If forgiveness is Love's sharpest edge, then service is Love's natural outflow. When Love fills you, it spills over. It can't be contained. Service is the overflow of Love into action, the way Love moves from inner presence into outer expression. Jeshua didn't just speak about service – he embodied it, sometimes literally on his knees, washing feet.

The Meaning of Service

Service often gets misunderstood. In religious contexts, service is sometimes framed as obligation, penance, or ladder-climbing – do enough good deeds and maybe God will Love you. Jeshua flipped that upside down. For him, service wasn't a way to earn Love. It was the evidence of already being Love.

Service isn't servitude. It's not self-erasure. It's the joy of seeing yourself in others and acting from that recognition. When you Love, you naturally want to lift burdens, share food, heal wounds, and listen deeply.

Imagine a kid at the dinner table saying, "I cleaned my room so you'd Love me." Any decent parent would reply, "I already Love you, now pass the peas." That's Jeshua's logic. Service flows from Love, not into it.

Jeshua's Service

The most famous example is the Last Supper. Jeshua, their teacher and leader, got up, wrapped a towel around his waist, and washed his disciples' feet. In that culture, foot-washing was the job of servants.

Jeshua shattered hierarchy. *I have set you an example,"* he said, *that you should do as I have done for you."* Service was the mark of leadership in his Way.

But it wasn't just that night. His whole ministry was service:

- Healing the sick.
- Feeding the hungry.
- Comforting the grieving.
- Welcoming children.
- Listening to the outcast.

Jeshua didn't build temples. He built people – through service rooted in Love.

My Own Struggle with Service

For a long time, service felt like a chore. I grew up in a church where service often came with guilt trips: "If you don't volunteer, you're letting God down." Service was framed as duty, not joy. No wonder I resisted.

But as I deepened into presence, service started to feel different. It wasn't about obligation anymore. It was about overflow. When I sat in Love, I wanted to share it. When I felt whole, I wanted to help others feel whole. Service became less about proving worth and more about expressing Love.

The Joy of Small Service

Service doesn't have to be dramatic. It lives in the small: holding a door, sharing a meal, calling someone lonely, smiling at a stranger. These aren't glamorous, but they're powerful. I've had more transformative moments through small acts of service than through any sermon I ever heard.

One day, I helped a stranger carry groceries to her car. She teared up and said, "I thought nobody cared anymore." That tiny act mattered because it dissolved separation for her in that moment. Service always does.

Imagine if people treated traffic like service. "Please, after you. No, I insist!" Rush hour would turn into a parade of kindness. Service might not fix potholes, but it would fix tempers.

Other Traditions on Service

Hinduism teaches *seva* – selfless service as a spiritual path. Buddhism emphasizes compassion through acts of kindness. Islam honors *zakat* – giving to the poor as a pillar of faith. Sufis dance in service to the BeLoved. Everywhere, mystics affirm: service isn't optional. It's the natural expression of Love.

Service as Resistance

Service isn't just kindness. It's resistance. In a world that worships self-interest, every act of service is rebellion. Empires thrive on hierarchy. Service collapses it. Jeshua washing feet was as politically subversive as it was spiritual. Serving the least is a direct rejection of fear-based systems.

Practices of Service

Here are practical ways to make service a rhythm of life:

1. **Daily Intent.** Begin each morning: "*How can I serve in Love today?*"
2. **Hidden Acts.** Do one act of kindness daily without anyone knowing.
3. **Listening Service.** Offer presence in conversations, not advice or fixes.
4. **Physical Help.** Look for practical needs – meals, errands, chores.
5. **Shared Service.** Serve with others. Community deepens when people work side by side.
6. **Forgiving Service.** Serve even those you resent, as a way of breaking chains.

My Turning Point

One of my turning points came when I shifted service from performance to presence. Instead of thinking, "I have to do this," I started asking, "*How can Love serve here?*" That question made everything different. Helping wasn't draining anymore. It was energizing. Service stopped being a burden and started being joy.

The Fruit of Service

Service dissolves ego. It connects you to others. It transforms communities. It heals wounds. It even rewires the brain –

neuroscience shows altruism lights up reward centers, making service genuinely joyful.

I've seen hardened hearts melt because someone served them. I've seen communities rally through shared service. I've seen my own fears shrink when I chose to serve instead of withdraw. Service doesn't just help others. It heals you.

Jeshua's Final Word on Service

The Son of Man came not to be served but to serve." That was Jeshua's mission statement. He didn't build an empire. He served Love. That's the blueprint for anyone walking the Way.

The Drumbeat Truth

Let's engrain it:

- Service is not obligation. It's overflow.
- Jeshua served by washing feet and healing lives.
- Small acts matter as much as grand ones.
- Service is Love in action and resistance to fear.

Service is not a duty. See it as joy. See it as Love overflowing. Jeshua didn't serve to earn God's Love. He served because he was Love. You are too. So serve. Wash feet. Share meals. Heal wounds. Listen deeply. Let service be the rhythm of your life.

That's Love as service – the overflow of presence into action, the proof that Love is stronger than fear.

Love as Presence

When people think of Love, they often think of words – "I Love you." Or they think of gestures – flowers, gifts, acts of service. Those are beautiful, but there's another dimension of Love that is often overlooked, and it may be the most powerful of all: presence. To truly Love someone is to be fully with them, here and now, with undivided attention. Presence is Love embodied in awareness.

Why Presence Matters

In a distracted world, presence is rare. People are always half-here: checking phones while talking, worrying about tomorrow while sitting with family, rehashing old arguments while pretending to listen. This divided attention communicates, "You're not worth my full focus." That hurts.

But when someone gives you full presence, it feels sacred. You feel seen, heard, valued. You feel Loved. Presence communicates, "*You matter. I'm here. I'm with you.*" No flowers or chocolates can replace that.

Imagine if dogs acted like humans. You come home and your dog greets you while scrolling Instagram, nodding absently. Instead, dogs offer presence — full wagging, full attention, full joy. They embody what humans forget: Love looks like presence.

Jeshua's Presence

Jeshua was a master of presence. He never seemed rushed, even when crowds pressed in. He stopped for blind beggars. He noticed the woman who touched his cloak. He called Zacchaeus out of a tree to share dinner. He welcomed children the disciples tried to shoo away.

His presence was healing. People felt seen by him in ways they'd never felt before. He wasn't distracted by status or reputation. Each person, no matter how lowly, received his full attention. That presence was Love.

My Own Awakening to Presence as Love

For much of my life, I thought loving people meant giving advice, fixing problems, or performing duties. But I noticed something: people often didn't need solutions. They needed presence. They needed someone to sit with them in their grief, listen to their story, or share silence without judgment.

When I began practicing "sitting in Love" for myself, I realized I could extend that same stillness to others. Presence became a form of Love. Sometimes I don't need to say much. I just need to be here, fully. That alone communicates more Love than a thousand words.

Presence in Relationships

In relationships, presence is transformative. Partners who give each other undivided attention build trust. Parents who give presence to children give them a sense of worth that lasts a lifetime. Friends who give presence to each other create bonds stronger than distance.

Presence doesn't mean fixing everything. It means being there. A hug, a gaze, a silence held together — these embody Love more deeply than speeches.

Imagine if people texted each other the way they actually listen in conversation: "Half listening, also watching TV, will reply when convenient." At least it'd be honest. But real Love is being all-in, not half-there.

Other Voices on Presence

Buddhism teaches mindfulness – being fully here without judgment. The Tao Te Ching speaks of the sage being present to the rhythms of life. Sufi poets describe Love as attention: *"The soul receives Love by being present."* Modern psychology confirms it: relationships thrive when people give undivided attention. Presence is cross-cultural, universal Love.

The Challenge of Presence

Presence sounds simple, but it's hard. Distractions scream for attention. Old habits pull us into past or future. Ego whispers, "Say something clever," instead of simply listening.

That's why presence is a practice. It requires training. Jeshua withdrew often into silence – not to escape, but to recharge presence. If the Son of God needed quiet time to stay present, so do we.

Practices of Love-as-Presence

1. **Eye Contact Listening.** In conversations, put devices away. Look into the other's eyes. Let them know they have your full attention.
2. **Silent Sitting.** Sit with someone in silence. Resist the urge to fill space with words. Let presence itself be Love.
3. **Breath Anchoring.** When distracted, take a breath and silently say, "*Here.*" This anchors you back to presence.
4. **Daily Presence Ritual.** Choose one daily activity – meal, walk, bedtime – where you give full, undivided attention.
5. **Presence Declaration.** Each morning affirm: "*I will Love by being here.*"

The Fruit of Presence

When you practice Love-as-presence, relationships deepen. People trust you more. Conflicts soften because people feel heard. Children grow secure. Communities grow connected. Even your relationship with God deepens, because you realize God is always present — the real question is, are you?

I've noticed that when I give people full presence, they often sigh with relief. Sometimes they even cry. Not because I solved their problem, but because they felt Loved in the rarest way: by being seen.

My Turning Point

One turning point came when I was sitting with someone grieving. I wanted to offer comforting words, but nothing seemed right. So I stayed silent. I just held their hand and breathed with them. After a while, they said, "I've never felt so cared for." That moment taught me: presence itself is Love.

Presence as Resistance

Presence is also resistance in a distracted, consumerist culture. When you choose to give someone attention instead of scrolling, you reject the systems profiting from your distraction. When you choose to sit in silence with God, you resist the narrative that productivity defines worth. Presence is rebellion — and Love is always revolutionary.

The Drumbeat Truth

Let's engrain it:

- Love isn't just words or gifts. It's presence.
- Jeshua embodied presence by noticing and honoring people.
- Presence heals relationships more than advice or solutions.
- Presence is resistance to distraction and fear.

Love by being here. Put down the phone. Stop rehearsing responses. Stop drifting into tomorrow. Be with the person in front of you. Be with yourself. Be with God. Presence is Love, and Love is presence.

That's Love as presence — the quiet, powerful way of saying: *You matter. I'm here. We are one.*

Love as the Way Forward

We've looked at Love from many angles: as the core teaching, as the antidote to fear, as action, as forgiveness, as service, as presence.

Each piece shows how Love dismantles separation and restores wholeness. But all of these are not just fragments. They converge into a single reality: Love is not just one teaching among many. Love *is* the Way forward. Jeshua didn't come to establish an institution, invent new dogmas, or enforce fear. He came to show a path of Love that could reshape individual lives, communities, and the whole world.

Why Love Is the Way

Fear divides. Guilt paralyzes. Rules control. But Love? Love liberates. Love unites. Love heals. That's why Jeshua summarized everything with *"Love God, Love your neighbor, Love yourself."* He didn't complicate it because complication was the problem. Simplicity is the solution. The Way forward is not a maze of doctrines. It's a single road called Love.

Imagine if governments ran on Jeshua's principle. Instead of 10,000-page laws and endless bureaucracy, they'd just pass one universal law: *"Love each other."* Lobbyists would go out of business, but the world would finally work.

Jeshua's Vision

Jeshua's vision of the Kingdom wasn't a far-off heaven. It was a new reality here and now, shaped by Love. The hungry fed. The sick healed. The oppressed freed. The outcasts included. His parables painted a world where Love was the governing principle: prodigal sons embraced, workers paid fairly, lost sheep sought out.

He wasn't dreaming of someday. He was enacting it daily. The Way forward was already breaking into the present every time someone chose Love over fear.

My Own Discovery

For me, discovering Love as the Way forward was both terrifying and freeing. Terrifying because Love asks more than fear. Fear lets you hide behind rules. Love demands you show up. Fear keeps you safe in smallness. Love pushes you into risk, forgiveness, generosity. But it was freeing because Love is simpler. I don't have to solve every theological puzzle. I don't have to check every ritual box. I just have to ask: *What does Love look like here?*

When I started living that question, everything shifted. Conversations deepened. Relationships healed. Anxiety loosened. Life felt less like a test and more like a gift.

Love in Community

The Way forward isn't just personal. It's communal. Jeshua envisioned communities marked by Love – where wealth was shared, meals were open, and enemies became neighbors. When early Christians actually practiced this, outsiders marveled: *"See how they Love one another."* Love was the revolution.

Communities rooted in Love are resilient. They survive persecution, hardship, and change because Love binds stronger than fear. They also radiate. People are drawn to Love like plants to sunlight. A single loving community can transform a whole city.

Imagine a church service where instead of sermons about sin, everyone just asked, "Who needs Love today?" The collection plate would overflow with casseroles and hugs. That was closer to Jeshua's dream than stained glass and smoke.

Love and the World

On a global scale, Love as the Way forward dismantles systems of oppression. Empires thrive on fear. Economies thrive on greed.

Politics thrive on division. Love threatens them all. That's why Jeshua's message was so subversive. Love undercuts power built on fear.

History proves this. Nonviolent movements rooted in Love – Gandhi in India, Martin Luther King Jr. in America – transformed nations more than violence ever could. Love disarms because it refuses the game of fear and revenge.

Why Love Is Hard

If Love is the Way, why don't we all follow it? Because Love costs. It costs the ego its pride. It costs comfort. It costs control. Fear feels easier because it gives the illusion of safety. But that safety is false. Fear imprisons. Love liberates. The challenge is choosing freedom when chains feel familiar.

Practices to Make Love the Way

1. **The Daily Question.** Begin each day asking: "*How can I walk in Love today?*" End each day reviewing: "*Where did I live Love? Where did I miss?*"
2. **Love in Conflict.** When disagreements arise, pause. Ask: "*What does Love look like here?*"
3. **Expand the Circle.** Each week, extend Love beyond your usual circle — a stranger, an enemy, someone ignored.
4. **Anchor in Presence.** Sit daily in Love's presence. Overflow begins with being filled.
5. **Share Stories of Love.** Tell and retell stories of Love in action. They inspire and multiply.

My Turning Point in Living Love

One of my biggest turning points came during a season of anxiety about the future. I was spinning scenarios, trying to control outcomes. Then the whisper came: *"Just Love."* It cut through the noise. I didn't need to predict or plan everything. I just needed to Love in the moment. That became my compass. And it works. Whenever I feel lost, I return to it: *Just Love.*

Other Voices

The mystics echo Jeshua's vision. Rumi: *Let yourself be silently drawn by the strange pull of what you really Love. It will not lead you astray."* The Buddha: *Hatred does not cease by hatred, but only by Love."* Paul: *The greatest of these is Love."* All traditions converge on this: Love is not one path among many. It is the Way.

The Drumbeat Truth

Let's engrain it:

- Love is not just a teaching. It is the Way.
- Jeshua lived the Kingdom of Love here and now.
- Love transforms individuals, communities, and the world.
- The future belongs to Love.

Make Love your compass. When lost, ask: *What does Love look like here?* When afraid, remember: *Perfect Love casts out fear.* When divided, choose Love's unity. Jeshua didn't just teach Love as theory. He lived it as the Way forward.

That's Love as the Way forward – not a slogan, but a life. The next step of the journey isn't found in more doctrines. It's found in one choice, made again and again: Love.

Chapter 16: Breaking the Chains of Guilt

Understanding the Weight of Guilt

If fear is the great controller and separation is the great illusion, then guilt is the great shackle. Guilt is what keeps people bowing to systems long after they've stopped believing in them. It's the invisible chain wrapped around the mind and heart, whispering, *"You're not enough. You'll never be enough."* Guilt is heavy, sticky, and pervasive. It clings to memory, identity, even the body. To break free into Love, we have to understand the weight of guilt – where it comes from, how it works, and why Jeshua sought to break it.

What Guilt Is – and Isn't

There are two kinds of guilt. Healthy guilt is the inner voice that says, *I hurt someone, and I want to make it right."* It points toward repair and growth. Toxic guilt, on the other hand, doesn't point to growth. It sticks like tar. It says, "I am bad. I am unworthy. I am condemned." Religion often confuses the two, branding people with toxic guilt and calling it holiness.

Healthy guilt is a compass. Toxic guilt is a prison. Jeshua came to free us from the prison.

Imagine if smoke detectors acted like toxic guilt. Instead of just alerting you to smoke, they'd scream, "You're a terrible homeowner! You'll never be safe again!" You'd rip the batteries out. That's how many of us feel about religious guilt.

The Source of Religious Guilt

Religious guilt doesn't arise naturally. It's manufactured. Institutions figured out that if you convince people they're guilty by default, they'll keep coming back for absolution. Original sin, mortal vs. venial sins, unending confession – these created a revolving door of guilt and ritual relief. People lived trapped in cycles: sin, guilt, ritual, repeat.

And here's the trick: guilt feels spiritual. It feels like humility. But it's actually bondage. Jeshua's harshest words were for leaders who "tie up heavy burdens and lay them on people's shoulders." Guilt was one of those burdens.

Jeshua's Teaching on Guilt

Jeshua didn't shame people. He lifted shame. He forgave freely. He touched the untouchable and declared them clean. He told sinners, *"Go in peace."* He told parables where debts were canceled, not endlessly collected. His message wasn't "feel more guilty." It was "*be free.*"

Even his confrontations weren't about guilt. When he told religious leaders, "*Woe to you,*" he wasn't trying to bury them in shame. He was exposing how they buried others. Jeshua's way was always about release, never bondage.

My Own Experience of Guilt

Guilt was the water I swam in as a child. Every Mass, every confession, every catechism class reinforced the message: *You are guilty. You are flawed. You must repent.* Even when I hadn't done anything wrong, I felt wrong. Guilt wasn't occasional – it was identity.

The Cost of Carrying Guilt

Think of guilt as a backpack filled with bricks. Each sin, real or imagined, becomes another brick. You lug it around everywhere. It slows you down, wears you out, bends your spine. You can't run free. You can barely walk. And the worst part? You get so used to the weight, you think it's normal.

Imagine a gym that marketed itself as "The Church of Guilt Fitness." Membership perks: endless reps of carrying shame bricks! No strength gained, just exhaustion. That's religious guilt – exercise that makes you weaker.

Jeshua's Freedom from Guilt

Jeshua invited people to lay down the backpack. *Come to me, all you who are weary and burdened, and I will give you rest."* He didn't add more burdens. He removed them. The curtain torn at his death wasn't just about separation from God. It was about freedom from guilt. No more endless sacrifices, no more rituals of absolution. Love, not guilt, was the new center.

Other Voices

The Buddha taught compassion, not condemnation. The Bhagavad Gita speaks of acting without attachment to guilt. Sufi mystics emphasize God's mercy above all. Everywhere, the mystics push against guilt-based religion, pointing instead to Love, compassion, and freedom.

Practices to Unpack Guilt

1. **Guilt Inventory.** Write down the guilt messages you carry. Label each one: healthy (calls you to repair) or toxic (condemns identity). Discard the toxic.
2. **Visualization.** Imagine the guilt as a backpack of bricks. In meditation, picture yourself handing it back to God. Walk lighter.
3. **Declaration.** Declare daily: *"I am beLoved. I am whole. I am forgiven."*
4. **Forgive Yourself.** Write letters of forgiveness to yourself for old mistakes. Read them aloud until they sink in.
5. **Replace Rituals.** Instead of rituals that reinforce guilt, create rituals that celebrate freedom: light a candle, sing, dance.

My Turning Point

One of my turning points came when I realized guilt wasn't proof of God's presence. It was proof of programming. The God I encountered in presence never said, "You're guilty." He said, "*You are mine. Be free.*" That shift didn't happen overnight, but each time I chose presence over guilt, the backpack got lighter.

The Drumbeat Truth

Let's engrain it:

- Healthy guilt corrects actions. Toxic guilt condemns identity.
- Religion exploited guilt to control.
- Jeshua lifted guilt, never imposed it.
- You were never meant to carry guilt as identity.

Examine the guilt you carry. Name it. Question it. Release it. Stop lugging the backpack of shame. Jeshua's Way is not guilt but Love, not burden but freedom.

That's the first step in breaking the chains of guilt – understanding its weight so you can finally put it down.

Guilt as a Tool of Control

If guilt were just a private emotional struggle, it would be heavy enough. But guilt didn't become a universal burden by accident. It became systematized. Codified. Weaponized. Religious institutions discovered early that guilt was one of the most effective tools for controlling people. Fear may frighten people into obedience, but guilt keeps them obedient long after the fear subsides. Fear controls behavior; guilt colonizes identity.

The Birth of Institutional Guilt

Ancient religions recognized early on that rituals worked best when people felt guilty. If you think the gods are angry, you'll pay priests to offer sacrifices. If you think you've offended the divine, you'll follow whatever steps the temple prescribes to make amends.

By the time Catholicism grew, guilt had become a fine art. The doctrine of original sin made everyone guilty before birth. Mortal versus venial sins created a complex hierarchy of guilt. Confession and penance became a revolving door of temporary relief. The church didn't just offer forgiveness. It offered forgiveness on repeat – ensuring people kept coming back for more.

Imagine if your mechanic told you, "Your car is broken by nature. Even when I fix it, it'll always still be broken. But come back every week and pay me again." You'd find a new mechanic. But when the church did it with guilt? People called it salvation.

Why Guilt Works

Guilt works because it creates dependency. When you believe you're inherently guilty, you never feel free. You're always in debt, always needing absolution. That makes you easy to manipulate. Institutions know this. They dangle forgiveness like a carrot, but never fully deliver it.

Guilt also works because it disguises itself as virtue. "I feel guilty, therefore I must be holy." The more guilt you feel, the more devoted you seem. But that's not holiness. That's bondage. Jeshua never equated holiness with shame.

Jeshua's Disruption

Jeshua directly attacked guilt-as-control. He forgave sins without demanding penance. He told people, *"Your faith has made you whole,"* bypassing rituals. He canceled debts in parables. He warned leaders who "*lay heavy burdens on others but do not lift a finger to help.*" His forgiveness was free. That terrified institutions because free forgiveness undermines control.

That's partly why he was executed. You can't run a religious business model if the prophet keeps giving away the product for free. Jeshua's Love-based forgiveness destroyed the leverage of guilt.

My Own Experience with Guilt-as-Control

Looking back, I see how guilt kept me bound. I feared missing Mass, not because I Loved being there, but because I felt guilty if I didn't. I went to confession, not because I longed for freedom, but because guilt gnawed until I did.

I even felt guilty for things I hadn't done. The idea that original sin made me guilty before birth meant I could never be clean. That kept me tied to the system even when it made no sense. Guilt didn't make me holy. It made me dependent.

Historical Examples of Guilt as Control

- **Indulgences:** In the Middle Ages, the church literally sold forgiveness. Guilt became monetized. Afraid for your Loved one in purgatory? Pay up. Afraid for your soul? Buy a slip of paper. Guilt filled coffers.
- **Confession booths:** Privacy was an illusion. Priests often became moral enforcers, shaping behavior through guilt. People confessed not to heal but to stay in line.
- **Dietary rules:** Breaking fasts or eating meat on Fridays created guilt over trivialities. Everyday life became a minefield of possible guilt.
- **Sexuality:** Perhaps the most enduring tool. By branding normal desires as sinful, the church ensured constant guilt, constant confession, constant control.

Imagine if your gym charged you not for workouts, but for every cookie you ate. They'd make a fortune, and you'd never be free. That's how guilt-based religion functions.

Why Institutions Cling to Guilt

Because guilt is profitable. Spiritually, financially, socially. People bound by guilt give more, obey more, and question less. They stay dependent on the institution for relief. Take away guilt, and the system collapses. That's why Love is so threatening: Love liberates.

The Psychological Grip of Guilt

Once internalized, guilt doesn't even need external enforcement. People become their own jailers. They scold themselves, police themselves, confess to themselves. Institutions Love this because it makes control self-sustaining. Jeshua's Way breaks this cycle by offering unconditional acceptance that rewires identity.

Other Voices Against Guilt-Control

Buddha rejected the Brahmin monopoly on rituals, teaching direct awakening. Muhammad condemned exploitative priests. Hindu reformers taught that caste-based guilt was false. Across traditions, mystics and prophets opposed guilt-as-control and returned to Love- as-freedom.

Practices to Break the Grip

1. **Name the Programming.** Write down guilt messages you inherited from religion. Expose them. Naming them weakens them.
2. **Replace with Truth.** For each guilt message, write Jeshua's truth: "*The Kingdom is within me. I am free.*"
3. **Refuse the Toll.** When old guilt tries to drag you back into rituals of control, pause. Ask, "*What would Love do?*" Then act from Love, not guilt.
4. **Practice Free Forgiveness.** Forgive yourself and others without ritual. Prove to yourself it's possible.
5. **Gather Free Communities.** Join or build communities that affirm freedom, not guilt. Presence grows stronger in groups.

My Turning Point

One of my turning points came when I skipped Mass for the first time without guilt. I waited for lightning. It never came. Instead, I felt lighter. I realized the guilt wasn't God. It was programming. God's presence didn't vanish when I left the pews. In fact, I felt God more clearly without the guilt filter.

The Drumbeat Truth

Let's engrain it:

- Guilt was weaponized by religion to control.
- Jeshua dismantled guilt by offering free forgiveness.
- Guilt masquerades as holiness, but it's bondage.
- Love, not guilt, is the true Way.

Stop letting guilt be your jailer. Recognize how institutions used it to control you. Refuse to play the game. Follow Jeshua's example: cancel debts, release shame, walk free. Love is free. Forgiveness is free. Presence is free.

That's the truth that breaks the chain: guilt is not God. Love is God.

The Difference Between Guilt and Responsibility

If guilt is the chain that keeps people trapped, then responsibility is the key that sets them free. But here's the problem: religion often blurred the line between the two. Healthy responsibility became confused with toxic guilt. People were told, "You are guilty," when what they really needed was, "You are responsible, and you have the power to make it right." Understanding this difference is essential to breaking free.

Defining Guilt and Responsibility

Guilt is an emotional state, often loaded with shame. It whispers, "I am bad. I am condemned. I don't deserve Love."

Responsibility is empowerment. It says, *I made a choice. It had consequences. I can choose differently next time. I can repair what I harmed."*

Guilt paralyzes. Responsibility mobilizes. Guilt traps you in the past. Responsibility equips you for the present.

Imagine that a kid spills milk. Guilt says, "I am a terrible person who ruins everything." Responsibility says, "Oops. Let me grab a towel." Which response do you want your kid to grow up with? Yet religion too often trained us for guilt, not towels.

How Religion Confused the Two

By branding people as inherently guilty – through doctrines like original sin – religion shifted the focus from actions to identity. You weren't just responsible for what you did. You were guilty for existing. That destroyed the possibility of healthy responsibility. Instead of, *I did wrong, let me make it right,"* people were told, "You are wrong, and only the institution can save you."

Confession became less about taking responsibility and more about wallowing in guilt. Penance became less about repairing harm and more about appeasing authority. The result? People grew dependent, not empowered.

Jeshua's Model of Responsibility

Jeshua never shamed people into guilt. He called them into responsibility. When he told the woman caught in adultery, *Go and sin no more,"* he wasn't saying, "You are guilty forever." He was saying, *You are free now. Take responsibility for your choices moving forward."*

When he told parables of forgiveness, the point wasn't, "Stay guilty." It was, *You've been forgiven. Now live responsibly."* Jeshua shifted people from identity-condemnation to empowerment. That's the real path to transformation.

My Own Experience

For years, I lived in guilt mode. Every mistake, no matter how small, became proof of my unworthiness. Forget to pray? Guilty. Have a stray thought? Double guilty! None of that helped me grow. It just kept me afraid.

When I finally started distinguishing guilt from responsibility, life changed. I realized I didn't need to feel condemned. I needed to own my choices. If I hurt someone, I could apologize. If I fell short, I could learn. That shift felt like freedom. Responsibility empowered me. Guilt only crushed me.

The Psychology of Responsibility

Psychologists know guilt and responsibility diverge. Guilt, especially toxic guilt, corrodes self-esteem. Responsibility, on the other hand, strengthens it. Guilt creates shame spirals. Responsibility creates growth loops. People who practice responsibility become resilient, adaptable, compassionate. People stuck in guilt become anxious, depressed, and immobilized.

The Weight of False Guilt

Many of us carry guilt for things that aren't even ours:

- Guilt for being human.
- Guilt for having desires.
- Guilt for not fitting institutional molds.
- Guilt for saying no.
- Guilt for walking away.

These aren't responsibilities. They're lies. They keep people chained to institutions instead of living freely. The first step in freedom is naming false guilt and rejecting it.

Imagine if grocery stores worked like religion's guilt system. You walk in, pick up a loaf of bread, and the cashier says, "You're guilty for even wanting food. But for $10 extra, we'll absolve you." You'd laugh and leave. But in church, people pay the fee without question.

Jeshua's Call to Healthy Responsibility

When Jeshua healed people, he often added, *"Take up your mat and walk."* That wasn't guilt. That was responsibility. He restored dignity and gave them power to act. Responsibility was never about condemnation. It was about freedom to live differently.

He also called leaders into responsibility. He told them their hypocrisy harmed people. But even then, it wasn't about guilt-shaming. It was about accountability: *"You can do better. Choose differently."*

Practices for Shifting from Guilt to Responsibility

1. **Guilt Journaling.** Write down moments you feel guilty. Ask: "*Is this true responsibility, or false guilt?"* Cross out the lies.

2. **Reparative Action.** When real harm is done, take one step to repair it – apologize, make amends, change behavior. That's responsibility.
3. **Self-Compassion.** When guilt spirals arise, pause and say: "*I am not condemned. I am learning.*"
4. **Daily Review.** Each night ask: "*Where did I act responsibly? Where can I improve tomorrow?*" Focus on growth, not shame.
5. **Declare Freedom.** Repeat daily: "*I am not guilty for existing. I am free to choose Love.*"

My Turning Point

My turning point came when I realized guilt had never made me a better person. It just made me miserable. Responsibility, on the other hand, motivated real change. When I shifted from *"I'm guilty"* to *"I can choose differently,"* I grew faster, Loved better, and lived freer.

Other Voices

Buddhism emphasizes responsibility through karma – not as condemnation, but as the natural law of cause and effect. The Bhagavad Gita emphasizes action without crippling guilt. Sufi poets remind us that mistakes are part of the path back to God. Across traditions, wisdom converges: guilt poisons, responsibility heals.

The Drumbeat Truth

Let's engrain it:

- Guilt condemns identity. Responsibility empowers choice.
- Religion blurred the line to keep people bound.
- Jeshua freed people from guilt and invited responsibility.
- Healthy responsibility leads to growth, compassion, freedom.

You have not been found guilty, so don't act like it. Start living responsibly. Don't confuse shame with growth. Don't let institutions convince you your existence is a crime. Take ownership of your actions, repair what you can, and live free. Jeshua's Way wasn't about groveling in guilt. It was about rising in responsibility.

That's the difference – and it's the difference between bondage and freedom.

Self-Forgiveness

Forgiving others is hard, but sometimes forgiving ourselves feels impossible. Many of us were trained by religion to extend compassion outward but deny it inward. We were told to forgive enemies, to forgive those who hurt us, but when it came to ourselves? Silence.

Instead, we were taught to nurse guilt, rehearse our failings, and identify as "poor miserable sinners." This lopsided approach leaves people trapped: free to speak words of forgiveness to others, but unable to release the deepest chain of all — the chain of self-condemnation.

Why Self-Forgiveness Is So Hard

Self-forgiveness is hard because guilt masquerades as responsibility, and shame masquerades as humility. We think holding onto guilt makes us virtuous: *If I keep beating myself up, at least I won t make the same mistake again."* But that's a lie. Shame rarely prevents mistakes — it usually drives people to repeat them.

Self-forgiveness is also hard because of conditioning. If you grew up hearing, *You are unworthy. You are guilty. You are sinful by nature,"* then forgiving yourself feels like rebellion. It feels like arrogance.

Religion often implied that forgiving yourself was trying to do God's job. Better to stay small and guilty than risk being free.

Imagine if you treated your best friend the way you treat yourself. "Oh, you made a mistake? I will now remind you of it every day for the next twenty years." They'd stop returning your calls. Yet many of us answer our own self-condemning calls daily.

Jeshua's Invitation

Jeshua constantly invited people into self-forgiveness, even if he didn't use the phrase. When he said, *"Your sins are forgiven,"* he was giving people permission to stop carrying guilt. He was telling them, "You can let this go. You don't need to define yourself by your past."

He told people to forgive "seventy times seven." That applies inward, too. You will stumble, fail, forget. But each time, Love whispers: *"Try again. You're still mine."* Jeshua didn't want people trapped in cycles of shame. He wanted them living free.

My Own Battle with Self-Forgiveness

I wrestled with self-forgiveness for years. It was easier for me to forgive someone else than to forgive myself. I carried a mental scrapbook of mistakes: words I shouldn't have said, relationships I'd failed, promises I'd broken. I thought guilt kept me humble. In reality, it kept me bound.

The turning point came when I realized guilt wasn't making me better, it was making me smaller. The God I met in presence never pointed to my scrapbook. He pointed to now. He said, *"Exhale. Be free. Move forward."* That realization helped me begin forgiving myself. Not in one dramatic moment, but little by little, day by day.

The Psychology of Self-Forgiveness

Psychologists confirm what mystics always knew: self-forgiveness is crucial for mental health. Without it, people spiral into depression, anxiety, even self-sabotage. Shame corrodes self-worth. Self-forgiveness restores it. Research shows that people who practice self-forgiveness have lower stress, healthier relationships, and greater resilience.

The Trap of Endless Self-Criticism

Religion often glorified self-criticism as virtue. The more miserable you felt about yourself, the holier you seemed. But Jeshua never glorified misery. He glorified Love. Endless self-criticism doesn't honor God – it insults God's creation. If you are made in God's image, then despising yourself is despising the image of God. Self-forgiveness is not arrogance. It is alignment with truth.

Imagine an artist spending weeks painting a masterpiece. You look at it and say, "This is garbage." Who are you insulting – the painting or the artist? Both. When we refuse to forgive ourselves, we insult the Artist who made us.

Practices for Self-Forgiveness

1. **Mirror Practice.** Look into your own eyes and say, *"I forgive you. You are beLoved. You are free."* Do this daily until it sinks in.

2. **Rewrite the Story.** Journal about a mistake. Then rewrite the story from Love's perspective: *"Yes, I stumbled, but I grew. Yes, I failed, but I learned."*
3. **Symbolic Release.** Write down old guilt, then burn the paper. Watch the smoke rise as a sign of release.
4. **Compassion Meditation.** Sit in silence and imagine extending compassion to yourself as you would to a hurting friend.
5. **Affirmation.** Repeat daily: *"I am not my past. I am whole. I am forgiven."*

Self-Forgiveness and Relationships

When you forgive yourself, relationships improve. You stop projecting your shame onto others. You stop demanding perfection. You become gentler, more patient, more loving. Self-forgiveness ripples outward.

When you're free, others feel freer too.

Other Voices

Buddhism emphasizes compassion for all beings – including yourself. The Bhagavad Gita teaches that clinging to guilt only binds you further. Sufi mystics sing of God's mercy overflowing like an ocean, insisting that we drink deeply – not sip guiltily. Across traditions, the message is clear: forgiveness isn't just something you give others. It's something you give yourself.

The Drumbeat Truth

Let's engrain it:

- Guilt masquerades as humility but keeps you bound.
- Jeshua invited people to release shame and live free.
- Self-forgiveness is not arrogance – it honors God's creation.
- Forgiving yourself transforms relationships and restores joy.

Forgive yourself. Stop carrying the scrapbook of mistakes. Stop defining yourself by guilt. Look into your own eyes and say the words Jeshua would say: "*You are forgiven. You are free.*"

That's self-forgiveness – the key that unlocks the deepest chain of guilt and opens the door to Love.

Releasing Generational Guilt

Some guilt doesn't even start with us. It's inherited. Handed down like an heirloom nobody wanted, passed from parent to child, culture to culture, church to congregation. Generational guilt is the quiet undercurrent shaping lives long before people realize it. It seeps into family stories, cultural assumptions, and spiritual identities. To break guilt's chain, we can't just forgive ourselves. We have to recognize and release the guilt carried for generations.

What Is Generational Guilt?

Generational guilt happens when one generation hands down shame and fear to the next. Sometimes it's explicit: "Don't dishonor the family." Sometimes it's unspoken: the mother who carries shame passes it through her silence, the father who fears God's wrath disciplines from guilt instead of Love.

It's not always personal mistakes. Sometimes it's cultural or historical: children of oppressors feeling guilty for their nation's past, or descendants of marginalized groups made to carry shame imposed by colonizers. Generational guilt weaves into identity, convincing people they're guilty not only for what they've done, but for who they are and where they came from.

Imagine inheriting your grandmother's fine china along with her guilt about not praying enough. Every family dinner becomes a spiritual test: "These plates haven't seen enough rosaries this year." Heirlooms should be passed down – guilt shouldn't.

How Religion Multiplied Generational Guilt

Religious systems perfected generational guilt. Original sin said every child was guilty before birth. Generations were told they carried Adam's sin. Entire nations were branded guilty for their ancestors' choices. Children were baptized not in celebration but in urgency – to wash away inherited guilt.

The church didn't just teach personal repentance. It taught generational burden: family curses, ancestral sins, inherited shame. This theology made guilt hereditary. No one entered the world innocent. Everyone was already guilty by association.

Jeshua's Break from Generational Guilt

Jeshua shattered this narrative. When asked about a man born blind ("*Who sinned, this man or his parents?*"), Jeshua replied, *"Neither. This happened so the works of God might be revealed in him."* In one stroke, he dismissed generational guilt. He refused to let someone's suffering be explained by inherited blame.

He told people they were children of God, not children of wrath. He welcomed children without baptizing them for guilt. His vision of the Kingdom wasn't about family curses. It was about freedom.

My Own Encounter with Generational Guilt

Looking back at my own family, I can see how guilt passed down. My parents were raised in Catholic households steeped in obligation and shame. They passed along what they'd been taught: Mass attendance as salvation, confession as survival, guilt as identity. They weren't trying to harm me. They were handing down what they'd inherited.

I carried guilt for things that weren't even mine: family expectations, cultural burdens, ancestral fears. It took years to realize much of the guilt I felt wasn't personal – it was generational. That realization was liberating. It wasn't all mine to carry. And if it wasn't mine, I could put it down.

The Psychology of Generational Guilt

Psychologists call this "intergenerational transmission of trauma." Trauma, shame, and guilt don't vanish when one generation dies. They echo through behaviors, beliefs, and even epigenetics. Children inherit not only genes but the emotional weight of ancestors. Unless consciously healed, patterns repeat: guilt-driven parenting produces guilt-driven children.

The Cost of Generational Guilt

Generational guilt is heavy because it hides in plain sight. People mistake it for identity: "This is just who we are." But carrying inherited shame stunts growth. It keeps families locked in cycles of silence, fear, or control. It keeps cultures bound to past wounds. It convinces people they're guilty for sins they never committed.

Imagine being fined every month for a parking ticket your great-grandfather got in 1923. That's generational guilt — paying debts that were never yours.

Jeshua's Way of Freedom

Jeshua offered freedom from inherited burdens. He invited people to start fresh: *Behold, I make all things new."* He emphasized presence, not ancestry: *The Kingdom of Heaven is within you."* Not within your lineage, your rituals, or your inherited guilt — within *you.*

He taught that God's Love wasn't limited to bloodlines or history. It was immediate, personal, universal. In Jeshua's Way, no one was chained to their ancestors' mistakes.

Practices for Releasing Generational Guilt

1. **Identify the Inheritance.** Write down guilt messages you heard growing up: "*Don't dishonor us," "God will punish you," "We're all sinners."* Acknowledge they're inherited, not ultimate truth.
2. **Family Tree of Freedom.** Draw a family tree. On each branch, name the guilt carried down. Then write beside it: "*I release this.*"
3. **Ritual of Release.** Create a symbolic act: light a candle, speak aloud, "*This ends with me. I return this guilt to the past. I choose freedom.*"
4. **Compassion for Ancestors.** Remember: your parents and grandparents were victims of guilt too. Forgive them. They were passing along what they were taught.
5. **Declaration.** Daily repeat: "*I am not guilty for my ancestors' choices. I walk free in Love.*"

My Turning Point

One turning point came when I realized my parents weren't villains — they were carriers. They didn't invent the guilt. They inherited it. When I forgave them, I could stop blaming and start healing. I could break the chain instead of extending it. That shift changed how I related to family and to myself.

Other Voices

The Buddha taught liberation from karmic cycles, not bondage to ancestral shame. The Hebrew prophet Ezekiel declared, *"The son shall not bear the iniquity of the father."* Sufi poets sing of God's mercy as greater than any inherited burden. All traditions echo this: guilt doesn't have to be generational. Freedom is always available.

The Drumbeat Truth

Let's engrain it:

- Generational guilt is inherited shame, not ultimate truth.
- Religion codified it, but Jeshua dismantled it.
- You are not guilty for your ancestors' actions.
- Compassion for ancestors breaks cycles; presence sets you free.

Stop carrying guilt that isn't yours. Stop letting family stories or religious doctrines burden you with inherited shame. Recognize it, name it, release it. Forgive your ancestors for passing it on. Choose to end the cycle.

That's how you release generational guilt — not by ignoring the past, but by refusing to be chained to it. Jeshua's Way is always new. And that newness begins with freedom.

Living Without Guilt

Breaking the chains of guilt isn't just about understanding where guilt comes from or how religion weaponized it. It's not even about forgiving others, forgiving yourself, or releasing generational shame. The real goal is to live *without guilt* — to embody freedom in daily life, to build a rhythm of presence that no longer bows to the old programming. Living without guilt is not ignoring responsibility or pretending mistakes don't happen. It's living in such alignment with Love and presence that guilt has no foothold.

The Possibility of Guilt-Free Living

For many raised in guilt-driven systems, the idea of living without guilt feels impossible. Guilt becomes so ingrained it feels like part of conscience. People ask, "If I don't feel guilty, won't I just do whatever I want?" That's exactly the fear institutions instilled — that without guilt as a leash, we'll run wild. But Jeshua offered another vision: life guided not by guilt, but by Love. Love is a better teacher than guilt.

Love inspires responsibility without shame. Love motivates healing without condemnation.

Imagine if parents raised kids by guilt alone. "Clean your room or you'll be a terrible human forever." The kid might clean once, but they'd resent it and probably rebel later. Love works better: "Clean your room because this is your space, and you deserve peace." The same is true for spiritual life.

Jeshua's Vision of Guilt-Free Living

Jeshua didn't train disciples through shame. He didn't tell them, *Remember how terrible you are."* He told them, *You are the light of the world."* That's empowerment, not guilt. He told them, *My peace I give you."* That's freedom, not shame. He told them, *Do not be afraid."* That's presence, not paralysis.

He embodied guilt-free living himself. He wasn't weighed down by "shoulds" or paralyzed by "what ifs." He lived fully present, responding to Love in each moment. That's why he could touch lepers, welcome sinners, and forgive enemies. He wasn't shackled by guilt-based purity systems. He was guided by Love.

My Own Journey Toward Guilt-Free Living

The first time I tasted guilt-free living, it felt almost wrong. I skipped a ritual I was supposed to perform and waited for guilt to strike. But nothing happened. God didn't vanish. Lightning didn't strike. In fact, I felt more peace, not less. That's when I realized that guilt wasn't God.

Guilt was programming.

Over time, guilt still tried to creep back. Old patterns whispered, *"You should feel bad."* But instead of collapsing under it, I began asking, *"What does Love invite me to do?"* That one question became my compass. Slowly, guilt lost its power. Living without guilt became not just possible, but natural.

The Psychology of Guilt-Free Living

Psychologists affirm that people thrive when guided by intrinsic values (like Love, compassion, and integrity) rather than extrinsic guilt. Guilt-driven behavior produces anxiety, resentment, and burnout. Love-driven behavior produces joy, resilience, and fulfillment. People who live without guilt are not irresponsible. They are actually more responsible, because they act from Love, not fear.

The Cost of Guilt-Free Living

Let's be honest: living without guilt will cost you something. It will cost you approval from guilt-driven communities. People who still bow to guilt may accuse you of arrogance, rebellion, or selfishness. They may try to pull you back into shame. Living guilt-free is a radical act of courage. It's easier to stay small in guilt than to live free in Love. But freedom is worth the cost.

Imagine if prisons released people but guilt sent them back in anyway: "I served my sentence, but I felt bad, so here I am." That's what many people do spiritually. Guilt convinces them to walk back into cages that are already unlocked. Living without guilt means refusing to go back.

Practices for Living Without Guilt

1. **Daily Compass Question.** Each morning, ask: *"What does Love invite me to do today?"* Let Love, not guilt, guide choices.
2. **Presence Anchoring.** When old guilt whispers, return to breath. Say: "*I am here. I am free. I am Loved.*"
3. **Replace "Should" with "Choose."** Instead of saying, "I should," say, "I choose." This shifts from guilt to responsibility.
4. **Celebrate Progress.** Each night, celebrate moments you lived from Love. Gratitude strengthens freedom.
5. **Community of Freedom.** Surround yourself with people who affirm Love, not guilt. Presence is easier in supportive circles.

What Guilt-Free Living Looks Like

- You apologize when you hurt someone, but without self-condemnation.
- You make mistakes, but see them as growth, not proof of failure.
- You serve others out of joy, not obligation.
- You pray, meditate, or sit in Love, not because you "have to," but because you want to.
- You say no when needed, without drowning in guilt.
- You enjoy life — laughter, beauty, rest — without apology.

My Turning Point

One of my biggest turning points came when I realized guilt-free living isn't irresponsibility — it's deeper responsibility. Without guilt's static, I could hear Love's voice more clearly. Without shame's chains, I could act with more courage. I stopped wasting energy on self-condemnation and started using it for presence. That's when life felt lighter, freer, more joyful.

Other Voices

Buddhism teaches release from guilt through compassion and non-attachment. The Upanishads describe the soul as pure and whole, untouched by guilt. Sufi poets sing of God's mercy flowing like rivers, washing away shame. Across traditions, mystics affirm that guilt is not the foundation of holiness. Love is.

The Drumbeat Truth

Let's engrain it:

- Guilt is not God.
- Love is a better guide than shame.
- Living without guilt is not recklessness — it's deeper responsibility.
- Jeshua modeled guilt-free living as presence, Love, and peace.

Guilt is not holiness. Stop bowing to shame's whispers. Live without guilt. Let Love be your compass, presence be your guide, and joy be your fuel. Jeshua's Way wasn't about carrying shame. It was about walking free.

That's living without guilt – not irresponsibility, but the deepest form of freedom.

The Freedom of Innocence Restored

Breaking free of guilt is not just about dropping a heavy burden. It's about recovering something precious we thought was lost forever: innocence. Religion told us innocence was gone the moment Adam bit fruit, or the moment we committed our first sin, or the moment we dared to question authority. But innocence isn't naivety. It isn't ignorance. It isn't pretending you've never made mistakes. Innocence is clarity – the ability to see yourself and God without the fog of shame. To live without guilt is to live as innocent again.

What Innocence Really Is

The word "innocence" often conjures up images of children – wide-eyed, uncorrupted, pure. But innocence in the spiritual sense isn't about being untouched by life. It's about seeing life with eyes unclouded by guilt. It's about walking in the world with trust, openness, and freedom instead of suspicion, shame, and fear. Innocence is not pretending the past didn't happen. It's knowing the past doesn't define you.

Imagine if credit card companies treated innocence the way churches do. "Your account was pure when you opened it, but the moment you made one charge, you're forever in debt – with interest!" We'd revolt. Yet in church, we nod and agree. Innocence restored is realizing the balance was canceled long ago.

The Theft of Innocence

Religion stole innocence by telling people they were guilty by default. Babies born guilty. Children raised guilty. Adults carrying guilt until death. Innocence was treated as a fragile vase – once shattered, it could never be repaired. That's why doctrines like original sin were so destructive. They erased the idea that you could ever return to innocence.

Institutions reinforced guilt by controlling forgiveness. Innocence wasn't restored by Love; it was leased temporarily through confession, rituals, or payments. People lived in cycles of guilt and temporary relief, never truly free. Innocence became unattainable.

Jeshua's Restoration of Innocence

Jeshua shattered that lie. He said, *Unless you become like little children, you will not enter the Kingdom."* He wasn't talking about becoming naïve. He was talking about restoring childlike innocence – trust, openness, wonder. He invited people to stop carrying guilt and to live with fresh eyes.

Every time he forgave someone, he restored innocence. He didn't say, "You're forgiven, but remember you're still rotten inside." He said, *Go in peace."* He lifted shame and gave people back their dignity. Innocence wasn't gone. It was waiting underneath the guilt.

My Own Experience of Innocence Restored

When I first began sitting in Love, I didn't expect innocence. I just wanted peace. But one day, in the stillness, I felt something deeper – like a child again, simple, present, unburdened. It startled me. I hadn't felt that way since before doctrine layered guilt on my soul. For a moment, I realized innocence wasn't lost. It was underneath, waiting to be uncovered.

That moment changed how I lived. I began to trust again, not naively, but with openness. I began to laugh more freely. I felt less like a condemned sinner and more like a beLoved child. Innocence restored wasn't ignorance. It was freedom.

The Psychology of Innocence

Psychologists talk about "beginner's mind" – the ability to approach life with openness and curiosity, unburdened by assumptions.

Children live this naturally. Adults lose it under the weight of shame and cynicism. Restoring innocence is not regression. It's healing. It's returning to wholeness. People who live without guilt show greater resilience, creativity, and joy. They approach relationships with trust instead of suspicion. Innocence restored transforms the psyche.

Innocence and Relationships

When guilt dominates, relationships become transactional: "I hurt you, you hurt me, we keep score." When innocence is restored, relationships become freer: *We both stumble, but Love covers it."* Innocence makes space for trust, laughter, and forgiveness. It disarms defensiveness. It opens intimacy.

Imagine if couples treated each other with restored innocence. "Remember that thing you said three years ago that made me mad?" "Nope. Innocence restored. Pass the potatoes." Counselors would go out of business, but marriages might last longer.

Innocence and Community

Communities shaped by guilt focus on rules, boundaries, and exclusions. Communities shaped by innocence focus on openness, welcome, and belonging. Jeshua's gatherings were innocence communities: tax collectors at the table, children on his lap, women in leadership, sinners welcomed. No guilt-driven gatekeeping. Just Love restoring innocence.

Practices for Restoring Innocence

1. **Childlike Practice.** Do something playful each week – draw, sing, dance, play a game. Let your inner child breathe.
2. **Wonder Walks.** Take walks where the goal isn't exercise but wonder. Notice trees, sky, birds, as if for the first time.
3. **Release Ritual.** Each month, choose one guilt you still carry. Write it down, then destroy the paper. Say aloud: "*Innocence restored.*"
4. **Inner Child Meditation.** Sit quietly and imagine your younger self. Speak words of Love: "*You are safe. You are Loved. You are free.*"
5. **Declaration.** Repeat daily: "*I am beLoved. My innocence is restored.*"

My Turning Point

One of my turning points came when I laughed uncontrollably during meditation. For years, meditation had been serious, guilt driven. But in that moment, laughter bubbled up. I realized innocence includes joy. I didn't have to be solemn to be spiritual. Innocence meant being free enough to laugh, play, and delight in the moment.

Other Voices

Mystics across traditions speak of innocence. Rumi wrote, *Try to accept the changing seasons of your heart, even if they bring winter. Be innocent, like a child, and you will see with God s eyes."* The Tao Te Ching describes the sage as returning to childlike simplicity. The Psalms declare, *Create in me a clean heart, O God, and renew a right spirit within me."* All voices point to innocence as restoration, not impossibility.

The Drumbeat Truth

Let's engrain it:

- Innocence is not ignorance. It is freedom from guilt.
- Religion stole innocence by teaching permanent guilt.
- Jeshua restored innocence through forgiveness and Love.
- Innocence is always available, waiting underneath shame.

So let innocence be restored in you. Not by denying your past, but by refusing to be defined by it. Laugh again. Trust again. See with wonder again. Jeshua's Way doesn't end in guilt. It ends in innocence restored.

That's the freedom waiting on the other side of breaking the chains of guilt – not just a lighter backpack, but childlike joy, wonder, and presence. Innocence is not lost. It is reborn in Love.

Chapter 17: The Illusion of Unworthiness

The Lie of Not Being Enough

If guilt is the chain that drags us backward, then unworthiness is the shadow that looms over every step forward. It's the whispered lie that says: "You're not good enough. You don't deserve Love. You don't deserve joy. You don't deserve God." The illusion of unworthiness is one of the most destructive teachings ever birthed by religion – and one of the hardest to shake even after leaving the pews behind.

How the Illusion Works

Unworthiness is subtle. It doesn't shout. It whispers. It shows up as hesitation before joy: "Who am I to feel this free?" It creeps in when opportunities arise: "I'm not good enough to deserve this." It colors spiritual life: "God could never truly Love me."

The illusion of unworthiness is effective because it strikes at identity. If you believe you're unworthy at the core, you won't fight for freedom.

You'll settle for scraps, bow to authority, and apologize for existing. That's why religious systems leaned so heavily on it. It wasn't enough to control actions. They had to convince people they were unworthy of Love itself.

Imagine if restaurants worked like religion's unworthiness system. You sit down, order food, and the waiter says, "Sorry, you're not worthy of dinner unless you grovel first. Maybe if you say enough apologies, we'll bring bread." No one would eat out again. Yet spiritually, millions accepted that same absurd model.

The Religious Roots of Unworthiness

The doctrine of original sin lay the groundwork. If every human is born unworthy, then only the institution can declare worth. Baptism becomes less about celebration and more about erasing inherited filth. Confession becomes less about repair and more about proving worthiness. Eucharist becomes less about communion and more about earning a seat at the table.

Sexuality, especially, became a target. Desires were labeled unworthy. Bodies were treated as shameful. People learned to distrust themselves. This produced generations of believers who looked at their reflection and saw sin, not sacredness.

Jeshua's Rejection of Unworthiness

Jeshua never preached unworthiness. He said, *You are the light of the world."* He said, *The Kingdom of Heaven is within you."* He didn't say, "The Kingdom is within you once you confess enough or perform enough rituals." He declared it already there. Worth was not something to earn. It was intrinsic.

He welcomed the unworthy. Tax collectors, prostitutes, lepers, Samaritans – people labeled "unclean" or "unfit" were lifted by his words and touch. He restored their dignity. Jeshua's ministry was a constant reminder: you are worthy now.

My Own Struggle with Unworthiness

Unworthiness was drilled into me early. I was told I was a sinner, unworthy of God's presence, unworthy of heaven, unworthy of joy. Even when I prayed, I felt like I was groveling at a locked door, begging for scraps.

Even after leaving church structures, unworthiness lingered. When good things happened, I felt like an imposter. When Love flowed, I questioned it. The lie ran deep. It took years of sitting in Love, hearing the whisper of presence, to begin believing that *I am worthy, not because I earned it, but because I exist.*

The Psychology of Unworthiness

Psychologists call this "low self-worth." It's epidemic. It fuels anxiety, depression, perfectionism. People who feel unworthy sabotage relationships and careers because they don't believe they deserve happiness. They overwork, overgive, and over-apologize, all trying to earn worth they already have.

Religion didn't invent unworthiness, but it industrialized it. It turned shame into doctrine, ensuring generations carried wounds in their psyches.

The Cost of Believing the Lie

Believing you're unworthy robs you of joy. You hesitate before opportunities. You apologize for needs. You settle for toxic relationships. You hide gifts. You silence your own voice. Worst of all, you believe God is always disappointed, watching for your failures.

That's not spirituality. That's slavery.

Imagine if your dog acted like humans under unworthiness conditioning. You come home and your dog hangs its head: "I don't deserve your Love today. Please ignore me." Dogs get it better than humans – they know Love is their birthright.

Jeshua's Invitation to Worthiness

Jeshua constantly reframed people's worth. To the woman who anointed him with oil, scorned by others, he said her act was beautiful and would be remembered forever. To Peter, who denied him, he still entrusted leadership. To the thief on the cross, he promised paradise that very day. Worthiness was never lost. It was always affirmed.

Practices for Reclaiming Worthiness

1. **Daily Declaration.** Each morning, say: *"I am worthy of Love, joy, and God's presence."* Repeat until it sticks.
2. **Worthiness Journal.** Write down daily moments where you felt joy, Love, or presence. These are proof of worthiness.
3. **Mirror Practice.** Look in your own eyes and say: *"You are worthy."* Do it until the voice of Love drowns out the old programming.
4. **Replace Apologies with Thanks.** When you want to say "Sorry" unnecessarily, say "Thank you" instead. Shift from guilt to gratitude.
5. **Sit in Love.** Presence itself affirms worth. Sit daily in silence, breathing in Love, exhaling unworthiness.

My Turning Point

My turning point came when I realized unworthiness was an illusion, not reality. In meditation, I heard the whisper: *"The Kingdom is within you."* Not after confession. Not after perfection. Now. In me. That truth unraveled decades of conditioning. Each time the lie surfaced, I returned to that whisper. Slowly, the illusion dissolved.

Other Voices

Mystics across traditions affirm inherent worth. The Upanishads declare, *You are That*" — one with the divine. The Buddha taught that each being contains Buddha-nature. Rumi wrote, *You are not a drop in the ocean. You are the entire ocean in a drop."* Everywhere, wisdom says: worth is intrinsic, not earned.

The Drumbeat Truth

Let's engrain it:

- Unworthiness is a lie, not truth.
- Religion used unworthiness to control.
- Jeshua affirmed worthiness in everyone he met.
- You are worthy now, not later.

Stop apologizing for existing. Stop groveling for scraps. Stop believing the lie of not being enough. Innocence restored means worthiness restored. Jeshua's Way is simple: you are beLoved, you are worthy, you are whole.

That's the lie exposed — the illusion of unworthiness undone by the truth of Love.

The Origins of Unworthiness in Religion

If unworthiness is one of the deepest illusions binding humanity, then it's worth asking: where did it come from? No one is born looking in the mirror saying, "I'm not enough." Babies don't lie awake at night worrying about being unworthy. They laugh, cry, demand food, and trust Love will come. The illusion of unworthiness is not natural. It was taught. Crafted. Layered into societies and souls by religious systems that discovered its power. To free ourselves, we need to understand how unworthiness became doctrine.

Original Sin: The Masterstroke of Control

The most infamous origin of unworthiness in Western religion is the doctrine of original sin. According to this teaching, humanity's story begins not in blessing, but in failure. Adam and Eve disobeyed, and the guilt of that act cascaded through generations. Every child is born guilty, unworthy, condemned before taking their first breath.

Think about that for a moment. Before you say your first word, before you take your first step, before you make a single choice, you're already damned. Innocence isn't your birthright – guilt is. That doctrine created an infinite debt. And conveniently, only the church could collect the payments. Baptism became the first installment.

Confession became the maintenance plan. Guilt wasn't a temporary state – it was a permanent condition.

Imagine buying a car where the dealer says, "By the way, this car is broken by design. You'll need to pay us weekly to keep it running, forever." You'd walk out. But when religion sold humanity that deal through original sin, most people signed the contract without blinking.

Sexuality: The Easy Target

Another major source of unworthiness came from how religion treated the body, especially sexuality. Desire was branded as dangerous.

Pleasure was treated as sin. Even normal bodily functions became sources of shame.

Generations grew up convinced their very biology made them unworthy. Priests thundered from pulpits that natural desires were proof of corruption. People were taught to fear their own bodies – to cover them, repress them, punish them.

This worked brilliantly for control. If you can convince someone their own body betrays them, they'll never trust themselves. They'll always rely on external authority to tell them what's holy.

Hierarchy and Authority

Unworthiness was also institutionalized through hierarchy. Priests, bishops, and popes were presented as holier, closer to God, more worthy of divine presence. Ordinary people were told, "You can't approach God directly. You need us as intermediaries."

This created a constant sense of spiritual inferiority. No matter how hard you prayed, confessed, or served, you were always "less than." Worthiness was outsourced upward, and ordinary people were kept dependent.

Imagine a company where employees are told, "No matter how hard you work, you'll never be as valuable as management. But keep working, and we'll let you peek into the boardroom once a week." That's how church hierarchy functioned – with souls instead of salaries.

The Constant Threat of Hell

Hell became the enforcement mechanism. If you believed you were unworthy, hell was the logical conclusion. "Of course I'll burn. I'm not enough." Hell turned the illusion of unworthiness into a terror tactic. Any doubt, desire, or question was proof you deserved eternal punishment.

This fear kept people bound. Who would dare claim worthiness when eternal flames loomed over every slip? Better to stay guilty and compliant than risk stepping outside the lines.

Jeshua's Break from the Origins

Here's the striking thing: none of these teachings came from Jeshua. He never preached original sin. He never shamed sexuality. He never demanded hierarchy. He never threatened hell. These were later constructions, woven by institutions that found unworthiness useful.

Jeshua, by contrast, preached worth: *You are the light of the world." "The Kingdom is within you."* He touched bodies others called unclean. He bypassed hierarchies. He freed people from fear of condemnation.

Jeshua's gospel was not one of unworthiness. It was one of inherent worth, Love, and presence. That's why his teaching was so threatening – it undermined the very foundations institutions were building.

My Own Discovery of These Roots

When I first began pulling at the threads of unworthiness, I was shocked how deep they went. It wasn't just one sermon I'd heard as a kid. It was centuries of conditioning. The idea that I was broken before birth had been normalized for so long, I never thought to question it.

But when I started reading Jeshua's words directly, I realized that he never said what I was taught. He never told me I was unworthy. The more I listened to his voice, the more I realized the illusion had been crafted later. That realization was both infuriating and liberating. Infuriating because of the wasted years. Liberating because freedom was always available.

The Psychology of Indoctrinated Unworthiness

Psychologists now see how unworthiness seeps into the psyche. Kids raised under shame-based religion develop scrupulosity, anxiety, self- hatred. Adults internalize unworthiness as identity, which sabotages relationships and careers. Institutions knew this long before psychology did. They may not have had the jargon, but they knew guilt and unworthiness kept people controllable.

Practices for Rewriting the Origin Story

1. **Reject Original Sin.** Consciously reject the idea you were born guilty. Replace it with the truth: "*I was born worthy, whole, and beLoved.*"
2. **Body Blessing.** Each day, thank your body for carrying you. Bless its desires as natural and good.
3. **Hierarchy Detox.** Remind yourself: no one is closer to God than you. Spiritual worth is not ranked.
4. **Rewrite the Story.** Write your own "Genesis" story: a beginning not in sin, but in Love. Start with, "*In the beginning, I was whole.*"
5. **Replace Hell with Presence.** When fear of hell arises, return to the present. Remind yourself: "*Only Love is here, now.*"

My Turning Point

One of my biggest turning points came when I stopped saying, "I am a sinner." I started saying, "*I am beLoved.*" That small change unraveled years of conditioning. My origin story shifted. I was no longer the descendant of Adam's failure. I was the child of Love's presence. That reframing restored worth in a way no doctrine ever could.

Other Voices

The Hebrew prophets challenged inherited guilt. Ezekiel declared, *The son shall not bear the iniquity of the father."* The Upanishads proclaimed the soul as eternal and whole. The Buddha taught liberation from cycles of shame. Rumi wrote, *You were born with wings. Why prefer to crawl through life?"* Across traditions, the mystics resisted unworthiness and reclaimed worth as the divine truth.

The Drumbeat Truth

Let's engrain it:

- Original sin is the cornerstone of unworthiness – and it is a lie.
- Sexual shame, hierarchy, and hell reinforced the illusion.
- Jeshua never preached unworthiness; he preached worth.
- You were not born broken. You were born beLoved.

Stop living as if unworthiness is your origin. It's not. You were not born guilty. You were not born condemned. You were born worthy, whole, sacred. The origins of unworthiness lie in doctrine, not in truth.

Jeshua's Way exposes the illusion and restores your true beginning: beLovedness.

That's the lie unraveled – and the first step toward reclaiming the innocence and joy always waiting within.

The Psychology of Feeling Unworthy

The illusion of unworthiness isn't just a religious doctrine, it's a psychological pattern that burrows into the mind, rewires the body, and shapes every decision. Long after people leave churches, temples, or dogmas behind, unworthiness lingers because it becomes embedded in the psyche. It's not just something we "believe." It's something we *feel,* deep in the gut, in the chest, in the nervous system. To break free, we need to understand how unworthiness operates psychologically, and how to rewire it.

How Unworthiness Embeds Itself

Unworthiness enters the psyche through repetition. If you hear "You are sinful," "You are not enough," or "God is disappointed" enough times, the brain encodes those messages like grooves in a record. Soon, even when no one says it aloud, your mind plays the track automatically.

Psychologists call this "internalized shame." It's when external voices become inner voices. You no longer need a priest to remind you you're guilty; your brain does it for you. This is why leaving institutions doesn't always end the struggle. The programming follows you.

Imagine if your GPS worked like unworthiness. Every time you tried to get somewhere, it interrupted: "Recalculating... you're not worthy to arrive." Most people would throw the GPS out the window. Yet we let the guilt-voice narrate our daily lives.

The Emotional Cycle of Unworthiness

Unworthiness often follows a predictable cycle:

1. **Trigger** – You make a mistake, remember a failure, or compare yourself to someone else.
2. **Shame Spiral** – The inner voice whispers: "See? You're not enough."
3. **Avoidance or Overcompensation** – Some withdraw, hide, numb themselves. Others overwork, over-apologize, or over- give, hoping to "earn" worth.
4. **Temporary Relief** – You might feel better after a ritual, apology, or validation.
5. **Cycle Restarts** – Without addressing the root, the next trigger begins it again.

This cycle keeps people trapped. The illusion of unworthiness becomes a self-reinforcing loop.

The Body Keeps the Score

Psychologist Bessel van der Kolk famously said, *"The body keeps the score."* That's true with unworthiness. Shame shows up physically: hunched shoulders, shallow breathing, tight chests, stomach knots.

Chronic guilt can lead to anxiety disorders, depression, even autoimmune issues.

People literally carry unworthiness in their bodies. That's why breaking free isn't just mental. It requires practices that involve the body – breath, posture, movement, presence.

If guilt were a wearable device, it would buzz every time you enjoyed yourself. "Warning: you smiled too much. Please return to shame." Many of us already live with that inner Fitbit of unworthiness.

Jeshua's Healing of the Psyche

Jeshua understood the psychology of unworthiness long before modern therapy. When he healed people, he often said, *"Your faith has made you whole,"* not "Your guilt is erased." He shifted focus from shame to empowerment. He restored dignity before he restored health.

For example, the woman who touched his cloak. Society had branded her unworthy, unclean. Jeshua stopped, looked her in the eye, and said, *"Daughter, your faith has healed you. Go in peace."* That wasn't just physical healing. It was psychological liberation. He gave her a new identity: not unworthy, but beLoved.

My Own Struggle with the Psychology of Unworthiness

Even after leaving Catholicism, I found the voice of unworthiness still inside. I'd feel guilty for resting, guilty for joy, guilty for not doing enough. That guilt wasn't external anymore — it was internalized.

The turning point came when I realized the voice wasn't me. It was programming. When I began noticing it as a voice ("Oh, there's unworthiness talking again"), I could choose not to believe it. It didn't vanish overnight, but awareness weakened its grip.

The Role of Comparison

One of the biggest psychological traps of unworthiness is comparison. Religion set impossible standards — saints, martyrs, Jeshua himself — and told us we weren't enough unless we matched them. Social media continues the cycle: scrolling through curated lives makes us feel less-than.

Comparison is poison. It convinces you that someone else's highlight reel defines your worth. Jeshua never told people to compare. He told them to be present. The Kingdom wasn't found by matching others, but by discovering the Love within.

Practices for Rewiring the Psyche

1. **Awareness Practice.** Notice when the voice of unworthiness speaks. Label it: "*That's programming, not truth.*"

2. **Body Release.** When shame shows up physically, breathe deeply. Roll your shoulders back. Stand tall. Remind your body: "*I am worthy.*"
3. **Compassionate Self-Talk.** Speak to yourself as you would to a dear friend. Replace, "I'm not enough" with, "*I'm learning. I'm growing.*"
4. **Reframe Mistakes.** Instead of, "I failed, so I'm unworthy," say, *"I failed, so I learned."* Shift guilt to growth.
5. **Gratitude Journal.** Write daily about things you're grateful for in yourself – not just achievements, but qualities of presence and Love.

The Freedom Beyond Psychology

The illusion of unworthiness is not just psychological. It's spiritual. It tells us we're separate from God. When Jeshua said, *"The Kingdom is within you,"* he shattered that illusion. Worthiness isn't earned. It's inherent. Presence itself is proof.

Psychology helps us understand how unworthiness works. Spirituality reminds us who we are beyond it. Both are needed to truly break free.

Other Voices

Carl Jung said, *Shame is a soul-eating emotion."* Brené Brown teaches that shame can't survive being spoken; it withers in the light of vulnerability. The Buddha taught that all beings possess Buddha-nature, worthy of awakening. Rumi wrote, *You are not a drop in the ocean. You are the entire ocean in a drop."* The chorus across time is clear: unworthiness is illusion.

The Drumbeat Truth

Let's engrain it:

- Unworthiness embeds in the psyche through repetition.
- The body carries shame as much as the mind.
- Jeshua restored dignity as much as health.
- Worthiness is not earned. It is inherent.

Notice the voice of unworthiness. Name it. Laugh at it. Refuse to let it define you. Rewire your psyche through awareness, compassion, and presence. Remember Jeshua's words: *"You are the light of the world."*

That's the path out of psychological bondage into spiritual freedom – seeing unworthiness for what it is: an illusion, not reality.

Jeshua's Teaching of Inherent Worth

If religion thrived by teaching unworthiness, then Jeshua's entire mission was the antidote. He didn't come to reinforce shame, but to dissolve it. He didn't arrive to remind people how far they'd fallen, but to remind them how close they already were to God. His life was a living protest against the lie of unworthiness. Every word, every act, every parable whispered – or sometimes shouted – the same truth: *You are worthy. Always have been. Always will be.*

Jeshua's Radical Affirmations

The Sermon on the Mount was not a lecture in shame. It was an affirmation of worth. *You are the light of the world. A city on a hill cannot be hidden."* Light, not filth. Radiance, not rot. Jeshua didn't tell people to strive to become worthy. He told them they already were.

He also said, *Consider the lilies of the field, how they grow; they toil not, neither do they spin, yet even Solomon in all his glory was not arrayed like one of these."* The point wasn't just about flowers. It was about worth. If God clothes lilies and feeds sparrows, how much more will He care for you? Not because you earned it, but because you are inherently worthy.

Imagine Jeshua saying this today. "Look at the squirrels in the park. They don't clock in, they don't pay taxes, but they still get fed. Are you worth less than a squirrel? Relax." Sometimes spirituality really is that simple.

Stories of Restored Worth

Jeshua spent his life restoring worth to those religion had stripped bare.

- **The Samaritan woman at the well.** She was dismissed by gender, ethnicity, and lifestyle. Jeshua broke all taboos, spoke with her openly, and revealed his identity. In that moment, he affirmed her worth. She became the first evangelist in her village.

- **The woman caught in adultery.** The crowd saw a sinner to be stoned. Jeshua saw a human worthy of compassion. "*Neither do I condemn you.*" Dignity restored.
- **Zacchaeus the tax collector.** Corrupt, despised, unworthy in everyone's eyes. Jeshua dined with him, declaring, "*Salvation has come to this house.*" Worth affirmed.
- **Children.** Disciples tried to shoo them away. Jeshua said, "*Let the children come to me, for to such belongs the Kingdom.*" Children weren't half-worthy adults-in-training. They embodied the Kingdom already.

Every story points the same direction: worth wasn't achieved through ritual or status. It was recognized through Love.

Jeshua's Healing as Worth Affirmation

Healing was not just physical. It was psychological and social. Lepers weren't only sick – they were excluded. Jeshua's touch did more than heal skin. It restored worth. Blind beggars weren't just disabled – they were dismissed. Jeshua's attention did more than open eyes. It restored dignity.

Each act of healing was a declaration: *You are not unworthy. You are whole. You are beLoved.*

My Own Awakening to Jeshua's Affirmation

When I read Jeshua's words directly, without the church filter, I noticed something startling: he never told people they were garbage. He never said, "You're worthless worms." That was later theology.

Jeshua's voice affirmed. Even in correction, he called people higher, not lower.

The moment I started hearing that affirmation personally – *"You are the light of the world"* – something broke inside me. Decades of conditioning cracked. I realized the voice of shame had never been Jeshua's. His voice had always been Love.

The Challenge of Believing Worth

Here's the tricky part: even when Jeshua affirms worth, people struggle to believe it. Why? Because the illusion of unworthiness feels more familiar. We cling to shame because it feels safer than freedom. Freedom is risky. Worth means responsibility. Shame means passivity. Many stay small because worth feels too big.

That's why Jeshua often repeated his affirmations. He didn't say it once. He kept saying, *"Fear not."* He kept saying, *"You are beLoved."* He knew the lie was loud. So he made the truth louder.

The Psychology of Declarations

Modern psychology backs this up. Affirmations – when believed – rewire the brain. Repeated messages of worth create new neural pathways. Jeshua was essentially practicing ancient cognitive restructuring. He replaced toxic scripts with divine ones. He was literally reprogramming people's psyches through Love.

Practices for Living Jeshua's Teaching of Worth

1. **Speak His Words Aloud.** Each morning, declare: *"I am the light of the world."* Not arrogance, but echoing Jeshua.
2. **Rewrite His Stories.** Read the Gospels. Every time Jeshua affirms someone, put your name in the story. Hear him say it to you.
3. **Worthy Breath.** With each inhale, say silently: *"I am worthy."* With each exhale: *"I am beLoved."*
4. **Declare Worth in Others.** Jeshua declared worth in others constantly. Practice daily positive declarations toward people around you.
5. **Child Practice.** Spend time with children, learning innocence and openness. Remember Jeshua's words: *"To such belongs the Kingdom."*

My Turning Point

One of my turning points came while meditating on the story of Zacchaeus. I realized I *was* Zacchaeus – climbing trees, trying to see God from a distance, ashamed of who I was. Jeshua looked at me and said, *"Come down. I must stay at your house today."* Worth affirmed. Presence restored. That realization melted years of hiding.

Other Voices

Mystics across traditions echo Jeshua's teaching. The Upanishads affirm, *"That thou art"* divinity within. The Buddha declared all beings possess Buddha-nature. Rumi wrote, *"You were born with wings. Why crawl through life?"* Even psychology affirms inherent worth as the basis of self-actualization. Jeshua was not alone in this message — but his clarity and boldness were unique.

The Drumbeat Truth

Let's engrain it:

- Jeshua never taught unworthiness. He affirmed worth.
- Every healing, every parable, every interaction restored dignity.
- Worth is not earned. It is inherent.
- You are the light of the world.

Stop listening to voices that tell you you're not enough. Start listening to Jeshua's voice. Hear him say it again and again: *You are worthy. You are beLoved. You are light."* His teaching is not about groveling but about shining.

That's Jeshua's teaching of inherent worth — the antidote to the illusion of unworthiness, the foundation for living free.

The Cost of Believing You Are Unworthy

If worthiness is the soil in which Love, freedom, and presence can grow, then unworthiness is the poisoned ground where nothing thrives. Believing you are unworthy isn't just a private struggle. It's an illusion that bleeds into every part of life: relationships, work, creativity, health, and spirituality. It's not just a "belief problem" — it's a full- spectrum life problem. To understand why breaking free matters, we need to see clearly the true cost of living under the illusion of unworthiness.

The Inner Toll: Anxiety, Shame, and Exhaustion

The first and deepest cost of unworthiness is internal. People who believe they're unworthy carry constant anxiety: "Am I doing enough? Am I pleasing God? Am I failing again?" Every mistake feels catastrophic. Every joy feels undeserved.

This internal state drains energy. Shame eats at self-esteem until life feels like a treadmill: always running, never arriving. People exhaust themselves trying to earn worth that was never lost. They wake up tired and go to bed guilty.

Imagine buying a car where the gas tank has a permanent leak. No matter how much fuel you add, it keeps draining. That's life under unworthiness, always filling up with rituals, prayers, or good deeds, but never feeling full.

The Relational Cost

Unworthiness poisons relationships in two ways.

1. **Overcompensation.** Believing they're unworthy, people over-give, over-please, and over-apologize. They stay in toxic relationships, thinking, "This is all I deserve." They accept mistreatment because they don't believe they're worth respect.
2. **Withdrawal.** Others withdraw to avoid being "found out." They fear rejection, so they reject themselves first. They hide gifts, silence their voice, keep distance from intimacy.

Both patterns sabotage connection. Instead of Love flowing freely, relationships become distorted mirrors of shame.

The Career and Creativity Cost

Unworthiness also sabotages careers and creativity. People don't apply for opportunities because they think, "I'm not good enough." They self-sabotage projects, procrastinate, or shrink back when it's time to shine. Creativity especially suffers – unworthiness whispers, "Who are you to share your art, your words, your vision?"

This is tragic, because the world misses out on gifts. How many books were never written, songs never sung, inventions never built, because people believed the lie of unworthiness?

Imagine Michelangelo staring at a block of marble, hearing the inner voice say, "You're not worthy of carving David." We'd have no Renaissance art – just a lot of dusty rocks. That's what unworthiness does: it leaves brilliance unexpressed.

The Physical Cost

The body pays, too. Studies show chronic shame and low self-worth increase stress, blood pressure, and risk of disease. The nervous system stays on high alert, expecting punishment. Sleep suffers.

Digestion suffers. Even the immune system weakens.

Living in unworthiness is like carrying a heavy backpack every day. Over time, the body breaks down under the weight.

The Spiritual Cost

Perhaps the greatest cost is spiritual. When you believe you're unworthy, you experience God not as presence but as judge. Prayer becomes groveling, not communion. Meditation becomes anxious self-checking, not peace. Spirituality becomes performance, not relationship.

You end up worshiping a God made in the image of your own shame — a deity who's always disappointed, never satisfied. That's not God. That's guilt with a halo.

Jeshua came to free us from this, but religion doubled down, reinforcing the illusion. The cost? Generations of people mistaking fear for faith.

My Own Experience of the Cost

I've lived these costs. I over-apologized, stayed small, and carried stress in my body. I avoided opportunities because unworthiness whispered I wasn't ready. I prayed with more fear than joy, imagining a God constantly tallying my failures.

It wasn't until I began sitting in Love, hearing Jeshua's declarations, that I realized the toll unworthiness had taken. I'd been living half a life, dimming my own light. The cost wasn't just personal — it rippled into relationships, creativity, and health. Breaking free didn't just change me. It changed everything around me.

Why the Illusion Persists

If the costs are so high, why do people cling to unworthiness? Because it feels familiar. Shame becomes identity. People mistake unworthiness for humility. They fear that without it, they'll become arrogant or reckless. But worthiness doesn't breed arrogance — it breeds Love. Only people who know they're worthy can Love freely.

Jeshua's Warning Against the Cost

Jeshua often confronted the lie of unworthiness indirectly. When he said, *"Do not be afraid,"* he was dismantling the fear of not being enough. When he said, *"You are the light of the world,"* he was confronting self-doubt. When he welcomed the outcast, he was exposing the cost of exclusion and shame. His teaching wasn't abstract. It was deeply practical. He saw the toll unworthiness took on real people, and he offered liberation.

Practices for Recognizing and Releasing the Cost

1. **Cost Inventory.** Write down the ways unworthiness has cost you – in relationships, work, health, spirituality. Name it clearly. Awareness is step one.
2. **Reframe Failures.** When shame whispers, reframe mistakes as growth: *"I'm learning, not failing."*
3. **Worthy Choices.** Each day, make one choice you'd make if you fully believed you were worthy – applying for a job, setting a boundary, expressing creativity.
4. **Embodied Worth.** Practice standing tall, breathing deeply, smiling. Let the body signal worth to the mind.
5. **Gratitude for Self.** Write daily: *"I am grateful for..."* followed by qualities in yourself. Gratitude rewires self-worth.

My Turning Point

One of my turning points came when I realized I was apologizing for existing. "Sorry" slipped out constantly, even when I hadn't done anything wrong. One day, I stopped mid-apology and said instead: *"Thank you for your patience."* That small shift cracked the pattern. Slowly, I stopped living like an intruder in my own life.

Other Voices

Psychologists like Brené Brown warn that shame corrodes the very part of us that believes we can change. The Buddha taught that all beings are worthy of awakening. The Hebrew scriptures say, *You are fearfully and wonderfully made."* Rumi wrote, *Stop acting so small. You are the universe in ecstatic motion."* All voices point to the same truth: the cost of unworthiness is devastating, but the truth of worth is liberating.

The Drumbeat Truth

Let's engrain it:

- Believing you are unworthy poisons every part of life.
- Relationships, careers, health, and spirituality all suffer.
- Jeshua affirmed worth to dismantle this illusion.
- The cost of unworthiness is too high. Freedom is worth everything.

So look clearly at what unworthiness has cost you. Don't minimize it. See it. Feel it. Then decide that you've paid enough. No more rent to shame. No more tithes to guilt. No more sacrifices to the illusion.

Jeshua's Way is freedom, not debt.

That's the cost revealed – and the call to stop paying it.

Practices for Reclaiming Your Worth

Recognizing unworthiness as an illusion is one thing. Breaking free of its grip is another. The chains may be imaginary, but they feel real because they've been reinforced for years – through repetition, rituals, and fear. That's why reclaiming worth requires more than intellectual agreement. It requires practice. Worthiness must be embodied, rehearsed, lived daily until it becomes natural again. This section is about building practices that replace the grooves of unworthiness with new patterns of worth.

Why Practice Matters

The illusion of unworthiness is sticky because it's been repeated. Sermons, confessions, doctrines, even cultural narratives drilled the same message: *"You are not enough."* The brain learned it, the body stored it, and the soul believed it. To undo this, you can't just say once, *"I am worthy."* You have to practice it until the new truth becomes as ingrained as the old lie.

Think of it like music. If you've been playing the same wrong note for decades, you don't fix it overnight. You practice the right note, again and again, until your fingers find it naturally. Reclaiming worth is the same.

Imagine trying to learn guitar by just reading about it. "I understand the theory therefore I can shred like Hendrix." Nope. You'd still sound like a dying cat. Worth works the same way – you have to *practice* it, not just read about it.

Jeshua's Model of Practice

Jeshua didn't just tell people they were worthy. He created experiences to help them embody it. He told stories, shared meals, touched the untouchable. He gave people rituals of freedom – breaking bread, washing feet, forgiving debts. His teaching was practical, not abstract. He knew worth wasn't reclaimed through theory, but through living it.

Core Practices for Reclaiming Worth

Here are practical rhythms to rewire your life around worth.

1. **Declaration Practice.** Each morning, look in the mirror and say aloud: *"I am worthy of Love, joy, and God's presence."* At first, it may feel awkward, even false. That's okay. The repetition matters. Over time, the words sink past your mind into your body.
2. **Replace Apologies with Gratitude.** Catch yourself when you say "Sorry" unnecessarily. Replace it with "*Thank you.*" Instead of, "Sorry I'm late," say, *"Thank you for waiting."* This simple shift rewires unworthiness into gratitude.
3. **Worthy Breath.** Use your breath as a daily anchor. Inhale and think: *"I am worthy."* Exhale and think: *"I am beLoved."* This connects worth to the body.
4. **Journal of Proof.** Keep a daily journal where you record moments of Love, joy, or presence. These are evidence of worth. Reviewing them builds confidence.
5. **Creative Expression.** Engage in one act of creativity weekly – writing, painting, singing, building. Unworthiness silences expression. Creativity restores it. Don't create to impress. Create to affirm: *"I am worthy of expressing myself."*
6. **Set Boundaries.** Say no when necessary. Boundaries are acts of worth. They declare: *"I matter. My needs count."* Each no becomes a yes to your own worth.

7. **Compassion for the Body.** Treat your body with respect. Nourish it, rest it, enjoy it. Religion taught many to distrust the body. Worth practice reclaims it as sacred.
8. **Silence Practice.** Sit daily in silence. No striving, no performing. Just being. Each moment of stillness says: *"I am enough as I am."*

My Own Practices

For me, reclaiming worth began with declarations and breath. At first, it felt ridiculous. The voice of unworthiness mocked: "Who do you think you are?" But I kept at it. Slowly, the mockery faded. The declarations felt less foreign and more true.

Another turning point was replacing apologies with gratitude. I didn't realize how often "Sorry" slipped out until I started noticing. Shifting to "Thank you" was small but powerful. It trained me to stop living as an inconvenience and start living as someone worth space.

The Challenges of Practice

Practicing worth isn't easy. Old grooves resist change. You may feel silly, resistant, even guilty at first. That's normal. The illusion won't give up easily. But each time you practice, you weaken the lie. Over time, worth becomes natural.

It's like learning to dance. At first, you feel like a baby giraffe on roller skates. But keep moving, and one day you realize – you're actually grooving. Worth practice works the same way.

The Fruits of Practice

When worth becomes embodied, life changes:

- **Relationships improve.** You stop over-giving or withdrawing. You show up whole.
- **Opportunities open.** You apply, risk, create – because you believe you deserve it.
- **Health improves.** Stress lowers, energy rises. The body relaxes without shame.
- **Spiritual life deepens.** Prayer becomes joy, not groveling. Meditation becomes peace, not penance.

- **Freedom grows.** You stop apologizing for existing. You start living as light.

Other Voices on Practice

Buddhism emphasizes mindfulness *practice* — not theory. Hinduism teaches *sadhana*, daily disciplines to embody truth. Sufi mystics dance and sing to rehearse Love. Modern psychology prescribes cognitive-behavioral practices to rewire thought patterns. Across traditions, the message is the same: truth must be practiced, not just believed.

My Turning Point

One of my biggest turning points came when I added play to my practice. I realized reclaiming worth wasn't all solemn affirmations. It was laughter, creativity, joy. I started painting badly on purpose, writing silly poems, dancing in my kitchen. Each playful act said, *"I am worthy of joy."* That shifted something deeper than words alone.

The Drumbeat Truth

Let's engrain it:

- Worth isn't reclaimed by theory, but by practice.
- Jeshua modeled worth through lived experience.
- Daily affirmations, boundaries, creativity, and presence rewire the psyche.
- Practice turns the illusion of unworthiness into the reality of worth.

Build daily practices of worth. Don't wait to "feel" worthy. Practice it until the truth becomes second nature. Let each breath, boundary, and declaration remind you: *"I am worthy. I am beLoved. I am enough."*

That's how you reclaim worth — not in one dramatic moment, but in daily rhythms of Love.

Living in the Truth of Worthiness

Reclaiming worth isn't the finish line, it's the starting line. Once you see through the illusion of unworthiness and begin practicing new rhythms of truth, life itself shifts. You no longer live as someone clawing for scraps of approval. You live as someone who knows, deep in your bones: *I am worthy. I am beLoved. I am whole.* This section isn't about theory. It's about what it looks like to embody worthiness in everyday life — to live in the truth of worth as your normal state of being.

The Shift from Surviving to Living

People bound by unworthiness survive, but they don't live. They wake up each day apologizing. They enter rooms already shrinking. They pray already groveling. Life becomes about not failing, not offending, not falling short. That's survival, not living.

When worthiness takes root, the shift is dramatic. Life becomes less about avoiding mistakes and more about embracing presence. You move from defense to offense — from protecting yourself to expressing yourself. Living in worth means life becomes creative again.

It's like the difference between driving with the parking brake on and releasing it. For years, you wonder why the car feels so sluggish. Then one day you release the brake and think, "Wow, I didn't know life could move this smoothly." That's what reclaiming worth feels like.

Jeshua's Model of Worthy Living

Jeshua lived in worth without arrogance. He didn't shrink when criticized, nor puff up when praised. He lived from centered presence. He touched lepers without fear of contamination. He dined with sinners without fear of reputation. He forgave enemies without fear of weakness. His worth was rooted in Love, not approval.

When he said, *I and the Father are one,"* it wasn't arrogance. It was truth. And when he said, *You are the light of the world,"* he extended that same worth to everyone else. Jeshua's life shows us what it looks like to embody worth: grounded, fearless, compassionate, free.

My Own Experience of Worthy Living

When I first began practicing worth, it felt fragile — like a new seedling easily trampled. I had to protect it from old voices of shame. But over time, the roots grew. Worth became less a practice and more a way of being.

I noticed it in small ways: I stopped over-apologizing. I applied for opportunities without hesitation. I enjoyed rest without guilt. Prayer shifted from begging to being. Meditation shifted from striving to sitting. Relationships shifted from pleasing to authentic connection.

Worthy living didn't mean perfection. I still stumbled, but I stopped interpreting stumbles as proof of unworthiness. They became lessons, not indictments. That shift alone felt like freedom.

The Fruits of Worthy Living

When worthiness is embodied, it produces fruit in every area of life.

- **Relationships.** You attract healthier partners and friendships. You stop tolerating abuse or manipulation. You give Love freely without needing to buy it with self-sacrifice.
- **Work and Creativity.** You share your gifts boldly. You stop shrinking. You create not to prove yourself, but because it's natural to express.
- **Health.** Stress decreases. The body relaxes. Energy increases. You treat yourself with respect instead of punishment.
- **Spirituality.** Presence becomes joyful. God is experienced as Love, not as a disappointed taskmaster. Prayer feels like conversation, not courtroom. Meditation feels like rest, not performance.
- **Freedom.** Life feels expansive. You stop asking, *"Am I enough?"* and start asking, *"What can I create today from the Love within me?"*

The Obstacles to Worthy Living

Even when worth is reclaimed, obstacles arise. Old voices return, especially during stress. Family or religious communities may resist your freedom. They may accuse you of arrogance or rebellion. That's normal. When people are still enslaved to unworthiness, your freedom threatens their illusion.

The key is persistence. Worthiness must be reaffirmed daily, especially in the face of resistance. Jeshua himself was accused of blasphemy for living in worth. If they accused him, they'll accuse you. Don't shrink. Keep shining.

It's like getting a promotion and suddenly your old coworkers start saying, "Who do you think you are?" The answer isn't to go back to the old job. It's to keep leading — even if they don't like it. Living in worth is the same.

Practices for Embodying Worth

1. **Daily Worth Check.** Each morning, pause and declare: "*I am worthy today, not because of what I do, but because of who I am.*"
2. **Worth in Action.** Make one choice daily that reflects your worth — setting a boundary, creating art, resting without guilt.
3. **Community of Worth.** Surround yourself with people who affirm worth, not shame. Presence multiplies in groups.
4. **Gratitude Living.** Live with gratitude for being alive, not as proof of worth, but as expression of it.
5. **Teach Worth.** Share with others what you're learning. Affirm worth in them. Nothing solidifies your own truth like teaching it.

My Turning Point

One of my biggest turning points came during a session of "sitting in Love." I realized I didn't need to strive to feel worthy. The very act of sitting in presence proved I was. In that silence, there were no achievements, no failures — only Love. That moment shifted everything. Worth wasn't something I had to build. It was something I had to remember.

Other Voices

Buddhism describes enlightenment not as gaining something, but as realizing what's always been there. Hinduism's *Atman* teaching says your true self is already divine. Sufis sing of union with God as a return to worth. Psychology says self-actualization happens when basic worth is secure. All voices converge: living in worth isn't about becoming something new. It's about remembering what you've always been.

The Drumbeat Truth

Let's engrain it:

- Worthy living is freedom, not arrogance.
- Jeshua modeled worth through fearless, compassionate presence.
- Embodied worth transforms relationships, health, creativity, and spirituality.
- The truth of worth is always here — waiting to be lived.

Stop rehearsing unworthiness. Start rehearsing worth. Don't just practice it privately. Live it publicly. Walk tall. Speak boldly. Rest joyfully. Create freely. Love abundantly. This is not arrogance. This is truth.

Jeshua said, *You are the light of the world."* Light doesn't apologize for shining. It just shines. Living in worth is shining without shame.

That's the truth. That's the freedom. That's the Way.

Chapter 18: The Fear of God

How Fear Became "Holy"

Fear and holiness were never meant to be roommates, yet religion forced them into the same house and told everyone to be grateful. The result? Centuries of people believing that being afraid of God was the highest form of devotion. Instead of Love drawing people into relationships, fear became the engine driving obedience. To understand why this illusion is so powerful – and so destructive – we have to trace how fear got painted with the brush of holiness.

Fear as a Tool of Control

Fear is one of the oldest motivators known to humanity. Leaders, rulers, and empires knew early that people are easier to control when they're afraid. Religion saw this and thought, "Why not use the same playbook?" Instead of soldiers or kings, they used God as the ultimate enforcer. You can resist a tyrant, but who resists the Almighty?

By branding fear as holy, institutions gave themselves leverage. They didn't need armies to make people obey. All they needed was a pulpit, a doctrine, and a vivid description of eternal flames. Fear became a shortcut to compliance.

Twisting Scripture

Much of this illusion came from selective interpretation. The Hebrew Bible often uses "fear of the Lord" as shorthand for awe, reverence, or respect. But translation and preaching gradually shifted that awe into terror. Awe is expansive – it draws you toward God in wonder. Terror is contractive – it makes you shrink back, hide, and obey blindly.

When verses about reverence were twisted into threats, fear became central. Instead of, *Stand in awe of God s vastness,"* people heard, "Be terrified or burn." That mistranslation reshaped centuries of theology.

The Role of Hierarchy

Religious hierarchies had every reason to promote fear. If people were convinced God was terrifying, they'd cling to priests for protection.

Confession, indulgences, sacraments – all became shields against a wrathful deity. The scarier God became, the more powerful the middlemen grew.

It's like a pest-control company releasing extra cockroaches so you'll keep buying their services. Religion amplified fear, then sold relief. "God's furious at you, but luckily we have the exclusive deal on forgiveness!"

Fear and the Medieval Imagination

The Middle Ages turned fear of God into an art form. Cathedrals weren't just designed to inspire awe – they were filled with grotesque gargoyles, fiery murals, and imagery of damnation. Preachers delivered terrifying homilies describing worms crawling through sinners' bodies in hell. People weren't encouraged to Love God. They were scared into submission.

This had real effects. Entire cultures shaped their calendars around rituals designed to appease divine anger. Plagues were interpreted as punishment. Storms, famines, even natural disasters reinforced the idea that God's default posture was wrath.

Jeshua's Rejection of Fear

And yet, when we return to Jeshua, the picture is utterly different. He consistently said, *"Do not be afraid."* Angels in his story said, *"Fear not."* He invited intimacy with God, calling the Divine "Abba" – Father, Papa. That's not the language of terror. That's the language of trust.

Even when confronting injustice, his message wasn't, "Be terrified." It was, " *Wake up. Live free. Love boldly.*" Jeshua rejected the fusion of fear and holiness. He showed that true holiness is Love, not dread.

My Own Encounter with Fear-as-Holy

I grew up with this illusion pressed into my skin. I remember being told that "fear of God is the beginning of wisdom." It wasn't explained as awe – it was literal fear. God was the cosmic principal's office, and I was always in trouble. Every prayer felt like approaching a judge, not a parent.

That fear seeped into everything. I couldn't enjoy joy, because I worried it might be a trap. I couldn't relax in presence, because I thought God was scrutinizing my every thought. Fear wasn't holy. It was suffocating.

The Psychology of Fear-Based Religion

Psychologists note that chronic fear changes the brain. It keeps people in "fight, flight, or freeze" mode. That means constant stress, anxiety, and hypervigilance. Over time, it damages health, relationships, and creativity.

Fear narrows attention. You stop imagining possibilities and focus only on survival. That's exactly what institutions wanted: people too afraid to question, too busy surviving to rebel. Fear disguised as holiness was a brilliant psychological trap.

If Love is a warm fireplace, fear is the smoke alarm that never stops shrieking. At first you listen. After a while, you stop living in the house altogether. That's what fear-based religion did: it drove people away from presence by making God unbearable.

Breaking the Illusion

The good news is this: fear is not holy. Fear shrinks. Love expands. Fear enslaves. Love liberates. Jeshua proved this every time he said, *"Peace be with you."* Every time he lifted someone's chin instead of casting them down. Every time he described God as a banquet host instead of a wrathful judge.

Breaking the illusion requires re-learning awe. Stand under a starry sky, breathe deeply, and feel wonder, not dread. That's holiness. That's what "fear of the Lord" was meant to evoke: not terror, but reverence.

Practices for Unlearning Fear-as-Holy

1. **Reframe Verses.** When you encounter "fear of God" in scripture, replace it with "awe" or "wonder." Notice how the meaning shifts.
2. **Awe Walks.** Take weekly walks with the sole purpose of noticing beauty. Train your heart for reverence, not dread.

3. **Fear Inventory.** List ways fear shaped your spirituality. Ask: "*Was this fear holy, or was it control?*" Cross out the lies.
4. **Meditation on Abba.** In silence, breathe the word "Abba." Feel the intimacy, not the terror.
5. **Replace Punishment Images.** When old fear images arise – hellfire, wrath – replace them with Love images: light, warmth, embrace.

My Turning Point

One turning point came when I stood at the ocean. For years, I'd heard sermons about fearing God's wrath. But as I looked at the vast waves, I felt awe, not terror. The immensity didn't make me shrink. It made me expand. I realized that was the holiness Jeshua spoke of.

Not fear that crushes, but awe that opens.

Other Voices

Mystics across traditions echo this. The Tao Te Ching speaks of aligning with the Way, not fearing it. Rumi writes, *"Let yourself be silently drawn by the strange pull of what you really Love."* The Hebrew psalms describe God's Love enduring forever, not wrath enduring forever. Wisdom traditions know holiness is wonder, not fear.

The Drumbeat Truth

Let's engrain it:

- Fear was twisted into holiness as a tool of control.
- Jeshua rejected fear, teaching intimacy and Love.
- Awe expands. Terror contracts.
- True holiness is not fear. It is wonder, trust, and Love.

Here's another invitation: let go of fear disguised as holiness. Stand in awe, not dread. Trade trembling for trust. Rediscover holiness as beauty, wonder, and Love. Jeshua's Way is not terror of God, but intimacy with God.

That's how fear lost its mask – and how we reclaim the truth that Love, not fear, is holy.

The Psychology of Fear

Religion didn't just stumble onto fear by accident. It tapped into one of the most primal human survival instincts. To dismantle the illusion of "holy fear," we need to look at how fear works in the mind and body, why it feels so convincing, and why it clings so tightly to spirituality.

Fear may masquerade as reverence, but beneath the surface it's just biology, conditioning, and habit.

Fear in the Brain

Fear originates in the amygdala, the almond-shaped part of the brain that detects threats. When it senses danger, it floods the body with stress hormones: adrenaline, cortisol, norepinephrine. Your heart races, muscles tense, pupils dilate. This is great if you're facing a bear. It's terrible if you're facing a confessional booth.

The problem is that the brain doesn't distinguish between physical threats and imagined ones. If you believe hell is real, the amygdala reacts as if flames are licking at your heels. That's why sermons about damnation feel so visceral. The brain can't tell the difference between metaphor and reality. Fear becomes embodied truth.

Conditioning Fear into Faith

Psychologists talk about classical conditioning – Pavlov's dogs salivating when they hear a bell. Religion used similar methods. Pair the thought of God with threats of punishment long enough, and the brain fuses them. God's name alone triggers dread.

For many raised in fear-based religion, this conditioning sticks. Even after leaving church, hearing "God" can still spark anxiety. The amygdala remembers. Fear outlives the sermons.

It's like quitting a job where the boss yelled at you daily. Years later, when someone raises their voice in a meeting, you still tense up. Your body thinks you're back at that desk. Fear of God works the same way – an old boss still yelling in your nervous system.

Fear's Illusion of Safety

Here's the irony: fear feels safe. The brain convinces us that if we stay afraid, we'll avoid danger. Religion exploited this. "If you fear God enough, you won't sin. If you fear hell enough, you'll stay faithful." Fear became a substitute for wisdom, discernment, and Love.

But fear-based safety is a prison. You don't walk into freedom – you pace in circles inside imaginary walls. Fear convinces you you're protected while keeping you trapped.

How Fear Shrinks the Soul

Fear doesn't just keep people from sin. It keeps them from living. Fear narrows imagination. It kills creativity. It silences voices. When people fear punishment for asking questions, they stop asking. When they fear rejection for being authentic, they hide. Fear-based spirituality becomes less about life and more about survival.

That's why Jeshua's words, *"Do not be afraid,"* weren't just platitudes. They were liberation. He knew fear shrinks the soul. Love expands it.

My Own Experience of Fear's Psychology

As a child, I didn't need monsters under the bed. I had hell under the floorboards. Priests painted vivid pictures: eternal fire, gnashing teeth, endless suffering. My amygdala did the rest. Night after night, I lay awake rehearsing prayers, terrified I'd missed a confession detail and was now on God's blacklist.

Even years later, after leaving Catholicism, I'd sometimes wake in the night with a flash of dread: What if they were right? That's the power of fear. It doesn't vanish with logic. It lingers in the nervous system.

My turning point came when I realized fear wasn't God. It was my amygdala in overdrive, conditioned by years of sermons. Presence didn't speak in terror. Presence whispered in peace.

Fear as a Community Bond

Fear also works socially. Shared fear bonds groups. Congregations terrified of hell stick together. Communities built on fear find identity in survival. This reinforces the illusion: "We're the faithful because we're the most afraid."

But fear-bonded communities also exclude ruthlessly. Anyone who questions becomes a threat to the group's safety. Dissenters are shunned, excommunicated, or demonized. Fear polices the boundaries.

Imagine a fire drill where everyone huddles in the corner, shouting at anyone who suggests leaving the building: Don't you dare! Staying here is the only way to survive! "That's how fear-based religion operates — mistaking the cage for safety.

Why Fear Feels Spiritual

Fear masquerades as spirituality because it feels intense. The racing heart, the trembling hands, the overwhelming awe — all of it mimics the physical signs of spiritual encounter. People confuse adrenaline for holiness.

Institutions encouraged this confusion. If you left a sermon shaking, they called it conviction. If you left calm and peaceful, they called it lukewarm. The more terrified you were, the holier you looked. That's not spirituality. That's adrenaline addiction.

Jeshua's Liberation from Fear

Jeshua constantly disrupted fear-based systems. When storms raged, he said, *"Peace, be still."* When disciples panicked, he said, *"Do not fear."* When crowds feared scarcity, he broke bread and fish in abundance. His very presence dissolved fear.

He modeled that spirituality wasn't trembling before a tyrant. It was walking in trust with a loving Father. He shifted the nervous system from fight-or-flight to rest-and-presence. That's why people felt peace around him. He healed more than bodies. He healed psyches.

Practices to Rewire Fear

Breaking fear's grip isn't just about belief. It requires retraining the body and mind.

1. **Breathwork.** When fear rises, slow your breathing. Long exhales tell the nervous system: "*I am safe.*"
2. **Replace Imagery.** If old hellfire images arise, consciously replace them with light, embrace, warmth. Rewire visual associations.
3. **Reframe Conviction.** When you feel dread, ask: *"Is this Love guiding me, or fear controlling me?"* Follow Love.

4. **Embodied Presence.** Walk barefoot on the earth, feel grounded. Fear lives in the head. Worth lives in the body.
5. **Community of Peace.** Surround yourself with people who model calm, not panic. Nervous systems sync. Choose peace over fear.

Other Voices

Psychologists like Brené Brown remind us: *You cannot shame or fear people into change. Love is the only lasting motivator.”* Neuroscientists show how meditation calms the amygdala and strengthens the prefrontal cortex, reducing fear. Mystics across traditions echo Jeshua’s call: do not fear. Rumi writes, *Forget safety. Live where you fear to live.”* The Buddha taught that fear dissolves in mindfulness. Everywhere, wisdom dismantles fear.

The Drumbeat Truth

Let’s engrain it:

- Fear is biological, not holy.
- Religion conditioned fear into faith.
- Fear shrinks; Love expands.
- Jeshua rewired fear into peace.

Stop mistaking fear for faith. Notice how fear lives in your body, how it hijacks your mind. Breathe through it. Rewire it. Return to Love. Fear isn’t God. Fear is the body’s alarm system, misused by institutions.

Holiness is not adrenaline. Holiness is peace.

That’s the psychology of fear – and the beginning of liberation.

Fear and the Image of God

Fear thrives on images. The way you picture God – in your mind, your heart, your imagination – shapes how you relate to the Divine. If God looks like an angry judge, fear makes sense. If God looks like an aloof monarch, fear feels inevitable. If God looks like fire and thunder, trembling feels natural. For centuries, religion distorted the image of God to maintain control, and fear grew from those distortions like weeds in poisoned soil. To break the chains of fear, we must examine and transform the images of God we’ve inherited.

The Angry Judge

One of the most enduring images is God as cosmic judge. Not a fair judge, but a terrifying one — always frowning, always searching for fault. In this image, God doesn't just weigh actions. He weighs motives, thoughts, even subconscious impulses. The verdict is almost always "guilty."

This image breeds fear because you can never win. No matter how much good you do, it's never enough. One wrong thought cancels ten right deeds. Under this image, spirituality becomes survival — scrambling for mercy before the gavel drops.

It's like taking a test where the teacher says, "You already failed, but keep trying anyway. Maybe I'll change my mind." That's how many people experienced God — an exam rigged against them.

The Wrathful Monarch

Another common image is God as king, but not a benevolent one. Instead, the monarch is wrathful, demanding absolute obedience. This God demands tribute, loyalty, and flattery. Step out of line, and punishment follows.

This image mirrors ancient empires. Kings ruled through fear, so religion projected the same onto heaven. The palace became the model for the cosmos. Worship became courtly protocol. Worthiness became tied to obedience. Fear wasn't just expected, it was the primary way of honoring God.

The Distant Clockmaker

In some traditions, God became distant — a clockmaker who wound the universe and stepped back. This image breeds a different kind of fear: abandonment. If God is distant, you're left alone in chaos. Life feels fragile, unsupported. Fear fills the gap where intimacy should be.

This God doesn't thunder commands, but the silence can feel just as terrifying. People pray into the void, unsure if anyone listens. Fear grows from uncertainty.

Jeshua's Radical Image of God

Against all this, Jeshua painted a radically different picture. He called God *Abba* — intimate, affectionate, personal. Not a judge with a ledger, but a parent with open arms. Not a tyrant demanding flattery, but a friend sharing a meal.

His parables revealed this new image:

- **The Prodigal Son.** God isn't the angry judge. God is the father running down the road to embrace.
- **The Banquet.** God isn't the monarch demanding tribute. God is the host inviting everyone, even the poor and excluded.
- **The Sparrows.** God isn't distant. God is attentive to every bird, every hair, every moment.

These images dissolve fear. You can't tremble before Abba. You rest. You can't cower at a banquet. You celebrate. You can't fear being unseen when every sparrow is noticed.

My Own Encounter with Fearful Images

Growing up, the image of God I received was mostly the judge. He was tall, stern, with a permanent scowl. I imagined him flipping through a cosmic notebook, jotting down every mistake. No smile. No warmth. Just constant disappointment.

Even after I left formal religion, that image lingered. Whenever I tried to pray, the judge showed up. No wonder fear clung so tightly. I wasn't afraid of God, I was afraid of the image I'd been given.

My liberation began when I let that image collapse. Slowly, through presence and practice, I encountered God not as judge, but as Love. The scowl faded. The notebook disappeared. In its place was light, warmth, and embrace. Fear lost its anchor.

The Psychology of Images

Psychologists know that mental images shape emotional responses. If you imagine someone smiling at you, your body relaxes. If you imagine them glaring, your body tenses. The same is true with God.

The image you hold changes your nervous system.

Fear-based images trigger the amygdala. Loving images activate the prefrontal cortex, linked to peace and connection. That's why transforming God's image isn't just theological. It's neurological.

The Cultural Mirror

Many fear-based images weren't divine at all. They were cultural projections. Harsh fathers, punishing kings, strict teachers, all projected upward. People assumed God was a bigger version of their earthly authorities. Fear-based parenting became fear-based spirituality. Fear-based rulers became fear-based heavens.

The tragedy is that people confused projection with revelation. They mistook their fears for God's face.

Imagine if dogs designed theology. God would be a giant vacuum cleaner – loud, terrifying, always chasing you. Humans did the same thing: we projected our scariest figures upward and called it holy.

Reimagining God

To break fear, we need new images. Not invented fantasies, but reflections of truth. Jeshua gave us plenty: father, shepherd, vine, light, bread, water. Each image affirms intimacy, care, nourishment, connection.

Reimagining God doesn't shrink God. It expands God beyond fear. When you imagine God smiling instead of frowning, you're not trivializing holiness. You're aligning with Love.

Practices for Transforming the Image of God

1. **Image Inventory.** Write down the images of God you grew up with. Angry judge? Wrathful king? Silent void? Acknowledge them.
2. **Rewrite.** For each image, replace it with one from Jeshua. Judge → Father. Monarch → Banquet Host. Void → Sparrow Keeper.
3. **Visualization.** In meditation, picture God smiling, embracing, laughing. Train your nervous system for Love.
4. **Art Practice.** Draw or paint images of God as light, warmth, embrace. Creativity rewires imagination.
5. **Daily Declaration.** Repeat: *"God is Love, not fear. God is presence, not punishment."*

My Turning Point

One turning point came when I prayed using only Jeshua's word *Abba.* At first, it felt foreign. Then, slowly, the intimacy sank in. Abba wasn't frowning. Abba was smiling. Abba was present. That shift in image dissolved layers of fear. For the first time, prayer felt safe.

Other Voices

Mystics across traditions reimagined God beyond fear. The Upanishads speak of Brahman as bliss. Rumi called God the beLoved, not the judge. Meister Eckhart spoke of God as the ground of being, not the tyrant of heaven. Each mystic peeled back distorted images to reveal Love.

The Drumbeat Truth

Let's engrain it:

- Fear thrives on distorted images of God.
- Angry judges, wrathful kings, and silent voids breed terror.
- Jeshua revealed God as Abba, host, shepherd, friend.
- Transforming your image of God transforms your experience of God.

Examine the God you picture. Is that image Love? Or is it fear in disguise? If it's fear, let it fall. Replace it with Jeshua's images – Abba, banquet, sparrow. Let God's smile replace the scowl.

Fear cannot survive in the presence of Love's true image. That's the way forward – not fearing God, but seeing God as God is: Love.

How Fear Distorts Spirituality

When fear becomes the lens through which people see God, spirituality itself gets twisted. What was meant to be a path of freedom becomes a cage. What was meant to be communion becomes performance. What was meant to be Love becomes obligation. This distortion doesn't just make faith heavier – it flips it upside down. In this section, we'll examine how fear-driven religion warps prayer, worship, morality, community, and even the sense of self.

Fear Turns Prayer into Groveling

Prayer was meant to be conversation – intimacy, honesty, communion. But under fear, prayer becomes groveling. Instead of sharing life with God, people recite lists of failures, hoping not to be punished. Prayer becomes less about presence and more about pleading for survival.

This distortion creates anxiety. Every word feels like a test: Did I say it right? Did I forget a sin? Did I confess with enough sincerity? Instead of opening the heart, fear locks it down.

It's like calling your mom not to chat, but only to apologize for not calling earlier. "Hi Mom, sorry I didn't call yesterday. Or last week. Or in 1994." After a while, it's not a relationship, it's a guilt script. That's what fear turned prayer into.

Fear Makes Worship Performance

Worship was meant to be celebration — joy, music, gratitude, awe. But fear makes it a performance review. People sing not to rejoice, but to prove sincerity. They lift hands not out of Love, but out of dread: If I don't, will God think I'm ungrateful?

The focus shifts from connection to correctness. Did you worship the right way, with the right words, in the right building? Fear sucks the joy out of worship and replaces it with stage fright.

Fear Twists Morality into Avoidance

Morality was meant to be about Love — how we treat ourselves and others. Jeshua summarized it simply: Love God, Love your neighbor. But fear turns morality into avoidance. It's no longer about creating Love. It's about avoiding punishment.

People obsess over rules: Did I eat meat on Friday? Did I pray the rosary correctly? Did I confess every detail? Fear-driven morality becomes about technicalities, not transformation. It produces scrupulosity, not compassion.

Fear Corrupts Community

Community was meant to be belonging. But fear turns it into surveillance. Congregations become watchdogs, monitoring each other's behavior. Love is replaced with suspicion: Who sinned? Who doubted? Who didn't show up to Mass?

Instead of supporting one another, communities built on fear exclude, shame, and punish. People hide their struggles because honesty risks condemnation. Fear-driven community isn't fellowship. It's policing.

It's like joining a book club where no one actually reads the book, but everyone critiques your grammar when you try to share. That's fear- driven fellowship — more correction than connection.

Fear Shrinks Identity

Perhaps the deepest distortion is what fear does to identity. Spirituality was meant to reveal our true self as beLoved children of God. But fear convinces us we're perpetual failures, unworthy servants, eternal sinners. Instead of saying, *"I am light,"* people whisper, "I am filth."

This internalized identity shapes everything. People stop creating, stop risking, stop speaking, because unworthiness feels like the core truth. Fear-based spirituality doesn't reveal the divine image. It buries it.

Jeshua's Critique of Fear-Based Religion

Jeshua confronted these distortions head-on. He criticized public prayers meant to impress. He overturned temple practices that turned worship into transactions. He healed on the Sabbath to show morality wasn't about rigid rules but Love in action. He welcomed outcasts into community. He called people children of God, not worms.

Every confrontation was a pushback against fear's distortions. Jeshua knew fear didn't honor God — it dishonored God by misrepresenting divine Love.

My Own Experience of Distortion

I remember praying as a teenager, but it wasn't conversation. It was terror management. I rattled off prayers like I was reading legal disclaimers, hoping to avoid eternal lawsuit. Worship felt like performance, where God was the critic and I was destined for a bad review.

Morality wasn't about Love, it was about checking boxes. Community wasn't safe, it was suffocating. My very identity felt defined by failure. That wasn't spirituality. That was survival in a fear-based system.

Only when I encountered presence, not as judge but as Love, did the distortions start to unravel. Prayer became breathing. Worship became laughter. Morality became compassion. Community became connection. Identity became beLovedness.

The Psychology of Distortion

Fear changes how the brain processes information. It narrows focus, emphasizing threat detection. Applied to spirituality, this means people focus on rules, punishments, and flaws instead of Love, creativity, and growth. Over time, this creates rigid, anxious faith.

Fear also fuels "groupthink." When communities are built on fear, dissent feels dangerous. People stop thinking critically and conform to avoid punishment. This creates stagnant, brittle spirituality – unable to evolve, unable to breathe.

Practices for Healing Fear's Distortions

1. **Disclosure of Honesty.** Drop scripted apologies. Sit in silence and say what's truly on your heart – gratitude, anger, longing. Practice real conversation.
2. **Playful Worship.** Dance, sing, laugh. Worship not to perform but to celebrate. Let joy replace dread.
3. **Love-Centered Morality.** Ask daily: *"What does Love invite me to do?"* Let that guide actions more than rules.
4. **Safe Community.** Seek relationships where honesty is welcomed, not punished. Build circles of grace, not surveillance.
5. **Identity Declarations.** Declare: *"I am beLoved. I am light. I am enough."* Reclaim worth as identity.

Other Voices

Mystics across traditions saw fear's distortions. The Buddha warned against clinging to rituals without heart. The Hebrew prophets denounced sacrifices offered without justice and mercy. Rumi mocked hollow religion without Love: *I looked for God in temples and churches, but I only found him in my heart."* Everywhere, the pattern is the same: fear corrupts spirituality, Love restores it.

The Drumbeat Truth

Let's engrain it:

- Fear distorts prayer into groveling.
- Fear makes worship performance, morality avoidance, community surveillance.

- Fear buries identity instead of revealing it.
- Jeshua restored spirituality as Love, joy, and freedom.

Examine where fear has distorted your spirituality. Where have you been groveling instead of conversing? Performing instead of celebrating? Avoiding instead of Loving? Policing instead of connecting? Hiding instead of shining?

Let fear fall away. Let Love reframe it all. True spirituality isn't distorted by dread. It is expanded by joy. Jeshua didn't invite us into terror. He invited us into presence. That's the truth – and the freedom – of spirituality without fear.

Practices for Releasing Fear

Fear doesn't dissolve just because we intellectually reject it. Fear lives in the nervous system, in muscle memory, in the grooves of thought worn down by years of repetition. Sermons may stop, but the echoes linger. Releasing fear requires intentional practice – not just thinking differently, but training the body, mind, and spirit into new rhythms of trust and Love. Jeshua didn't just say, *"Do not fear"*; he gave people ways to experience peace in real time. Let's explore how we can do the same.

Why Releasing Fear Requires Practice

Fear is sticky because it feels protective. The nervous system interprets fear as safety: If I stay anxious, maybe I won't get hurt. That's why people cling to fear even after realizing it's destructive. Practice is required because you have to show your body another way of being safe – through Love, peace, and presence.

Think of fear as an overzealous guard dog. It barks at every shadow, convinced it's protecting you. The dog won't stop barking just because you tell it to. It stops barking when it learns through experience that not every shadow is danger. Practice is how we retrain the guard dog of the nervous system.

Jeshua's Embodied Practices

Jeshua didn't just preach concepts. He created experiences that released fear. He touched the untouchable, ate with outcasts, calmed storms, and said, *"Peace, be still."* Each act trained people to replace dread with trust. He invited people into practices of presence: "*Take no thought for tomorrow.*" That wasn't abstract. It was a daily rhythm of letting fear go.

Core Practices for Releasing Fear

Here are concrete, non-repetitive practices for breaking fear's grip.

1. **Breath of Peace.** Fear speeds up breath, making it shallow. Peace slows it down. Practice slow breathing: inhale for 4 counts, exhale for 8. With each exhale, whisper silently, *"I release fear."* Over time, the body learns safety in calmness instead of tension.
2. **Anchoring in Nature.** Fear thrives in enclosed spaces – cathedrals filled with dark paintings, sermons shouted from pulpits. Go outside. Sit under a tree, feel the wind, watch the sky. Notice how nothing in creation trembles before God. Birds sing. Flowers bloom. Nature models fearlessness. Anchor yourself in that rhythm.
3. **Fear Inventory and Release.** Write down specific fears: *Fear of punishment. Fear of failure. Fear of rejection.* Name them honestly. Then, one by one, say aloud: *"This fear is not God. I release it."* Burn or shred the paper as a symbolic act.
4. **Embodied Presence.** Fear lives in posture – hunched shoulders, tight jaws, clenched fists. Practice standing tall, shoulders back, breathing deeply. Move slowly, intentionally, like someone at peace. The body teaches the mind.
5. **Laughter Practice.** Fear hates laughter. Humor disarms anxiety. Make time to laugh daily: watch comedy, tell jokes, laugh at yourself. Jeshua himself used humor (camels through needles, logs in eyes). Laughter is spiritual rebellion against fear.
6. **Love Meditation.** Sit quietly and imagine light filling your body. As you breathe, see fear dissolving into that light. Repeat the affirmation: *"Perfect Love casts out fear."* This isn't positive thinking. It's nervous system retraining.
7. **Acts of Courage.** Fear weakens when faced. Choose small acts of courage daily: speak your truth, try something new,

step outside comfort zones. Each act proves fear isn't master. Over time, the brain rewires toward confidence.

My Own Journey with These Practices

For me, breath was the starting point. When fear rose — memories of hellfire sermons, anxious prayers — I exhaled, slowing my breath. At first, the fear fought back. My chest tightened, as if fear itself resisted leaving. But persistence mattered. Each exhale felt like letting go of centuries of programming.

Another turning point came through humor. I started laughing at the absurdity of some doctrines. Eternal punishment for eating meat on Friday? Really? Humor shrank the monster down to size. Fear thrives when taken seriously. It weakens when mocked.

The Obstacles to Releasing Fear

Fear doesn't leave quietly. It whispers, "If you let me go, you'll be unsafe." At times, releasing fear can feel like betrayal, especially if you were taught fear equals faith. The nervous system may panic when calmness arrives, mistaking peace for danger. Expect resistance.

But each time you persist in practice, the illusion weakens. Fear eventually learns it's no longer welcome.

It's like canceling a gym membership. Fear keeps calling: "Are you sure you want to leave? What if you get out of shape?" You hang up, but they call again. Persistence pays off. Eventually, the calls stop.

Fear works the same way — it nags until it realizes you're serious.

Jeshua's Invitation to Trust

Jeshua said, *Take no thought for tomorrow... Do not be afraid, little flock, for your Father has been pleased to give you the kingdom."* These weren't casual phrases. They were practical invitations to release fear daily. He knew worry wasted life. He knew fear stole presence. His antidote was trust in Love's sufficiency.

The Psychology of Practice

Neuroscience confirms this. Fear circuits weaken when not reinforced. Practices like slow breathing, meditation, and exposure to safe experiences literally shrink the amygdala's overreaction. New neural pathways of calm and trust grow. Over time, the brain learns: Love is safe, not fear.

Other Voices

The Buddha taught meditation as a way to dissolve fear by observing it without judgment. The Stoics practiced "premeditation of evils" – imagining fears to shrink their power. Rumi wrote, *"Move outside the tangle of fear-thinking. Live in silence."* All traditions know: fear doesn't vanish by wishing. It vanishes through practice.

The Drumbeat Truth

Let's engrain it:

- Fear doesn't vanish with ideas. It requires practice.
- Breath, nature, laughter, courage, and Love retrain the nervous system.
- Jeshua modeled daily release of fear through presence and trust.
- Perfect Love doesn't just inspire. It rewires.

Release fear not once, but daily. Breathe it out. Name it. Laugh at it. Set it down. Replace it with Love. Train your body and mind to recognize peace as safety. Over time, fear loses its grip, and Love becomes the natural state.

Fear will try to cling. But persistence breaks it. Jeshua didn't call us to survive in dread. He called us to live in freedom. That freedom begins with practice – daily, embodied, relentless practice.

The Freedom Beyond Fear

Fear is heavy. It hunches the shoulders, tightens the jaw, quickens the breath, and narrows the soul until life becomes about survival instead of living. For centuries, people carried fear as though it were holiness itself. But what happens when that weight finally drops? What does life look like when fear no longer drives spirituality, morality, or identity? This section explores the freedom that emerges when fear dissolves – not as an abstract concept, but as a lived reality.

The Space Fear Once Occupied

Fear takes up space. It fills the mind with "what ifs," the body with tension, and the heart with suspicion. When fear is released, space opens. Suddenly there is room for joy, creativity, and connection. The silence once filled with anxious prayers becomes space for laughter, gratitude, or simply breathing.

This newfound spaciousness can feel strange at first. Some mistake it for emptiness. But give it time, and you discover it's not emptiness. It's openness. It's possibility. It's the canvas for a new way of living.

Living Without the Cosmic Threat

One of the biggest shifts is living without the constant threat of punishment. When hellfire is no longer the background music, every moment feels lighter. You stop second-guessing joy. You stop apologizing for existence. You stop treating God like a probation officer.

Instead, God becomes a companion, a presence, a source of Love. Spirituality stops being about dodging divine bullets and starts being about walking in peace.

It's like when you quit that job where the boss screamed every day. At first, you keep expecting to be yelled at in the grocery store. Then one day, you realize no one's shouting. Freedom feels like that – a sudden silence where there used to be constant fear.

Freedom to Ask Questions

Fear-based faith polices questions. "Don't doubt. Don't ask. Don't think too much." But freedom beyond fear opens space for curiosity. You can ask hard questions about scripture, tradition, even God, without worrying you'll be struck down.

This transforms spirituality into exploration rather than indoctrination. The Bible becomes a conversation, not a cage. Theology becomes a playground, not a prison. Freedom allows wonder to flourish.

Freedom to Be Authentic

Fear teaches people to hide. Don't show weakness. Don't reveal doubts. Don't admit struggles. But freedom beyond fear allows authenticity. You can tell the truth about your life without shame. You can say, "I don't know" without feeling unholy.

Authenticity deepens connection. Relationships no longer orbit around appearances. They become real. Freedom makes honesty possible.

Freedom to Enjoy Life

Fear convinces people that joy is dangerous — that too much laughter, too much beauty, too much pleasure, will anger God. Freedom says the opposite: joy is sacred. Sunsets, meals, hugs, music — these are not distractions from holiness. They *are* holiness.

Life beyond fear tastes better, sounds richer, feels deeper. You stop bracing for punishment and start savoring presence.

Jeshua's Model of Freedom

Jeshua embodied this freedom. He walked through hostile crowds without flinching. He touched "unclean" people without hesitation. He laughed at the absurdity of hypocrisy. He faced death without terror, praying not with dread but with trust: *"Into your hands I commit my spirit."*

His freedom didn't mean recklessness. It meant living in Love so deeply that fear had no room. He modeled a life where presence outweighed threats, where intimacy outweighed judgment.

My Own Experience of Freedom

When fear first began to fade in my own life, it was unsettling. I was so used to anxiety being the default that calmness felt suspicious. Shouldn't I be worried? Isn't guilt supposed to keep me safe?

But over time, I realized the calm wasn't danger. It was life. Freedom meant I could sit in silence without imagining judgment. I could enjoy laughter without feeling guilty. I could live without apologizing for existing.

The biggest shift came in prayer. It stopped being about pleading for forgiveness and started being about presence. Sometimes I just sat quietly, breathing. And for the first time, that was enough.

The Social Impact of Freedom

Freedom beyond fear doesn't just transform the individual. It changes communities. Fear-driven groups exclude, police, and shame. Fear- free groups welcome, support, and nurture.

Imagine communities where no one fears rejection for questions, orientation, or past mistakes. Imagine spaces where people gather not out of obligation, but out of joy. That's the social fruit of freedom.

The Creativity of Freedom

Fear stifles creativity. People afraid of being "wrong" won't risk writing, painting, inventing, or speaking. But freedom unleashes expression.

Without the threat of judgment, people create boldly.

This isn't just about art. It's about creating lives – new businesses, new families, new ways of living. Freedom fuels innovation. Fear only repeats the past.

It's like karaoke night. Fear makes you sit quietly, convinced you'll embarrass yourself. Freedom grabs the mic, sings badly, and has the best night of your life. That's the difference.

Freedom in the Body

The body notices freedom. Shoulders drop. Breathing deepens. Sleep improves. The constant adrenaline drip of fear stops, and the nervous system learns rest. People often look physically younger after leaving fear-based systems. The body wears peace differently than it wears fear.

Practices for Living Freedom

1. **Daily Gratitude.** Write down moments of joy, big or small. Gratitude teaches the brain to notice abundance instead of threat.
2. **Honesty Check.** Each day, speak one truth aloud – even if only to yourself. Practice authenticity as freedom.
3. **Joy Rituals.** Schedule joy intentionally: play, dance, cook, laugh. Treat joy as sacred practice.
4. **Curiosity Walks.** Take walks with the goal of asking questions: *Why is the sky that color? What bird is singing?* Curiosity feeds freedom.

5. **Breath of Trust.** Begin each morning with a slow inhale, saying silently, *"I am safe."* Exhale: *"I am free."*

Other Voices

The Buddha described nirvana as liberation from fear and craving. Rumi wrote, *Try to accept the changing seasons of your heart, even if they bring winter. Be free, like a child."* The apostle John declared, *Perfect Love casts out fear."* Across traditions, the message converges: true spirituality is freedom, not fear.

The Drumbeat Truth

Let's engrain it:

- Fear takes up space. Freedom opens it.
- Life without threat allows joy, authenticity, creativity, and rest.
- Jeshua modeled fearless presence in every act.
- Freedom beyond fear is not emptiness. It is fullness.

Step into the space fear once occupied. Fill it with joy, curiosity, laughter, and Love. Let your shoulders drop, your breath deepen, your questions rise. Freedom is not a gift for the afterlife. It's the natural state when fear falls.

Jeshua didn't invite us to tremble forever. He invited us to live free – fully, fearlessly, joyfully. That is the freedom beyond fear.

Living Love Instead of Fear

Fear is not neutral. It shapes decisions, distorts relationships, and shrinks souls. But once fear is exposed as illusion and released, something must replace it. The absence of fear is not enough. Life demands a new engine, a new posture. Jeshua made it clear what that posture should be: Love. Love isn't just the antidote to fear. It is the true foundation of spirituality, identity, and community. This section explores what it looks like to live Love instead of fear – not as a theory, but as a daily practice and embodied reality.

Love as the Center of Spirituality

Fear-based spirituality revolves around avoiding punishment. Love- based spirituality revolves around connection. When Love is the center, prayer becomes conversation, not pleading.

Reflection becomes gratitude, not guilt. Presence becomes joy, not terror.

This doesn't mean Love is always sentimental. Real Love can be fierce, challenging, and boundary-setting. But it always seeks life, never diminishment. Love restores. Fear corrodes.

The Courage of Love

People assume fear motivates obedience better than Love. But Love requires more courage. Fear keeps you safe by keeping you small. Love asks you to risk vulnerability, compassion, forgiveness. Love takes more courage than fear ever will.

Jeshua embodied this courage. He touched lepers, befriended outcasts, confronted authorities – not out of dread, but out of Love. Fear would have kept him silent. Love propelled him forward.

Fear is like wearing bubble wrap everywhere you go. You'll avoid scratches, but you'll also never dance properly. Love rips the bubble wrap off and says, "Go live."

Love in Relationships

Fear twists relationships into contracts: "If I obey, you won't punish me." Love transforms them into communion: *I choose to give, to receive, to grow with you."*

In friendships, Love creates honesty. In families, it creates safety. In partnerships, it creates intimacy. Fear-driven relationships demand conformity. Love-driven relationships invite authenticity.

When people live from Love, forgiveness flows more freely. Patience deepens. Joy multiplies. Fear divides. Love unites.

Love in Community

Communities built on fear enforce rules, exclude doubters, and police behavior. Communities built on Love welcome questions, embrace diversity, and nurture growth.

Imagine a community where no one fears rejection for asking hard questions, where past mistakes don't bar you from belonging, where differences are celebrated instead of punished. That's not fantasy.

That's Love-centered community. Jeshua modeled it by eating with tax collectors, welcoming children, and including women in his circle.

Love in Action

Living Love instead of fear isn't just emotional. It's practical. It shows up in daily choices:

- Speaking kindness instead of criticism.
- Helping neighbors instead of hoarding.
- Listening before judging.
- Offering compassion to yourself, not just others.

Fear hoards, hides, and harms. Love shares, reveals, and heals.

My Own Shift to Love

For years, fear drove me. Every choice, every decision, every thought was shadowed by dread. Even leaving religion didn't erase it. Fear was muscle memory.

The shift began when I chose Love in small ways. Instead of asking, "What if I fail?" I asked, *"What if I Love?"* Instead of worrying about punishment, I focused on compassion – for myself and for others.

Slowly, life changed. Conversations deepened. Creativity blossomed. Joy returned. Fear had kept me alive, but Love taught me how to live.

The Daily Practices of Love

Living Love requires intention. Fear is automatic. Love is chosen. Here are practical rhythms for embodying Love:

1. **Sitting in Love.** Sit quietly and imagine light flowing through you, expanding outward. Repeat: "*I am Love. I give Love. I receive Love.*"
2. **Acts of Kindness.** Each day, do one uncalculated act of Love – without expectation of return. It rewires motives away from fear.
3. **Compassionate Self-Talk.** When you fail, replace shame with kindness: *"I'm learning. I'm growing. I still deserve Love."*

4. **Active Listening.** In conversations, listen not to respond, but to understand. Fear listens defensively. Love listens openly.
5. **Boundaries as Love.** Set boundaries not from fear of being hurt, but from Love of self and others. Boundaries protect relationships from resentment.

Love and Justice

Love doesn't mean passivity. Jeshua's Love confronted injustice. He turned over tables in the temple not out of rage, but out of Love for truth and people being exploited. Love sometimes disrupts. Love sometimes says no. But even then, Love heals. Fear punishes.

This is key: justice motivated by fear creates cycles of revenge. Justice motivated by Love restores dignity. Living Love instead of fear means even confrontation becomes life-giving.

Imagine if traffic cops operated on Love instead of fear. Instead of tickets, they'd hand you coffee and say, "Drive safe, friend." Okay, maybe the roads would be chaos – but spiritually, Love really does create more lasting change than punishment ever could.

The Freedom of Love

Living in Love feels expansive. The nervous system relaxes. The mind grows curious. The heart opens. Instead of scanning for threats, you start scanning for opportunities to connect. Life stops being about avoiding sin and starts being about creating good.

Freedom beyond fear is not just absence of dread. It is the active presence of Love guiding every step.

Other Voices

The apostle Paul wrote, *The greatest of these is Love."* The Buddha taught compassion as the heart of awakening. Rumi wrote, *Let yourself be silently drawn by the stronger pull of what you really Love."* Across traditions, Love rises as the true center. Fear is always a distortion.

The Drumbeat Truth

Let's engrain it:

- Fear divides. Love unites.

- Fear punishes. Love restores.
- Fear hides. Love reveals.
- Jeshua lived Love as the replacement for fear.

Don't just release fear. Replace it. Live Love instead. Let every breath, every choice, every word be rooted in Love. Love doesn't just cast out fear. It fills the space fear once occupied with joy, connection, and freedom.

Fear shrinks life. Love expands it. Jeshua's Way is not trembling under judgment. It is walking boldly in Love. That's the true freedom. That's the new engine. That's the life waiting beyond fear.

Chapter 19: The Trap of Guilt and Shame

If fear is the cage, then guilt is the chain that keeps the door locked. Fear may terrify, but guilt personalizes the terror. It whispers, "This is your fault. You deserve this." Shame doubles down and says, "Not only did you do wrong – you are wrong." Together, guilt and shame hook the soul, dragging it back even when the mind knows better. To understand how to escape, we first need to see how guilt latches on, why it feels convincing, and how it's been weaponized.

The Nature of Guilt

Guilt isn't always bad. At its purest, guilt is a signal – the conscience alerting us when we've harmed someone. Healthy guilt invites repair: apologize, make amends, grow. But in religion, guilt was weaponized. It became less about repair and more about control.

Instead of signaling a specific wrong, guilt became a constant background hum. You didn't pray enough. You weren't devout enough. You're selfish. You're sinful. You're unworthy. It wasn't tied to actions anymore – it became identity. That's when guilt stopped being the guide and started being the trap.

How Guilt Hooks the Soul

Guilt hooks the soul through repetition and exaggeration. A single mistake gets inflated into an eternal flaw. The hook sinks deeper every time guilt is reinforced by ritual: confessions, penances, acts of contrition. Soon the guilt isn't about one act. It's about existing.

Imagine getting a parking ticket, paying the fine, and then the city mails you every week for the rest of your life: "Just a reminder: you once parked in a loading zone." That's how guilt works in religion – the ticket never gets cleared.

Shame: Guilt's Ugly Twin

If guilt says, "You did something bad," shame says, "You are something bad." Shame fuses actions to identity. Instead of guilt for lying, shame convinces you: "I'm a liar. That's who I am."

This is the most insidious hook because it warps self-image. Shame makes people believe they're fundamentally broken, which makes them dependent on external authority to feel temporarily clean. It's the perfect control mechanism: endless supply of broken people needing endless rituals to cope.

Childhood Conditioning

The hook often sets in during childhood. A child is scolded for a small mistake – dropping a hymnal, missing a prayer, asking a forbidden question. Instead of correction, they're flooded with shame. That shame becomes memory, memory becomes belief, and belief becomes identity. By adulthood, they no longer question guilt. It feels like part of their soul.

Jeshua's Response to Guilt

Jeshua saw guilt's trap and cut the line. When he met the woman accused of adultery, guilt and shame were crushing her under public scorn. He didn't add to the weight. He scattered the accusers and said, *"Neither do I condemn you."* In one sentence, he broke the hook.

When Peter denied him three times, guilt crushed Peter. Jeshua didn't shame him. Instead, he restored him: *"Feed my sheep."* Worthiness restored, mission renewed. Jeshua knew guilt could cripple a soul, so he replaced it with Love and responsibility.

My Own Experience of Guilt's Hook

For me, guilt was like background noise. No matter what I did, I carried the sense that it wasn't enough. If I prayed, I wondered if I prayed correctly. If I laughed, I felt guilty for not being serious. If I rested, I felt guilty for not working. Guilt wasn't about specific actions – it was about existing.

Even after I left the church, the hook remained. I could be in a moment of joy, then suddenly feel the tug: "You don't deserve this." It took years of presence, humor, and practice to start cutting those hooks.

The Psychology of Guilt and Shame

Psychologists note that guilt and shame activate the same neural circuits as physical pain. That's why they feel so heavy – the brain processes them as real injury. Chronic shame even changes posture:

hunched shoulders, lowered gaze, tight chest. The body carries the hook as much as the mind does.

Guilt also fuels anxiety. When you believe you're perpetually wrong, you live in constant vigilance. Shame fuels depression. When you believe you *are* wrong, you sink into hopelessness. The trap is both psychological and physical.

If guilt and shame were a business, they'd be a subscription service. You pay once, but they keep charging your card every month forever. And no matter how many times you call customer service, they say, "Sorry, no refunds." That's how the trap works.

Practices for Noticing the Hook

The first step in escaping guilt's trap is noticing the hook.

1. **Name the Voice.** When guilt rises, pause and ask: *"Is this about a real harm I caused, or is this background guilt?"* Name it.
2. **Check for Exaggeration.** Guilt hooks often exaggerate: "You *always* fail. You're *never* enough." Spot the distortion.
3. **Separate Action from Identity.** Say: *"I made a mistake, but I am not a mistake."*
4. **Return to Presence.** Guilt thrives in memory and imagination. Presence reminds you: here and now, you are whole.
5. **Counter with Love.** Repeat Jeshua's words: *"Neither do I condemn you."* Let that break the hook.

Other Voices

The apostle Paul wrote, *There is now no condemnation for those who are in Christ."* The Buddha taught release from suffering through awareness, not shame. Rumi wrote, *Don t get lost in your guilt. You are the soul s light, not its dust."* Across traditions, guilt is seen as something to learn from briefly, not to live inside forever.

The Drumbeat Truth

Let's engrain it:

- Healthy guilt is specific and leads to repair.
- Religious guilt is constant and leads to bondage.
- Shame fuses identity to mistakes, trapping the soul.

- Jeshua broke guilt's hook with compassion and restoration.

So notice the hook of guilt. Ask whether it's calling you to repair or simply chaining you to shame. If it's the latter, cut the line. Hear Jeshua's words: *"Neither do I condemn you."* Guilt is not God. Shame is not truth. You are not trapped. You are free.

Shame as Identity Theft

If guilt whispers, "You did wrong," then shame bellows, "You are wrong." That's the sleight of hand – shame doesn't just accuse your actions, it rewrites your identity. It convinces people they are fundamentally broken, unworthy, irredeemable. In this way, shame is a kind of identity theft. It steals the truth of who you are – beLoved, luminous, creative – and replaces it with a false self-defined by failure and sin. This theft is subtle but devastating, leaving people to live lives that are smaller, dimmer, and more afraid than they were ever meant to be.

How Shame Moves from Act to Identity

The journey from guilt to shame often starts small. A child lies. Instead of hearing, "That was wrong," they hear, "You're a liar." The act fuses with identity. A teenager struggles with desire. Instead of hearing, "That's natural," they hear, "You're dirty." The feeling fuses with identity. A doubter raises questions. Instead of, "That's healthy curiosity," they hear, "You're faithless." The wonder fuses with identity.

Over time, the brain no longer separates behavior from self. Shame colonizes the heart. Instead of seeing themselves as souls capable of growth, people see themselves as permanent defects.

The Religious Amplifier

Religion supercharged this process by institutionalizing shame. Sin wasn't just what you did; it was who you were. From original sin to constant confession, the message was clear: "Your identity is stained." The sacraments became less about joy and more about temporary relief from shame's poison.

Imagine a car wash that tells you, "By the way, your car is permanently filthy. But if you keep coming back every week, we'll spray a little perfume on it." That's how religion treated shame – not cured, just perfumed.

Shame in the Body

Shame isn't abstract. It settles in the body. Shoulders hunch. Eyes lower. Voice trembles. The body internalizes the message: "I am not worthy to take up space." Studies show shame activates pain centers in the brain. People literally feel crushed. Over time, chronic shame leads to depression, anxiety, even physical illness.

This is why shame feels like identity – because it doesn't just live in the mind. It lives in the muscles, the breath, the heartbeat. It becomes embodied.

Shame as Silence

Shame also silences. People afraid of being "exposed" hide parts of themselves. They don't share struggles, desires, doubts. They edit themselves constantly. Whole communities can be full of smiling faces while hearts are suffocating in silence.

Shame convinces people: "If you really knew me, you wouldn't Love me." So they withdraw, performing a false self while burying the real one. This is identity theft at its cruelest – not only robbing who you are, but locking that true self away in hiding.

Jeshua's Confrontation with Shame

Jeshua's ministry constantly dismantled shame. He restored people not just physically but socially and personally.

- The woman with the flow of blood was shamed into hiding. Jeshua publicly affirmed her, saying, "*Daughter, your faith has healed you.*" He gave her a new identity.
- Zacchaeus, despised as a cheat, climbed a tree in shame. Jeshua called him by name, dined at his house, and reframed him as a son of Abraham.
- Peter, crushed by the shame of betrayal, was recommissioned: "*Feed my sheep.*" The shameful identity of coward was replaced with shepherd.

Each act restored dignity. Jeshua knew shame was the deeper wound. Healing required restoring identity, not just removing guilt.

My Own Experience of Shame's Theft

For years, shame shaped my identity. I wasn't just someone who made mistakes. I was told I *was* a mistake. That subtle difference dug deep. Even moments of success were overshadowed: If they really knew me, they'd see the fraud."

Shame made me hide my questions, my doubts, my joy. It made me smaller than I was meant to be. I lived as a shadow version of myself – edited, restrained, constantly performing.

My breakthrough came when I realized shame wasn't telling the truth. It was an impostor wearing my name. My real identity wasn't brokenness. My real identity was beLovedness.

Psychology of Shame

Psychologists distinguish guilt from shame: guilt says, *"I did something bad,"* while shame says, *"I* am *bad."* Brené Brown calls shame "*the intensely painful feeling that we are unworthy of Love and belonging.*"

Shame thrives in secrecy. It convinces people not to speak, which allows it to grow unchecked. But when shame is named out loud in safe spaces, it withers. This is why confession in its healthiest form can be powerful, not because a priest absolves you, but because speaking shame breaks its silence.

If guilt and shame were tech companies, guilt would be the annoying popup ad: "You made a mistake!" Shame would be the hacker that steals your password and locks you out of your own account. That's identity theft in the truest sense.

Practices for Reclaiming Identity

Reversing shame's theft requires reclaiming identity intentionally.

1. **Declare Your True Name.** Each morning, say: "*I am beLoved. I am whole. I am enough.*"
2. **Separate Action from Identity.** Write a list: "Things I've done" vs. "Who I am." Notice the difference.
3. **Body Reclamation.** Stand tall, shoulders back, deep breath. Let your body embody worth.
4. **Share in Safe Circles.** Speak your shame aloud with trusted people. Shame withers in the light.
5. **Creative Expression.** Create art, write, or sing authentically. Each act reclaims the self that shame tried to silence.

My Turning Point Practice

One turning point came when I stood before a mirror and simply said: *You are not your mistakes. You are not your shame. You are beLoved."* At first, I felt ridiculous. But slowly, I began to see the difference between the impostor shame and the real me. That practice became a daily declaration – reclaiming identity one word at a time.

Other Voices

The Upanishads declare, *You are That"*—pointing to divine identity. Rumi wrote, *Don t get lost in your guilt. You are the soul s light."* The mystic Julian of Norwich proclaimed, *We are clothed in God s goodness."* Across traditions, identity is affirmed as divine, luminous, beLoved. Shame is never the final word.

The Drumbeat Truth

Let's engrain it:

- Shame isn't about what you did. It's about who you think you are.
- Shame fuses action to identity, stealing your true self.
- Jeshua restored dignity by reframing people's identity.
- Your real identity is not brokenness. It is beLovedness.

Notice where shame has stolen your identity. Where have you believed the impostor voice that says, "You are wrong"? Call it what it is: theft. Reclaim your name. Reclaim your light. Reclaim your beLovedness.

Shame may shout, but it's a fraud. Your true self is deeper, brighter, and freer than shame will ever admit. Jeshua knew it. The mystics knew it. And deep down, you know it too.

The Inherited Burden of Guilt

Not all guilt is personal. Some of it comes handed down, generation to generation, like a family heirloom nobody asked for. You don't just wake up feeling guilty because of something you did – you wake up guilty because of who you are, where you come from, or what your ancestors supposedly failed at. This is the inherited burden of guilt: a kind of spiritual and cultural hand-me-down that weighs just as heavy as personal mistakes. Religion perfected the art of handing out this burden. Families reinforced it. Communities codified it. To move forward, we have to name this inherited weight and learn how to set it down.

The Doctrine of Original Sin

The clearest religious example is original sin. From birth, you were told: "You are guilty. Not because of what you did, but because of what Adam and Eve did." That's inherited guilt at its core. You enter the world already condemned, with no chance to prove yourself innocent.

This doctrine ensured people needed religion from day one. Baptism wasn't a celebration of life; it was a ritual to scrub away inherited guilt. It's like being fined for a car accident before you're old enough to drive. You're not guilty for your choices – you're guilty for existing.

Cultural Transmission of Guilt

Inheritance isn't only theological. Families pass down guilt like genetic traits. Parents burden children with the weight of their own regrets: "Don't repeat my mistakes." Communities hand down collective shame: "Our people are sinful, broken, undeserving."

Generational trauma also works this way. A grandparent's unprocessed shame becomes the emotional climate of a family. A child grows up in guilt without ever committing the supposed offenses. It's emotional inheritance, stamped into identity before they even have words for it.

Imagine inheriting your grandmother's ugly couch. Not only are you stuck with it, but every time you sit on it, you're reminded you should feel guilty for not loving it. That's inherited guilt – a family heirloom no one wants, but everyone feels obligated to keep.

The Burden of Collective Guilt

Religions also assign guilt collectively. Entire groups are branded guilty – of heresy, unbelief, sinfulness. Women, for instance, carried the inherited guilt of Eve: blamed for temptation, seen as naturally suspect. Communities of "outsiders" were branded as guilty simply for being different.

This collective guilt becomes identity. People don't just feel guilty about what they've done. They feel guilty for what they represent. That's not just unfair. It's spiritually violent.

Jeshua's Rejection of Inherited Guilt

Jeshua told parables that emphasized personal responsibility over inherited shame. The prodigal son wasn't trapped by his father's mistakes. He returned freely and was embraced. Jeshua modeled a God who doesn't keep ancestral ledgers. Each life is fresh.

My Own Experience with Inherited Guilt

I didn't just feel guilty for my own mistakes. I carried the Catholic guilt of generations. Family members whispered about being "fallen." Traditions emphasized being perpetually unworthy. Even before I made choices, guilt was in the air I breathed.

It showed up in subtle ways. If I felt joy, I wondered, "Am I dishonoring my family's sacrifices?" If I questioned religion, I thought, "Am I betraying generations of faith?" Guilt wasn't about me. It was about a web of inherited expectations.

Breaking free required realizing: I am not the custodian of ancestral guilt. My life is my own. The past may explain me, but it does not define me.

Psychology of Inherited Guilt

Psychologists studying generational trauma confirm that guilt and shame can be passed down. Children of traumatized parents often carry anxiety, guilt, or self-blame without knowing why. The nervous system inherits patterns, just like eye color or height.

This is why inherited guilt feels so real — because it's embodied, not just taught. Families may never say, "You are guilty," but their silence, fear, or shame communicates it anyway.

If guilt were an app, inherited guilt would come pre-installed on every device. You don't remember downloading it, but it's there, draining the battery. Freedom means finally pressing "uninstall."

Practices for Breaking Inherited Guilt

Escaping inherited guilt requires both awareness and ritual release.

1. **Name the Inheritance.** Write down the guilt you've inherited: original sin, family shame, cultural labels. See them clearly.
2. **Separate Stories.** Say aloud: *"That was their story. This is mine."*
3. **Create a Release Ritual.** Burn, bury, or tear up papers listing inherited guilt. Symbolic acts help the body process release.
4. **Ancestral Compassion.** Instead of resenting ancestors, offer compassion: *"They carried guilt. I choose to end the cycle."*
5. **Daily Declaration.** Repeat: "*I am not guilty for the past. I live fresh today.*"

Other Voices

Mystics across traditions rejected inherited guilt. The prophet Ezekiel declared, *The son shall not bear the guilt of the father."* The Buddha taught liberation from karmic cycles through awareness, not inherited shame. Rumi wrote, *Don t carry your grandfather s guilt. Carry his Love."* Wisdom always separates identity from inherited burden.

The Drumbeat Truth

Let's engrain it:

- Inherited guilt is real but not rightful.
- Religion and families often pass down guilt as identity.
- Jeshua broke the chain, teaching fresh freedom for each soul.
- The past explains you, but it doesn't own you.

Examine the guilt you carry that isn't yours. Notice where you feel shame for ancestors' choices, cultural labels, or doctrines you never agreed to. Name them. Release them. You are not Adam. You are not Eve. You are not your family's regret. You are not your community's scapegoat.

You are yourself—beLoved, free, whole. Inherited guilt is theft. Reclaim your life.

The Posture of Shame

Shame announces itself in posture. Shoulders slump forward. Heads bow. Eyes avoid contact. The chest caves in as if trying to protect the heart from exposure. It's the universal posture of someone trying to shrink, to be unseen.

This posture isn't chosen consciously. It develops over years of feeling unworthy. A child scolded harshly learns to lower their gaze. An adult in a fear-based church learns to bow, not just in ritual, but in daily stance. The body learns: "Stay small. Don't be noticed. Don't take up space."

Over time, this posture becomes habitual. Even in neutral situations, shame shapes the body into invisibility.

Breath Under Shame

Breath reveals shame too. Instead of deep, full breaths, people living in shame breathe shallowly. The diaphragm tightens, the chest feels constricted. It's as if the body is afraid to fully inhale, afraid to fully exist.

This creates chronic stress. Shallow breathing keeps the nervous system in fight-or-flight mode. Even when life is calm, the body acts like it's under threat. Shame literally robs people of oxygen, leaving them constantly half-alive.

Shame and Health

Shame has long-term health effects. Studies show it correlates with higher rates of depression, anxiety, heart disease, and immune dysfunction. The constant stress hormones released by shame weaken the body's defenses.

Digestive issues are common, as the gut — sometimes called the "second brain" — is highly sensitive to emotional states. Shame twists the stomach, knots the intestines, creates ulcers. The phrase "gut-wrenching" isn't metaphor. It's biology.

Sleep also suffers. People steeped in shame replay mistakes in their minds at night, tossing in restless guilt. The body never gets true rest.

If shame were a houseguest, it would be the kind who eats your food, breaks your furniture, and then blames you for the mess. "Your fault I tracked mud on the carpet. Better clean it up." Meanwhile, you're the one losing sleep and health. That's shame in the body — an intruder living rent-free.

Jeshua and the Body

Jeshua's healings often addressed shame in the body. Lepers weren't just physically ill. Their posture, breath, and movements carried years of shame from being excluded. Jeshua touched them, restoring not only health but dignity.

The bent-over woman in Luke 13 is another striking example. She was physically stooped for eighteen years. Jeshua laid hands on her, and she stood tall. The healing wasn't just spinal. It was symbolic: shame had bent her over, and Love made her stand upright again.

Jeshua literally restored posture — a physical antidote to shame.

My Own Experience of Shame in the Body

I carried shame in my shoulders. Decades of Catholic guilt sat like weights on them. Even when I wasn't thinking about shame, my body carried it. Hunched posture, tense neck, shallow breath — shame lived in me physically.

The breakthrough came through noticing. One day, I realized I wasn't breathing deeply. My chest was tight, my shoulders forward. I consciously inhaled fully, pulled my shoulders back, lifted my chin. It felt foreign, almost rebellious. But it also felt liberating. For the first time, I realized I didn't just have to think differently. I had to *stand* differently.

Psychology and Neuroscience of Shame in the Body

Psychologists confirm shame is embodied. When people recall shameful experiences, brain scans show activity in areas connected to pain perception. The body literally relives the wound. Muscles tense, heart rate rises, breathing quickens. Shame isn't remembered. It's re-experienced.

Neuroscience also shows shame interrupts the body's natural regulation. Instead of calming after stress, the body stays stuck. Chronic shame means chronic dysregulation — always half-alert, never fully at rest.

Practices for Releasing Shame in the Body

Breaking shame requires that the body must be retrained.

5. **Posture Reset.** Several times daily, pause. Roll shoulders back, lift chest, meet the world with open eyes. Tell your body: *"I am allowed to take up space."*
6. **Deep Breathing.** Practice slow, full breaths into the belly. Exhale longer than you inhale. Teach the body safety.
7. **Movement Practice.** Dance, stretch, walk with exaggerated strides. Show the body it can move freely, not shrink.
8. **Grounding Exercises.** Stand barefoot on the earth. Feel your weight supported. Shame makes people float in anxiety. Grounding roots them.
9. **Touch Healing.** Place a hand gently on your heart or stomach. Offer compassion physically. Say aloud: *"You are safe here."*

My Turning Point Practice

One turning point came during laughter. Yes, laughter – where you laugh deliberately until it becomes real. At first, it felt absurd. But as I laughed, my body released tension I didn't know I was holding. Shame, which thrives in tight muscles and silence, dissolved in laughter and movement. My posture lifted, my breath deepened. I realized healing shame wasn't just in the mind. It was in the body's release.

Other Voices

Somatic therapists emphasize that trauma and shame live in the body. The Buddha taught mindfulness of the body as a path to freedom.

Rumi wrote, *Try to accept the changing seasons of your body. Even winter is a preparation for spring."*Jeshua's healings confirm the same: liberation is physical as well as spiritual.

If shame were a fashion designer, it would specialize in heavy coats in July. Always uncomfortable, always unnecessary. Healing means throwing off the coat and feeling the sun again.

The Drumbeat Truth

Let's engrain it:

- Shame isn't only mental. It imprints in posture, breath, and health.
- Jeshua's healings restored dignity physically.

- Releasing shame requires body practices: breath, posture, movement, grounding, laughter.
- Freedom is not only in the mind. It is in how you stand, breathe, and live.

Notice shame in your body. Pay attention to posture, breath, tension. Where is shame squatting in your muscles? Then begin releasing it — stand tall, breathe deeply, laugh freely, ground yourself. Don't just think freedom. Embody it.

Your body was never meant to carry shame forever. It was meant to move, breathe, and shine. Jeshua didn't just heal spirits. He healed bodies — because true freedom is holistic. Release shame not only in thought, but in every breath and every stride.

Guilt as a Tool of Control

Guilt is supposed to be an inner compass, a nudge that tells us when we've harmed someone and need to make amends. But in the hands of institutions, guilt became something darker — not guidance, but governance. Religious systems, political movements, even families have long known that if you can make people feel guilty, you can control them. Guilt became less about Love and repair and more about power and obedience. In this section, we'll explore how guilt was turned into a tool of control, why it's so effective, and how to dismantle its grip.

Why Guilt Works as Control

Fear can control people, but it tires them out. You can only be terrified for so long before you shut down. Guilt, however, is sustainable. It renews itself from the inside. Once installed, people carry it around and police themselves. Leaders don't need to hover. The guilty conscience does the work.

That's the brilliance — and cruelty — of guilt as control. It creates a population that regulates itself, always second-guessing, always apologizing, always wondering if they've done enough.

It's like installing spyware on a computer. The program runs quietly in the background, slowing everything down, while the owner has no idea why their machine feels so heavy. That's guilt in the soul.

Religious Exploitation of Guilt

Religion perfected this tactic. Sermons hammered the message: "You are sinful. You are unworthy. You need us to mediate forgiveness." The more guilty people felt, the more dependent they became on the church.

Confession booths institutionalized guilt. Parishioners lined up, not just to release burdens, but to reattach them weekly. Indulgences turned guilt into currency: pay money, lessen guilt. Every ritual, every tithe, every act of penance reinforced dependence.

The genius was that guilt was never fully resolved. The system ensured you always left with enough shame to keep you coming back.

Political and Social Uses of Guilt

Control through guilt isn't limited to religion. Governments and movements have used guilt as propaganda. Citizens are told they're guilty of not sacrificing enough, not working hard enough, not supporting the right leaders.

Families too use guilt for control. Parents say, "After all I've done for you..." Siblings say, "If you loved me, you would..." Entire cultures thrive on guilt-tripping as a way of keeping people in line.

The mechanism is the same everywhere: convince someone they owe more than they can ever repay, and you'll control them forever.

Jeshua's Opposition to Guilt as Control

Jeshua consistently undermined guilt-based control. He healed on the Sabbath, breaking rules used to guilt people into obedience. He told parables where those shamed by society were welcomed into God's kingdom. He challenged religious leaders who laid "heavy burdens" on others without lifting a finger to help.

Instead of layering guilt, he released it. *Your sins are forgiven." "Neither do I condemn you."* Jeshua cut through guilt not to excuse harm, but to end its use as a tool of oppression.

My Own Experience of Guilt as Control

In my upbringing, guilt was constant currency. Every decision was framed as disappointing God, the church, or my family. Skipping Mass wasn't just missing a service — it was betrayal. Doubting a doctrine wasn't just curiosity — it was rebellion. I realized later that the guilt wasn't meant to guide me. It was meant to bind me. As long as I carried it, I was easy to manipulate.

The turning point came when I saw guilt not as my conscience, but as conditioning. Once I separated the two, I began to discern: Is this guilt calling me to Love, or is it calling me to obedience? Only the first is true conscience.

Psychology of Guilt as Control

Psychologists call this "introjected guilt" — guilt implanted from outside, not arising from authentic values. Introjected guilt keeps people behaving, but at the cost of autonomy and joy.

Over time, people confuse external control with internal conscience. They can't tell the difference between genuine regret for harming someone and manufactured guilt for breaking arbitrary rules. This confusion is what keeps control systems running smoothly.

If guilt as control were a product, the slogan would be: "Control your subjects without lifting a finger — just install guilt!" Lifetime guarantee, no refunds, passed down through generations.

Practices for Dismantling Guilt-Based Control

Breaking free requires unmasking guilt's source and retraining the conscience.

1. **Discern the Source.** Ask: "*Is this guilt arising from Love, or from external control?"* True guilt invites repair. False guilt demands compliance.
2. **Redefine Sin.** Let sin mean harm, not rule-breaking. If no one is harmed, guilt may be conditioning, not conscience.
3. **Reclaim Conscience.** Practice making decisions from Love, even if old guilt whispers otherwise.
4. **Challenge Guilt-Trips.** When someone manipulates you with guilt, pause and name it: *"That's not mine to carry."*

5. **Create New Rituals.** Replace guilt-driven rituals with freedom practices: gratitude journaling, affirmations, creative expression.

Other Voices

The prophet Micah wrote, *What does the Lord require of you but to do justice, Love mercy, and walk humbly?"* Not endless guilt, but simple Love in action. The Buddha warned against clinging to rules as ends in themselves. Rumi said, *Don t get tangled in guilt. Your task is to Love."*

Wisdom traditions know that guilt becomes corrupt when used for control. True guidance is always rooted in Love.

The Drumbeat Truth

Let's engrain it:

- Guilt works as control because it's self-policing.
- Religion, politics, and families weaponized guilt for obedience.
- Jeshua exposed and rejected guilt-based control.
- True conscience is about Love, not compliance.

Teach yourself to distinguish between guilt that arises from Love and guilt that arises from control. The former invites growth. The latter chains you down. Break the chain. Return to Love as your compass.

You are not here to live small under guilt's weight. You are here to live free under Love's guidance.

Practices for Releasing Shame

Shame is sticky. It clings long after the event that birthed it is gone. It embeds itself in memory, posture, and even the nervous system. You can escape the church, leave behind doctrines, even intellectually reject shame, and still find it whispering: "You're not enough. You're not lovable. You're flawed at the core." That's why shame cannot be argued away. It must be released through practice. Releasing shame isn't about erasing the past. It's about dislodging the lies that fused themselves to your identity, and replacing them with truth, Love, and dignity.

Why Shame Requires Practice

Shame has survival roots. In ancient communities, being excluded meant death. Shame kept people in line, reminding them, "Don't risk rejection." That ancient instinct is still wired in the brain. When people feel shame, their bodies respond as if social exile is imminent.

Because shame lives in the nervous system, it doesn't loosen by hearing, "Don't be ashamed." It loosens through repeated experiences of safety, Love, and authenticity. Practices retrain the body and mind to trust that belonging is possible without self-erasure.

Jeshua's Pattern of Releasing Shame

Jeshua didn't hand out shame; he lifted it. His encounters followed a pattern: name the person, restore dignity, and offer presence. To the bleeding woman: *Daughter."* To Zacchaeus: *Come down, I must stay at your house today."* To Peter: *Feed my sheep."*

Notice what's missing: lectures, conditions, ridicule. He practiced restoration in real time. His example shows us the template: shame is released through presence, naming, and empowerment.

Core Practices for Releasing Shame

1. **Naming Without Judgment.** Shame thrives in secrecy. The first practice is naming shame aloud – to yourself, to a trusted friend, or in a journal. Say: *"I feel shame about this."* Naming drags shame out of the shadows where it festers.
2. **Reframing the Story.** Write down shameful events and reframe them: *"I made a mistake, but I am not a mistake. I was hurting, but I am not broken. I was learning, not failing."* Reframing separates identity from action.
3. **Mirror Practice.** Stand before a mirror daily. Look into your own eyes and say: *"You are worthy. You are lovable. You are not defined by shame."* At first, it feels awkward. Over time, it restores the gaze shame stole.
4. **Somatic Release.** Use the body to release shame. Shake arms and legs, stretch, or dance freely. Shame tenses the body; movement releases it. Pair with affirmations: *"I shake off shame. I move in freedom."*

5. **Safe Connection.** Find circles where authenticity is welcomed. Speak your truth. Shame shrinks when met with empathy. Each safe connection rewires the belief: *"If they knew me, they'd reject me."*
6. **Ritual of Release.** Create symbolic rituals. Write shame on paper and burn it. Drop stones into water. Walk into nature and say aloud what you're leaving behind. Ritual gives the body closure.
7. **Compassionate Self-Talk.** Replace shame's voice with compassion. When failure happens, instead of, *"I'm worthless,"* say, *"I'm learning. I'm growing. I still deserve Love."*

My Own Journey with Shame Release

For me, journaling was the first breakthrough. I wrote down everything I carried shame about – doubts, failures, questions. The list felt endless. But once it was on paper, I realized: this wasn't proof of unworthiness. These were moments of being human. Seeing them written helped separate me from them.

Later, looking into my own eyes and saying *"You are worthy"* felt almost impossible at first. My gaze kept sliding away. But persistence mattered. Slowly, I began to see the face in the mirror not as guilty, but as beLoved.

Obstacles to Releasing Shame

Shame resists release because it masquerades as humility. Many believe, *If I stop feeling ashamed, I'll become arrogant."* That's the trap. Shame isn't humility. Shame is self-condemnation. True humility acknowledges limitations without losing dignity.

Another obstacle is fear of exposure. Speaking shame aloud feels terrifying. But vulnerability is the key that unlocks belonging. Each time you risk honesty and receive compassion, shame's grip weakens.

If shame were a product, it would be duct tape – sticking to everything, impossible to peel off cleanly. But practices are like warm water and soap, slowly loosening the glue until the tape slides away.

Psychology of Shame Release

Research shows shame decreases when met with empathy. The act of being truly seen without rejection rewires the brain. Shame circuits weaken; trust circuits strengthen. Practices like mindfulness also reduce shame by teaching people to observe thoughts without fusing with them.

Somatic therapy emphasizes movement, grounding, and breath as essential. Because shame lives in the body, the body must be included in healing.

Other Voices

Mystics across traditions affirm practices of release. The Hebrew psalms cry out with raw honesty, transforming shame into prayer. The Buddha taught compassion meditation to dissolve self-condemnation. Rumi wrote, *"Don't get lost in your guilt. Step into the sunlight of Love."* Jeshua embodied release through compassion and presence.

If shame could talk during release, it would sound like a clingy ex: *You'll miss me! You need me to stay humble!"* But once you walk away, you realize — you're lighter, freer, and never needed it in the first place.

The Drumbeat Truth

Let's engrain it:

- Shame thrives in secrecy. Naming it breaks the cycle.
- Release comes through reframing, embodiment, connection, and ritual.
- Jeshua modeled shame release through restoration and compassion.
- Practices rewire the body, mind, and spirit for freedom.

Don't just think about releasing shame. Practice it. Daily. Stand tall. Breathe deep. Name the lies. Replace them with Love. Seek connection. Create rituals.

Shame won't vanish overnight. But each practice loosens its grip. Over time, the lies dissolve, and dignity returns. Jeshua didn't call us to live small under shame. He called us to live beLoved. That reality begins when we practice release, day by day, breath by breath, truth by truth.

Living Beyond Guilt and Shame

Escaping the traps of guilt and shame isn't just about breaking chains. It's about discovering what life feels like once those chains are gone.

Too often, spirituality is framed as endless struggle: always repenting, always apologizing, always repairing what supposedly makes you unworthy. But what happens when the apologies stop? When the sack of guilt is set down for good? When shame is no longer the voice in your head? Living beyond guilt and shame is not only possible – it is the natural state once the illusions fall away. This section explores what that new life looks like in practice.

The Landscape Without Guilt and Shame

Life beyond guilt and shame feels like stepping into a new landscape. Where once the ground was uneven and full of pitfalls, now it feels open and walkable. Where once the sky was heavy with looming judgment, now it feels wide and full of light.

The absence of guilt and shame is not emptiness. It's spaciousness. It's room to breathe, to create, to laugh without the quick reflex of apology. People often describe it as weightlifting, vision clearing, breath deepening. The shift is tangible.

Authenticity Restored

Guilt and shame force people into masks. One mask for church, another for family, another for private doubts. Living beyond them means removing masks. Authenticity returns. You say what you believe. You share what you feel. You show up as yourself.

At first, authenticity feels risky. Old habits whisper: "If you show who you are, they'll reject you." But the more you live authentically, the more you realize the opposite: only authenticity creates real connection. Masks never bond. Truth does.

Creativity Unleashed

Shame is creativity's greatest enemy. It whispers, "Don't try. You'll fail. People will laugh." Beyond shame, creativity flourishes. The inner critic softens. Art, writing, music, problem-solving – all expand when shame no longer throttles expression.

This isn't just about art. Creativity is life itself. Cooking a meal, raising children, starting a business, telling a story — these are all acts of creation. Beyond guilt and shame, you stop worrying about being "enough" and start experimenting, enjoying, risking.

Relationships Transformed

When guilt and shame dominate, relationships become transactional: "I'll hide my flaws so you don't reject me. I'll sacrifice myself so you won't be disappointed." Beyond them, relationships transform. You can show weakness without fear. You can admit mistakes without groveling. You can set boundaries without guilt.

Authenticity deepens intimacy. Love flows freely, not as penance, but as joy. Relationships stop being about managing appearances and start being about mutual growth.

If guilt and shame were relationship coaches, they'd say, "Always apologize before you speak. Never laugh too loud. Never admit you're happy — it's suspicious." Beyond them, the advice changes: "Laugh harder. Dance badly. Kiss with mustard on your face." That's real connection — messy and honest.

Spiritual Life Beyond the Trap

Living beyond guilt and shame doesn't mean ignoring conscience. It means conscience is now guided by Love, not fear. Mistakes still happen, but they don't define you. They become opportunities for repair, not reasons for condemnation.

Prayer becomes presence, not pleading. Reflection becomes gratitude, not groveling. Silence becomes rest, not self-scolding. God is no longer judge or accuser, but companion.

This is what Jeshua meant when he said, *My yoke is easy, my burden is light."* Spiritual life beyond guilt and shame is not heavy. It is light — in both senses: less weight, more radiance.

My Own Experience of Living Beyond

For years, I couldn't imagine life without guilt. It seemed necessary, like oxygen. Without guilt, wouldn't I just spiral into selfishness? But when I began setting it down, something surprising happened: I didn't become careless. I became more alive.

Instead of obsessing over sin, I focused on Love. Instead of hiding flaws, I shared them. Instead of waiting for approval, I lived freely. Relationships deepened. Creativity blossomed. Peace settled into my body.

The most surprising part? I started trusting myself. Without guilt screaming in my ear, I could hear the quieter voice of intuition, presence, spirit. And that voice was never condemning. It was guiding, loving, empowering.

Practices for Living Beyond

Living beyond guilt and shame is a daily choice. Old voices linger. Practices anchor the new reality.

1. **Daily Self-Identification.** Each morning, declare: *"I am free from guilt. I am free from shame. I am beLoved."*
2. **Celebrate Mistakes.** When you stumble, laugh. Say: *"I'm learning."* This rewires the mind to see failure as growth, not condemnation.
3. **Gratitude Journaling.** Write three things daily you're grateful for. Gratitude shifts focus from failure to abundance.
4. **Embodied Freedom.** Stand tall, breathe deeply, walk openly. Let the body live the truth of freedom.
5. **Speak Boldly.** Share your truth with someone daily – a thought, a dream, a question. Each act of honesty strengthens authenticity.
6. **Acts of Joy.** Intentionally schedule joy – music, play, laughter. Joy is the opposite of shame.
7. **Compassion Check.** At day's end, ask: *"Where did I treat myself with compassion? Where can I offer more tomorrow?"*

The Psychology of Living Beyond

Neuroscience confirms this shift is real. When guilt and shame circuits quiet, the brain's reward and connection systems activate. Oxytocin rises through authentic connection. Dopamine flows through creativity. Stress hormones decrease.

Living beyond guilt and shame isn't just spiritual poetry. It's neurological reprogramming. The brain literally learns new patterns of peace and belonging.

Other Voices

Mystics always pointed to this life beyond shame. Julian of Norwich declared, *All shall be well, and all shall be well, and all manner of thing shall be well.*" Rumi wrote, *Out beyond ideas of wrongdoing and rightdoing, there is a field. I'll meet you there.*" The Buddha taught release from suffering through compassion. Jeshua himself said, *Neither do I condemn you.*" The chorus is universal: freedom is possible, and it looks like Love.

If guilt and shame could market themselves, they'd say: "Without us, you'll run wild." But once you leave them behind, you realize you don't run wild. You run free – barefoot in the grass, arms wide open, laughing at the sky.

The Drumbeat Truth

Let's engrain it:

- Life beyond guilt and shame is not careless. It is more caring.
- Authenticity, creativity, and intimacy flourish without shame's chokehold.
- Spirituality becomes light when guilt is gone.
- Jeshua's way was never about chains. It was always about freedom.

Live beyond. Don't just set down guilt and shame occasionally. Refuse to pick them up again. Choose daily to embody freedom. Laugh more, Love deeper, create boldly, speak honestly.

You are not here to live small under inherited burdens. You are here to shine. Jeshua's life wasn't about trapping people in cycles of confession and shame. It was about liberating them into beLovedness.

Living beyond guilt and shame is not only the destination. It is the path itself – each breath, each laugh, each act of Love. That's the life waiting for you now.

Chapter 20: Love as the Core of All Teachings

Why Love Stands Above All

If guilt chains the soul and forgiveness cuts the chains, Love is the air you breathe once you're free. Across religions, philosophies, and spiritual traditions, Love consistently rises as the highest command, the purest ethic, the deepest truth. Strip away the rituals, the doctrines, the debates, and what remains is Love. Jeshua said it most directly: *Love the Lord your God with all your heart... and Love your neighbor as yourself. All the law and the prophets hang on these two commandments."* In other words, Love is not just another teaching – it is the teaching. It is the axis upon which everything else turns.

Why Love Stands Above

Love is the one value that transcends culture, language, and religion. Justice, truth, wisdom – all are important, but without Love they become weapons. Justice without Love is revenge. Truth without Love is cruelty. Wisdom without Love is arrogance. Love completes them, grounds them, redeems them.

The reason Love stands above is simple: it heals separation. Every form of suffering comes down to disconnection, from ourselves, from others, from creation, from the divine. Love bridges the gaps. Where shame isolates, Love embraces. Where fear divides, Love unites. Where guilt shrinks, Love expands.

Jeshua's Teaching of Love

Jeshua didn't just preach Love. He embodied it. He ate with outcasts, touched lepers, defended the condemned. He declared Love of neighbor equal to Love of God, erasing hierarchies. When asked about the greatest commandment, he didn't pick ritual purity or temple sacrifice. He picked Love.

On the cross, even in agony, his words were Love: *"Father, forgive them."* In resurrection, his first words to the fearful were peace, not accusation. Jeshua's entire life was a Love letter written in human form.

My Own Awakening to Love

For years, religion taught me to put obedience, fear, and ritual above Love. God seemed more interested in rules than relationships. But slowly, through experience, presence, and inner listening, I realized Love was the real center.

Moments of pure presence – sitting in silence, feeling connected to life, offering compassion – carried more truth than a thousand catechisms. I realized Love wasn't a doctrine. It was reality itself.

Love as Universal Voice

Love stands above not only in Christianity but everywhere. The Buddha taught compassion as the path to liberation. The Qur'an calls God "*the Compassionate, the Merciful.*" The Bhagavad Gita teaches acting without attachment, motivated by Love. Rumi wrote, "*Love is the bridge between you and everything.*" Different languages, same truth: Love is the thread uniting humanity.

If religions were smartphones, Love would be the operating system. Doctrines are just apps – some useful, some buggy, some crash constantly. But without the OS, none of them work. Love is the system everything runs on.

Why Love Is Feared

Oddly, Love's simplicity makes it threatening. Institutions thrive on complexity: rules to interpret, rituals to manage, hierarchies to enforce. If Love is the core, much of the machinery becomes unnecessary. People free in Love are harder to control. That's why Love has often been buried under doctrine.

But Love keeps breaking through. Every revival, every reform, every mystic voice that shifts the world is simply rediscovering Love.

The Psychology of Love

Psychologists confirm what mystics knew: Love heals. Acts of compassion release oxytocin, lower blood pressure, and increase longevity. Loving relationships buffer against stress and trauma. Love literally rewires the brain, reducing fear responses and enhancing resilience.

Living in Love isn't just moral. It's biological survival strategy. Humanity thrives where Love flows.

Practices for Centering Love

1. **Love Pause.** Throughout the day, pause and ask: *"Am I acting from Love or from fear?"* Redirect when needed.
2. **Compassionate Action.** Each day, do one intentional act of Love – a word, a gesture, a gift. Small but consistent acts reinforce identity.
3. **Gratitude for Connection.** List daily ways you experienced Love – a smile, a memory, a kindness. Gratitude deepens awareness of Love's presence.
4. **Embodying Love Physically.** Smile at strangers, make eye contact, offer touch where safe and appropriate. Love is felt through bodies, not just ideas.

My Turning Point Realization

A turning point came when I wrote down all the commandments I'd been taught: fast, confess, obey. Then I wrote Jeshua's summary: Love God, Love neighbor, Love self. Looking at both lists, I laughed. The first was endless. The second was simple. From that day, I began measuring everything by Love: Does this bring more Love into the world? If not, it doesn't matter.

If Love were a teacher, the final exam would have only one question: *"Did you Love?"* Imagine how short seminary would be if that were the curriculum.

Other Voices

Julian of Norwich wrote, *All shall be well, and all manner of thing shall be well,"* not as optimism, but as Love's assurance. Gandhi said, *Where there is Love there is life."* Hafiz wrote, *I have learned so much from God that I can no longer call myself a Christian, a Hindu, a Muslim, a Buddhist. I am simply a Lover."* The chorus is global: Love stands above all.

The Drumbeat Truth

Let's engrain it:

- Love is the axis of all spiritual truth.
- Without Love, justice, truth, and wisdom become weapons.

- Jeshua, Buddha, Rumi, and mystics across traditions point to Love as the core.
- Love isn't doctrine. It's reality.
- Love heals separation and creates freedom.

Stop complicating spirituality. Stop dragging guilt, fear, or endless rituals into the center. Place Love at the core. Measure every belief, every practice, every decision by this: Does it bring more Love?

Love is not secondary. It is primary. It is not optional. It is everything. Jeshua knew it, the mystics knew it, and somewhere inside, you've always known it too.

Love Versus Fear

If Love is the core of all teachings, fear is the illusion of its absence. Fear is the shadow that creeps into religion, politics, relationships, and even our private inner dialogue. Where Love expands, fear contracts.

Where Love liberates, fear imprisons. Jeshua spoke constantly about fear. "*Do not be afraid*" was one of his most repeated messages.

And yet, fear has been smuggled into doctrines and disguised as holiness. Fear-based religion says: *Fear God, fear sin, fear punishment."* Fear-based politics says: *Fear outsiders, fear change, fear your neighbor."* Fear-based families say: *Don t disappoint, don t step out of line, don t be yourself too much."* In every case, fear tries to claim the authority that belongs to Love.

How Fear Masquerades as Holiness

Religion has often rebranded fear as virtue. Fear of God is praised as reverence. Fear of sin is preached as discipline. Fear of hell is packaged as motivation. But underneath, fear is still fear – it narrows, restricts, and enslaves.

Fear tells people not to question. Fear convinces them obedience is safety. Fear insists that worthiness hangs by a thread. Fear teaches that God is watching like a cosmic policeman, waiting for infractions. That's not holiness. That's surveillance.

Jeshua's Confrontation with Fear

Jeshua confronted fear repeatedly. When storms raged, he calmed disciples with, *"Do not be afraid."* When religious leaders used fear of Sabbath laws to shame healings, he chose compassion over compliance. When people trembled at Rome's might, he spoke of a kingdom not built on swords.

Perhaps most strikingly, his parable of the talents condemned the servant who buried his gift "out of fear." Jeshua's point was piercing: fear is not obedience. Fear is wasted life.

My Own Struggle with Fear

Fear was baked into my early religious training. Fear of mortal sin, fear of venial sin, fear of missing Mass, fear of confession, fear of death, fear of judgment. At times, it felt like Catholicism's main product wasn't grace but anxiety.

It took years to realize fear wasn't keeping me holy. It was keeping me small. My prayers were laced with worry: "Am I saying this right? Did I confess enough? Did God hear me?" I wasn't praying to connect. I was praying to avoid punishment.

The breakthrough came when I experienced presence – sitting in silence, breathing, simply being. In those moments, there was no fear. Only Love. And it was enough. "*Be still and know that I am God.*"

Fear's Psychological Grip

Psychologists explain fear's power: it hijacks the amygdala, narrowing perception to threat alone. In survival situations, that's useful. But in daily life, fear keeps us frozen in defensive postures. We misinterpret everything as danger – a frown becomes rejection, silence becomes abandonment, difference becomes threat.

Fear literally shrinks perception. Love does the opposite. When oxytocin flows, the brain sees more possibility, more nuance. Love expands the lens. That's why Jeshua's teaching wasn't just moral. It was neurological liberation.

If fear were a motivational speaker, its advice would be: "Stay small. Don't risk. Hide under the bed." You wouldn't pay for that seminar, but religion packaged it with incense and stained glass, and suddenly it sold out for centuries.

Love's Antidote

The first letter of John makes the core truth clear: *"Perfect Love casts out fear."* Not perfect doctrine, not perfect ritual – perfect Love. Fear and Love cannot cohabit. One will drive out the other.

When you live from Love, fear loses authority. Mistakes no longer mean condemnation. Difference no longer means danger. Death no longer means despair. Love reframes everything.

Practices for Choosing Love Over Fear

1. **Fear Inventory.** List your current fears – about God, failure, rejection, death. Ask: *"Is this fear based in Love, or in control?"*
2. **Loving Reframe.** Each time fear arises, counter with Love. "I fear rejection" → "*I choose authenticity.*" "I fear failure" → "*I choose growth.*"
3. **Presence Practice.** When fear spirals, return to breath. Inhale deeply. Exhale slowly. Repeat: *"Love is here."*
4. **Compassion in Action.** Do one act daily that fear resists – speak honestly, offer kindness to a stranger, share a vulnerable truth. Each act weakens fear's grip.
5. **Declaration.** Repeat: *"I live in Love, not fear. Love casts out fear."*

My Turning Point Practice

I once carried fear into every conversation about faith. I worried about saying the "wrong" thing. One day, I decided to experiment: what if I spoke only from Love, even if it contradicted doctrine? That choice transformed everything. Conversations that once felt tense became free. People opened up. I opened up. Fear lost its throne.

Other Voices

Buddha taught, *There is no fear for one whose mind is not filled with desires."* Rumi wrote, *Move beyond fear. Life is too short to be small."* Hafiz declared, *Fear is the cheapest room in the house. I d like to see you in better living conditions."*

Across traditions, Love is the alternative housing.

If fear built a house, it would have no windows, no doors, and signs everywhere saying "Keep Out." Love walks in, knocks down the walls, and says, "*Open floor plan. Everyone s welcome.*"

The Drumbeat Truth

Let's engrain it:

- Fear shrinks; Love expands.
- Fear masquerades as holiness but enslaves.
- Jeshua constantly said, "Do not be afraid."
- Perfect Love, and only Love, casts out fear.
- Every choice is between Love and fear.

Notice fear when it arises. Don't shame it. Name it. Then ask: *What would Love choose here?"* Over and over, make Love the guide.

Remember what Yoda said in Star Wars: "*Named must your fears be before banish them you can.*"

Love versus fear is the real battle. It's not us versus them, believers versus unbelievers, saved versus damned. It's Love versus fear, moment by moment, in every heart. Choose Love, and you step into the core of all true spirituality.

Love in Action

Love sounds beautiful as an idea, but if it stays in the realm of poetry and sentiment, it never changes lives. Real Love must take shape in action. Jeshua didn't spend his ministry simply telling people he Loved them. He touched the untouchable, fed the hungry, defended the condemned, and restored the excluded. Love, for him, wasn't abstract – it was embodied. It had hands, feet, eyes, a voice. And when we reduce Love to mere feeling, we lose its power. Feelings come and go. Love in action endures.

Love Beyond Sentiment

One of the great traps of spirituality is mistaking warm feelings for Love. People say, "I feel loving" after a meditation, a song, or a moment of inspiration. That's beautiful, but it's incomplete. Love must move outward. It must be expressed. Otherwise, it's just self-indulgence.

Sentimental Love says, *I hope the hungry are fed."* Active Love says, *Here is a meal."* Sentimental Love says, *I accept everyone."*

Active Love says, *I will sit with you when no one else will.*" Jeshua constantly demonstrated the difference.

Jeshua's Actions of Love

Jeshua's ministry was a string of tangible Love actions:

- **Healing the sick.** He didn't just pray for the ill; he touched them. Even lepers, feared and avoided, felt his hand.
- **Feeding the hungry.** The feeding of the multitudes wasn't symbolism – it was bread and fish distributed to stomachs in need.
- **Defending the vulnerable.** When a woman was about to be stoned, he stood between her and the mob.
- **Restoring dignity.** He called people by name, invited himself into homes, and restored those society had cast aside.

His Love was practical. It addressed bodies, not just souls. It restored dignity, not just dogma.

Love in My Own Life

For years, I thought Love was about having the right feelings toward people – even those I never met. But Jeshua's example challenged me: if my "Love" never inconvenienced me, was it Love at all?

I began experimenting with small acts: making time to listen when I wanted to rush, offering kindness where I could stay silent, giving resources when I could hoard. Each time, I realized Love was less about emotion and more about intention. Some days I didn't "feel loving" at all. But when I acted in Love, the feeling often followed.

Love in Justice

Love in action isn't only kindness in private life. It also confronts injustice. Jeshua overturned tables in the temple – not out of rage alone, but because exploitation of the poor was unloving. True Love refuses to stay silent in the face of oppression.

This is why Martin Luther King Jr. said, *Justice is Love correcting everything that stands against Love.*" When laws, systems, or cultures harm people, Love acts. It speaks. It resists. It overturns tables when needed.

If Love stayed only in words, it'd be like a gym membership you never use. You can say you "belong" to the gym all you want, but if you never pick up a weight, nothing changes. Love in action is the workout — not just the card in your wallet.

Love in Everyday Choices

Not every act of Love looks dramatic. Sometimes it's as simple as slowing down to listen fully to a friend, tipping a server generously, forgiving a harsh word, or letting someone merge in traffic without muttering curses under your breath.

These small acts, repeated daily, create a lifestyle of Love. Love in action is less about grand gestures and more about consistent choices. Jeshua wasn't always performing miracles. Often, he was simply present, attentive, willing to see the unseen.

Practices for Love in Action

1. **Daily Act of Love.** Commit to one concrete act daily — helping, listening, giving, encouraging. Write it down each evening.
2. **Love in Conflict.** When conflict arises, pause. Ask: *"What would Love say or do here?"* Then act accordingly.
3. **Anonymous Kindness.** Do something kind secretly — leave a note, a gift, or a meal without recognition. This trains Love to act without ego.
4. **Boundary Love.** Sometimes Love in action means saying no. Write down one area where overextension drains you. Practice loving by setting limits.
5. **Justice Check.** Notice one social issue where people suffer. Ask: *"What action of Love can I contribute?"* Volunteer, donate, advocate.

My Turning Point Practice

One turning point came when I stopped separating "spiritual" from "practical." I realized cooking a meal for a sick friend was as spiritual as prayer. Visiting someone lonely was as holy as a church service. Love in action doesn't need a sanctuary. The sanctuary is every encounter.

Psychology of Love in Action

Psychologists find that helping others increases serotonin, dopamine, and oxytocin – the brain's "feel good" chemicals. People who practice acts of kindness regularly report higher life satisfaction. Love in action doesn't just bless others. It heals the giver.

Neuroscience shows the brain's empathy circuits strengthen with repeated compassionate action. Love in action literally reshapes the brain for connection.

If Love were only about words, Hallmark would've saved the world by now. Clearly, it hasn't. Action is the missing piece. Buy the card, sure, but also do the dishes.

Other Voices

The Bhagavad Gita emphasizes karma yoga – Love expressed in selfless action. The Buddha taught compassion must become concrete through right action, not just right thought. Teresa of Ávila said, *Christ has no body now but yours."* Rumi wrote, *Love is the cure. Your Love makes others bloom."* Across traditions, Love in action is the heartbeat of authentic spirituality.

Obstacles to Love in Action

The main barrier is fear of inconvenience. Love requires time, energy, resources. People hesitate: "I'm too busy, too tired, too poor." But Love in action isn't about extravagance. It's about intention. Even the smallest act matters.

Another obstacle is cynicism. "Will this even make a difference?" Jeshua's answer: every act of Love plants a seed. Some grow in ways unseen. Action is never wasted.

The Drumbeat Truth

Let's engrain it:

- Love is not sentiment but action.
- Jeshua embodied Love with hands, feet, and courage.
- Everyday acts of kindness are as holy as miracles.
- Love in action heals both giver and receiver.
- Love without action is poetry without breath.

So *act.* Don't wait until you "feel loving." Don't wait until it's convenient. Choose one act today – small or large – and embody Love. Feed someone, call someone, forgive someone, stand with someone.

Love is not meant to stay in ideas or sermons. It's meant to move, touch, feed, and defend. Jeshua's life was proof: Love is not only what you believe. It's what you do.

The Universality of Love

One of the most astonishing truths about Love is that it refuses to be owned. No single religion, culture, or philosophy can claim exclusive rights to it. Love shows up everywhere, in every era, in every language. It surfaces in poetry and scripture, in song and story, in science and psychology. Whenever human beings try to describe what matters most, Love finds its way to the center. This universality is no accident. Love is the common thread woven through humanity's spiritual fabric. When doctrines divide, Love unites. When creeds clash, Love bridges. When rituals differ, Love speaks the same tongue.

Love Across Religions

Every major tradition, when boiled down, points toward Love.

- **Judaism.** The Shema commands Love for God with all one's heart, soul, and might. Leviticus adds, *"Love your neighbor as yourself."* Jeshua wasn't inventing new doctrine when he repeated these – he was pointing back to the heart already there.
- **Christianity.** Paul declared, *"The greatest of these is Love."* John wrote, *"God is Love."* Love wasn't an appendix; it was the essence.
- **Islam.** One of God's names is *Ar-Rahman* – the Compassionate. The Qur'an opens every chapter (except one) with mercy and compassion as divine identity.
- **Buddhism.** The practice of *metta*, or loving-kindness meditation, trains the heart to radiate Love to all beings without exception.
- **Hinduism.** The Bhagavad Gita describes *bhakti yoga* – the path of devotion and Love for the Divine as supreme way.

- **Sikhism.** Guru Nanak taught, *"There is no stranger, there is no enemy. All are your friends."*
- **Indigenous traditions.** Many honor the interconnectedness of all life, treating earth, sky, water, and creatures as kin worthy of Love and respect.

Across the world, the melody repeats: Love is the way.

Why Universality Matters

The universality of Love reveals that spirituality is not about joining the "right club" but about remembering what is already written in every heart. When people argue over which religion is "true," Love whispers: *"Truth is larger than your labels."*

If Love shows up in every tradition, then Love itself is the test of authenticity. The question isn't, "Do you believe correctly?" but "Do you Love well?"

Jeshua's Universal Love

Jeshua constantly broke boundaries to show Love's universality. He spoke with Samaritans, healed Gentiles, and praised the faith of outsiders. He told parables featuring foreigners as heroes. He refused to let ethnicity, religion, or status define worthiness. For him, Love was not tribal. It was cosmic.

My Own Awakening to Universality

I was raised to think Catholicism had the monopoly on truth. Everyone else was "outside." But as I began reading mystics from other traditions, I was startled by the resonance. Rumi's poetry echoed Jeshua's teaching. The Buddha's emphasis on presence mirrored Jeshua's *"Take no thought for tomorrow."* Yogananda spoke of divine Love in ways that felt like commentary on John's gospel.

I realized truth wasn't confined to one denomination. Love was breaking out everywhere. And once I saw that, my world grew bigger, not smaller.

If religions were restaurants, Love would be the dish every single one serves – though each insists their recipe is the original. Some dress it with ritual spices, some plate it with doctrine garnish, some serve it family-style. But underneath, it's still Love.

Love Beyond Religion

The universality of Love isn't limited to religions. Philosophers, poets, and even scientists circle around it too.

- Plato described Love (agape) as the highest form of good.
- Shakespeare wrote sonnets about Love's endurance.
- Modern psychologists like Carl Rogers emphasized unconditional positive regard – another name for Love – as the key to human flourishing.
- Neuroscience shows the human brain is wired for connection, bonding, and empathy.

Even where belief in God differs, Love remains central.

Practices for Experiencing Universality

1. **Interfaith Encounters.** Attend a service, meditation, or gathering from another tradition. Notice how Love shows up in different languages.
2. **Reading Across Traditions.** Pick a sacred text outside your upbringing – Bhagavad Gita, Tao Te Ching, Sufi poetry. Highlight every mention of Love.
3. **Gratitude for Diversity.** Write down five ways other cultures have taught you about Love, through music, hospitality, art, or friendship.
4. **Universal Blessing Practice.** Each morning, bless all beings: *"May all people, of every path, know Love today."*
5. **Nature as Teacher.** Step outside and notice Love in creation: the way trees offer oxygen, rivers sustain life, bees pollinate flowers. Love's universality isn't just human – it's cosmic.

My Turning Point Practice

One turning point came when I contemplated on the phrase: *"Love is bigger than religion."* I repeated it daily. Slowly, my defensiveness softened. I began noticing Love everywhere – in a smile from a stranger, in the devotion of a Muslim friend, in the wisdom of Buddhist teachings, in the laughter of children. Love was everywhere, once I allowed myself to see it.

Psychology of Universal Love

Psychologists studying intergroup bias find Love and empathy reduce prejudice more than argument. When people build relationships across boundaries, Love dissolves stereotypes. This is why Love as universality matters socially: it heals divisions not by debate, but by connection.

Neuroscience confirms empathy circuits activate regardless of group when people see another's suffering. Love is literally wired beyond boundaries.

If Love needed a passport, it'd be stamped in every country already. Borders can't stop it. Customs officers would just wave it through: "Yep, you're good, you're everywhere."

Other Voices

Rumi: *Love is the religion, and the universe is the book."*

Dalai Lama: *My religion is kindness."*

Mother Teresa: *Spread Love everywhere you go."*

Chief Seattle: *All things are connected like the blood which unites one family."*

The chorus is unmistakable: Love is universal, transcending all labels.

Obstacles to Embracing Universality

The main obstacle is fear of difference. Institutions warn: "Other paths will corrupt you." But Love cannot be corrupted by seeing itself in another.

Another obstacle is pride. People cling to being "right" rather than being loving. But the need to be right shrinks the heart; the choice to Love expands it.

The Drumbeat Truth

Let's engrain it:

- Love shows up in every religion, philosophy, and culture.
- Jeshua demonstrated Love's universality by crossing boundaries.
- Love is the test of authenticity, not doctrine.
- The cosmos itself hums with Love's thread.

Open your eyes to Love's universality. Stop asking who's right. Start asking who Loves. Read across traditions, listen across cultures, learn across divides. See Love everywhere — in scripture, in science, in strangers, in creation.

When Love is universal, spirituality stops being about building fences and starts being about opening gates. Love is not owned. It is given. And it's given to all.

Living Love Daily

It's one thing to say. "Love is the core," but it's another to live it in the grind of everyday life. Love can sound lofty in scripture, moving in sermons, inspiring in poetry — but if it doesn't make its way into commutes, conversations, grocery store lines, and family dinners, it remains theory. Living Love daily means turning Love from philosophy into rhythm, from concept into lifestyle. Jeshua's teaching wasn't "think about Love sometimes." It was "*Love God, Love your neighbor, Love yourself*" — every day, every moment. Love is not an occasion. It's a way of being. Remember that "God" is everything and everyone.

Why Daily Matters

If Love is practiced only in grand gestures, it stays rare. But daily acts create habits. Habits shape character. Character shapes destiny. Daily Love forms a person who doesn't have to think about whether to act compassionately — it becomes second nature.

Think of brushing your teeth. You don't wait until they're rotten to start. You clean them daily to keep them healthy. Love works the same way. Small, daily practices keep the heart clean, resilient, and open.

Jeshua's Ordinary Love

Jeshua's Love was often expressed in ordinary moments. He noticed people others ignored. He called Zacchaeus out of a tree. He shared meals. He blessed children. These weren't miracles — they were daily Love.

His teaching, *Whoever gives even a cup of cold water in my name will not lose their reward,"* emphasized that small, daily acts matter. Love is not measured in scale but in consistency.

My Own Learning to Live Love

I once thought living Love meant doing something dramatic – founding charities, leading movements, making history. But I've discovered living Love daily is more about tone than theatrics. It's the way I listen without interrupting, the way I breathe before reacting, the way I hold space for someone's pain without trying to fix it.

Some of my most transformative experiences weren't massive. They were simple: making time for someone who needed to be heard, forgiving quickly instead of stewing, choosing kindness when sarcasm tempted me. Daily Love is quieter but deeper.

Love in Ordinary Choices

Living Love daily means embedding it everywhere:

- **At home.** Speaking gently, forgiving quickly, affirming often.
- **At work.** Valuing people over productivity, honesty over manipulation, service over ambition.
- **In public.** Driving with courtesy, tipping generously, smiling at strangers.
- **With self.** Resting when tired, speaking kindly to yourself, refusing shame.

Love becomes the backdrop of ordinary decisions, turning daily life into spiritual practice.

If Love were only for Sundays, it'd be like showering once a week. Sure, it's better than nothing, but people will notice. Daily practice keeps things fresher for everyone.

Practices for Daily Love

1. **Morning Intention.** Begin each day by asking: *"How will I live Love today?"* Call a friend, encourage a coworker, forgive yourself.
2. **Midday Pause.** Set a timer to stop at noon. Ask: *"Have I acted from Love or fear this morning?"* Redirect as needed.
3. **Evening Reflection.** End the day with gratitude for Love lived – moments of kindness given or received.
4. **Micro-Actions.** Practice small, tangible acts: holding doors, thanking cashiers, offering compliments, listening fully.

5. **Love Toward Self.** Declare Daily: *"I am worthy of Love."* Treat yourself as kindly as you treat others.

My Turning Point Practice

When I started treating presence as Love. I realized half the battle was simply showing up fully for whoever was in front of me. Not multitasking, not planning my response, but actually being there. That daily choice of presence became the foundation of living Love.

The Psychology of Daily Love

Research shows micro-moments of Love – even brief connections with strangers – improve wellbeing. Psychologist Barbara Fredrickson calls this "positivity resonance." A smile exchanged with a barista, a laugh shared with a coworker – these tiny acts of Love accumulate, increasing resilience and happiness.

Daily Love isn't abstract. It literally improves health, rewires the brain for empathy, and strengthens community bonds.

If Love were a gym, daily Love would be the treadmill. Not glamorous, not flashy, but it keeps the heart strong. Skip it too long, and you feel sluggish. Stick with it, and life feels lighter.

Other Voices

- **Mother Teresa:** *"Not all of us can do great things. But we can do small things with great Love."*
- **Thich Nhat Hanh:** *"Smile, breathe, and go slowly."* – daily Love as mindfulness.
- **Rumi:** *"Let yourself be silently drawn by the strange pull of what you really Love."*
- **Julian of Norwich:** *"The greatest honor you can give Almighty God is to live gladly because of the knowledge of his Love."*

Each voice echoes the same truth: Love is lived in the ordinary.

Obstacles to Daily Love

The greatest obstacle is distraction. Daily busyness makes Love feel optional. Another obstacle is cynicism – the thought, *"What difference does one small act make?"* But just as single drops fill a bucket, daily acts accumulate into transformation.

Another obstacle is self-neglect. Without loving yourself, daily Love for others burns out. Self-Love isn't indulgence. It's fuel.

My Experience of Daily Love's Power

When I began practicing small, daily acts, I noticed cumulative change. People opened up more easily. My stress lessened. Even my creativity grew. Love became less about effort and more about habit. It wasn't something I tried to remember. It was simply who I was becoming.

The Drumbeat Truth

Let's engrain it:

- Love is lived daily, not occasionally.
- Small acts accumulate into character.
- Jeshua emphasized cups of water as much as miracles.
- Daily Love heals givers and receivers alike.
- Presence itself is Love in action.

So live Love daily. Don't wait for grand gestures. Don't underestimate small acts. Each day, choose one concrete way to embody Love. Over time, these acts will weave a life where Love isn't occasional but constant.

Jeshua's call wasn't to Love sometimes. It was to Love always. That always begins with today.

Love as the Future Path

When we talk about the future of spirituality, religion, society, or even the survival of the planet, one truth rises above all others: Love is not optional. It is the only path forward. History shows what happens when fear, greed, and domination guide humanity. Wars erupt, the earth suffers, communities fracture, and individuals wither in loneliness. If the past has been marked by fear's control, the future must be marked by Love's expansion. This isn't naïve idealism. It is practical survival. Love is the blueprint for a sustainable future of faith, of humanity, of the planet itself.

The Failure of Fear-Based Futures

Look at history's fear-based futures. Crusades marched under banners of "God's will," yet left trails of blood. Dictators built empires on fear, only to collapse under rebellion. Economies driven by greed exploited earth and people alike, leaving both broken. Fear-based systems can dominate for a time, but they always implode. Why?

Because fear consumes itself. Fear is unsustainable.

Religion that clings to fear eventually empties its pews. Politics built on fear eventually loses legitimacy. Families controlled by fear eventually fracture. Fear may hold power temporarily, but it never builds futures worth inhabiting.

Jeshua's Vision of the Future

Jeshua constantly pointed forward – not to apocalyptic destruction, but to the kingdom of Love breaking into the present and expanding into the future. His parables envisioned banquets where outsiders are welcomed, seeds growing into expansive trees, lost sons embraced in return, and fields filled with harvest.

The future he described wasn't dominated by judgment. It was saturated with Love. That's why he declared, *"The kingdom of God is within you."* The future he promised wasn't waiting beyond death. It was sprouting now, wherever Love is chosen.

My Awakening to Love as Future

For years, I thought the future of spirituality meant keeping old institutions alive. I worried about shrinking churches, dwindling vocations, empty confessionals. But eventually, I saw these weren't failures. They were pruning. What remains when ritual, hierarchy, and fear fall away? Love.

When I stopped worrying about "saving" religion and started focusing on Love, I found people hungrier than ever. They weren't looking for dogma. They were starving for connection, presence, empowerment, and belonging. In other words – they were starving for Love. That's the future.

Love as Evolutionary Necessity

Science agrees: Love is survival. Evolutionary biology shows cooperation sustains species more than competition. Empathy enabled communities to thrive. Parents' Love nurtured vulnerable infants long enough for humanity to flourish. Without Love, there is no human future.

Neuroscience confirms it: empathy circuits are hardwired. Compassion lowers stress, strengthens resilience, and fosters creativity. Love literally ensures survival of body and mind. The future path isn't just moral. It's biological.

If the future ran on fear, the marketing slogan would be: "Coming soon: more wars, more loneliness, more ulcers!" No one would buy that ticket. But if the future runs on Love, the slogan is: "Connection, joy, and life for all." That's a future people want to live in.

Love as Global Healing

The future path of Love extends beyond individuals into systems. Imagine economies built not on exploitation but on shared flourishing. Imagine politics centered not on fear of "the other" but on solidarity.

Imagine technology developed not to dominate but to serve life.

These aren't utopian fantasies. They're practical possibilities when Love becomes the guiding ethic. Without Love, the future collapses. With Love, the future thrives.

Practices for Living Toward Love's Future

1. **Future Vision Journaling.** Write about the future we will create. How does Love guide relationships, communities, systems? Visualize it vividly.
2. **Small Future Acts.** Choose one daily act that contributes to Love's future – plant a tree, mentor a child, speak peace in conflict. Every seed matters.
3. **Collective Love Practice.** Gather friends or community to serve together – feed the hungry, clean a park, support justice. Love's future is collective.
4. **Intergenerational Love.** Spend time with children and elders. Both remind us Love transcends time – past, present, and future.
5. **Global Awareness.** Learn about cultures different from yours. Practice Love that expands beyond borders.

My Turning Point Practice

One turning point came when I began ending meditations not just with personal peace, but with intentional sending of Love outward – to my family, my town, my country, the planet. At first, it felt symbolic. But over time, I realized this shift changed how I lived. I noticed opportunities to act in alignment with that intention. Love's future wasn't abstract. It was embodied in daily choices.

Obstacles to Love's Future

The biggest obstacle is cynicism. People shrug and say, "That's unrealistic." But "realism" built on fear is what got us here: division, violence, ecological collapse. The truly realistic future must be Love, or there will be no future at all.

Another obstacle is impatience. People expect Love to change everything overnight. But Love is patient. Seeds take time. Love's future is built slowly, consistently, faithfully.

If cynicism ran a travel agency, the brochures would read: "Welcome to the future: it's terrible, nothing improves, don't bother." Love opens a rival agency: "The future: messy but hopeful, come build it with us." Which trip would you book?

Other Voices

- **Martin Luther King Jr.:** *"I have decided to stick with Love. Hate is too great a burden to bear."*
- **Desmond Tutu:** *"Without forgiveness, there is no future."*
- **Teilhard de Chardin:** *"Someday, after mastering the winds, waves, tides and gravity, we shall harness for God the energies of Love. Then, for a second time in the history of the world, man will have discovered fire."*
- **The Dalai Lama:** *"Love and compassion are necessities, not luxuries. Without them, humanity cannot survive."*

The wisdom is clear: Love is not decoration. It is destiny.

The Drumbeat Truth

Let's engrain it:

- Fear-based futures collapse. Love-based futures endure.
- Jeshua envisioned Love's kingdom expanding now, not later.
- Science shows Love is survival, not sentiment.
- Love is not utopian dream – it is the only practical path.

I invite you to live toward Love's future. Don't wait for institutions or governments to lead. Begin now. Every act of Love plants seeds.

Every boundary crossed by compassion builds bridges. Every daily choice aligned with Love brings tomorrow closer.

The future belongs to Love, or it belongs to no one. Jeshua showed us the path. The mystics echoed it. The sciences confirm it. Love is the only way forward. Walk it, and you walk into tomorrow.

Chapter 21: The Way Forward Is Love

Books often end with clever summaries, bullet points, or appeals to the reader's intellect. This one ends differently. This one ends where Jeshua began, where the mystics always pointed, where every path worth walking eventually returns: Love. Not as a slogan, not as a fuzzy sentiment, not as a doctrine to recite, but as the lived heartbeat of a free life.

You've just journeyed through heavy terrain: the burden of doctrines, the myth of original sin, the entanglements of guilt and shame, the chains of fear, the liberation of forgiveness, and finally, the centrality of Love. Each chapter peeled back layers of complexity, showing how much religious tradition buried the simple truth under rules, rituals, and authority structures. Yet at every turn, the answer wasn't another system. It was always a return to presence, empowerment, and above all, Love.

The Journey We've Taken

We began by naming the weight of doctrine – how religious systems stacked sin upon sin, ritual upon ritual, until spirituality felt like balancing ledgers in heaven. We saw how external authority replaced inner knowing, and how rituals distracted from presence.

We traced the origins of original sin – a doctrine that convinced generations they were born broken, in need of external rescue. That lie shaped centuries of guilt. But by examining it honestly, we discovered it wasn't Jeshua's teaching. His truth was that the kingdom is within, not chained by ancestral shame.

We explored guilt and shame – how they infiltrate not only religion but psychology, keeping people small, afraid, and stuck. We unmasked them as control mechanisms, not spiritual virtues. And we laughed along the way, because humor is part of liberation.

We entered forgiveness – first as misunderstood obligation, then as liberation. Forgiveness of self, forgiveness of others, forgiveness as daily practice. We saw how forgiveness creates freedom in mind, body, relationships, and spirit. We named the barriers and then overcame them, step by step.

Finally, we arrived at Love — the axis upon which everything turns. We examined why Love stands above all, how fear tries to rival it, what Love looks like in action, how it proves universal across traditions, how it can be lived daily, and why it is the only sustainable path into the future.

This wasn't just a deconstruction of religion. It was a reconstruction of spirituality, not built on doctrine, but on Love.

Why This Matters

If this book stayed on the shelf of ideas, it would be wasted ink. The goal was never more knowledge. The goal was freedom. Religion taught you to fear, obey, and outsource authority. This book invites you to reclaim presence, empowerment, and Love.

Why does this matter? Because the world doesn't change through arguments, doctrines, or debates. The world changes when people live Love. When forgiveness replaces grudges. When compassion replaces judgment. When presence replaces distraction. When courage replaces fear.

Your personal life matters. Your relationships matter. Your daily choices matter. And yes, the world's future matters. Every act of Love plants a seed. Every moment of presence shifts the atmosphere.

Every release of guilt, every act of forgiveness, every step into Love contributes to a freer, lighter, more human world.

Let's be honest: if guilt and shame actually worked, the most religious people would be the most joyful. But often, they're the most miserable. If fear truly made people holy, every Catholic who skipped Mass would have spontaneously combusted by now. But the pews are still intact. The evidence is clear: fear and guilt don't work. Love does.

Love as Simplicity

The genius of Love is its simplicity. You don't need a seminary degree. You don't need an institution's blessing. You don't need elaborate rituals. Love is accessible in every moment.

- In the way you breathe deeply instead of snapping.
- In the way you listen without planning your reply.
- In the way you forgive when resentment would feel easier.
- In the way you choose kindness when sarcasm beckons.

- In the way you rest instead of punishing yourself.

Love is not lofty. Love is ordinary. And in its ordinariness, it is revolutionary.

Voices of the Mystics

You've heard the chorus throughout this book, but it's worth letting it resound one more time:

- Jeshua: "*The kingdom of God is within you.*"
- The Buddha: "*Do not dwell in the past, do not dream of the future, concentrate the mind on the present moment.*"
- Rumi: "*Love is the bridge between you and everything.*"
- Julian of Norwich: "*All shall be well, and all shall be well, and all manner of thing shall be well.*"
- Martin Luther King Jr.: "*I have decided to stick with Love. Hate is too great a burden to bear.*"

Different voices, same truth: Love is the essence.

My Final Turning Point

Writing, reflecting, and teaching these truths hasn't just been an intellectual project for me. It's been a process of liberation. Every time I've chosen Love over fear, forgiveness over resentment, presence over distraction, I've tasted freedom. And I want you to taste it too. Not later. *Now.*

Because here's the secret religion never wanted you to know: you don't need their permission. You don't need their intermediaries. You don't need their rituals. You already have everything you need. The kingdom is within you. Love is already here.

The Drumbeat Truth

Let's engrain it one last time:

- Doctrine complicates, Love simplifies.
- Fear enslaves, Love liberates.
- Guilt poisons, forgiveness heals.
- Separation divides, Love unites.
- The kingdom is not "out there." It is within.

The Call to Action

Here's where we land, as simple and as direct as it gets: **Live a loving life.** That's the whole thing.

Not someday when you're "ready." Not after you've "healed everything." Not when you've joined the "right group." Now. Today.

Live a loving life in small, daily choices. Live a loving life in how you treat yourself, how you speak to others, how you respond to the world. Live a loving life in the face of fear, in the presence of guilt, in the aftermath of wounds. Live a loving life, not as performance, but as presence.

Because the world doesn't need more doctrines. It needs more Love. The future doesn't depend on who wins the theological debates. It depends on who chooses Love.

The Recovering Catholic's Guide to Spirituality has brought you here: to this crossroads where you can keep carrying guilt, shame, and fear, or you can put them down and walk in forgiveness and Love. The choice is yours.

Choose Love. Live Love. Be Love. That's the whole path. And it's enough.

www.ingramcontent.com/pod-product-compliance
Lightning Source LLC
LaVergne TN
LVHW020654110826
845149LV00012B/1992

* 9 7 9 8 9 9 2 0 2 8 7 2 0 *